John Ker

Lectures on the History of Preaching

John Ker

Lectures on the History of Preaching

ISBN/EAN: 9783337003128

Printed in Europe, USA, Canada, Australia, Japan

Cover: Foto ©Lupo / pixelio.de

More available books at **www.hansebooks.com**

LECTURES

ON THE

HISTORY OF PREACHING

BY THE LATE

REV. JOHN KER, D. D.,

Professor of Practical Training in the United Presbyterian Church.
Author of
Sermons; "The Psalms in History and Biography," &c.

EDITED BY

REV. A. R. MACEWEN, M. A., BALLIOL, B. D., GLASGOW.

INTRODUCTION BY REV. WM. M. TAYLOR, D. D., LL. D.

New York :
A. C. ARMSTRONG & SON,
714 BROADWAY.
1889.

INTRODUCTION.

THE author of these Lectures stood in the very front rank of the preachers both of his country and his age. His first volume of Sermons, republished on this side of the Atlantic under the title of "The Day Dawn and the Rain," and originally issued in Edinburgh in 1869, as "Sermons by Rev. John Ker," is now in its thirteenth edition in Great Britain, and has attracted the attention and called forth the commendation of the best critics. The discourses which it contains are characterized by originality of thought, simplicity of style, and a certain quiet power that carries conviction without any straining after effect. His lines of method are all natural without being obvious, and his movement along these is always singularly easy and delightful. The same qualities distinguish his second volume, which, though published after his death in 1886, is a worthy companion of the first, and has already taken its place among the homiletic models of our times.

For many years before his death a nervous break-down in health incapacitated him for regular pulpit work. But, at the reorganization of the Theological Seminary of the United Presbyterian Church of Scotland, he consented to attempt the performance of the duties of the chair of Practical Training for the Ministry, and these he continued to perform, with marked acceptance, till his sudden and lamented decease.

As a man he possessed large stores of varied information, ample scholarship, thorough acquaintance with literature, a true poetic temperament, and sound common sense, while these were all pervaded by the devoutest piety and the sweetest modesty. There was always about him a great amount of reserve force. He never seemed to be making an effort, and, eloquent as his discourses were, they were delivered in a pleasant, conversational manner, which won its way and did its work almost before the hearer was aware. These qualities appeared in his work in the professor's chair, as well as in that which he did in the pulpit. His department was new, and he had to act in it the part of a pioneer. But it was one for which his whole previous history had been a preparation, and to which he devoted the maturity of his powers. He went into it with all his heart, and in this volume we have a specimen of the manner in which he dealt with, at least, one part of the field which had been intrusted to him. The opening Historical Lectures, without being exhaustive, are eminently rich, and his treatment of the German Pulpit, which forms the main part of the work, is, so far as we know, the fullest which has yet been given in the English language. It is not, strictly speaking, a work on Homiletics, but the purpose of the Professor is never once lost sight of, and his criticisms on the men who come up before him for review are often more valuable than direct disquisitions on the making of sermons would have been, while his *obiter dicta* are always both incisive and suggestive ; so that, as a recent critic has said, "For thoughtful preachers, this volume would prove more helpful than most helps for the pulpit." To the careful study of all such, we heartily commend the work.

March, 1889. WM. M. TAYLOR.

EDITORIAL PREFACE.

A FEW words of preface are required to explain the relation of these Lectures to Dr. Ker's other work, since his own request—the one act of his life which his friends regret—prevents the publication of any memoir or biography.

In the year 1875, among other changes in the Theological Hall, the United Presbyterian Church resolved to institute a professorship, which should not be tied down to any one department of theology, but should attend to the training of students in its more practical aspects, with special regard to preaching and pastoral work. Such a Chair exists under some name in every complete Theological College, although in some churches, as had previously been the case in

the United Presbyterian Church, it is combined
with the charge of a departmental subject. The
title chosen was the *Chair of Practical Training
for the Work of the Ministry;* and, in 1876, Dr.
Ker was elected by the Synod as its first occupant.

For some years he had been laid aside from· his
Glasgow pastorate, and, although he could not now
refuse duties so congenial to him, he declined to be
called a "professor," and accepted the appointment
on the understanding that he should have such
freedom as his health required, in regard to the
amount and the duration of his work.   Through
God's kindness, however, he was enabled, with
short interruptions, to discharge the full duties of
the Chair for ten years ; and when he died on the
4th of October, 1886, he was preparing for the
work of another session.

It was left to a large extent in Dr. Ker's own
hands to determine the scope and even the subjects
of his lectures. He had no precedent to guide him,
nor any rule beyond the understanding that his
work was to bear directly on the actual duties of
the pastorate. While always careful to observe
this limit, he so exercised his freedom as to secure
constant variety. At one time he lectured upon
the Public Worship of the Church, upon Prayer and

Praise and the relation of these to the Sermon. At another time he lectured upon Family Visitation and Family Prayer, upon the Care of the Young, and upon general Pastoral Superintendence. He discussed the different conceptions of the Church of Christ as a Society, contrasting the Roman Catholic and the Protestant conceptions, indicating the faults of each, and showing the bearing of such points upon the minister's relation to the work of his own and other denominations. Again, he reviewed the Principles of the United Presbyterian Church, the Forms of Process, and the business of Sessions and other congregational agencies. He occupied several lectures in showing the bearing of University studies upon the minister's work, and the advantage to which a preacher may turn his reading in general literature. Indeed, each year seemed to open out to him some new aspect of his office; he was constantly planning and writing new lectures ; so that very few of his lectures were repeated more than twice or thrice.

It will thus be seen that the Lectures on the History of Preaching represent only a fragment of his work, and that they consider the subject with a distinctly practical aim. The selection of them from his manuscripts is due to the fact that owing to the nature of the subject they were more closely reduced to writing than the others, and that they deal with a subject of interest to the general Christian public.

Besides lecturing upon such topics as we have mentioned, Dr. Ker occupied alternate lecture-hours in instruction of a less formal and more conversational kind. Prescribing texts and topics' to the students, he asked them to prepare skeletons of sermons, or sermons, and discussed such exercises in the class. Sometimes he asked them to suggest divisions or plans on the spur of the moment, or after quarter of an hour's reflection ; and he carried out a similar method with regard to other ministerial duties. These are the hours which have left the most lasting impress upon his pupils ; for while he never failed to show his rare combination of critical acumen with appreciation of the freshness and independence of younger minds, it was then that he gave freest scope to his own genial intellect, and revealed most plainly his unfailing spirituality and elevation of tone. Such work, although it leaves the deepest mark on men, cannot be preserved except in living characters.

With regard to the twenty-one Lectures which

are included in this volume, readers will find that
the first seven of them form part of a larger plan
than is carried out in those which follow. They
deal with the general history of the Church prior
to the Reformation, while Lectures IX.-XXI. are
occupied exclusively with the history of German
Protestantism. In the first lecture, Dr. Ker
indicates his intention of dealing with the preaching of the other branches of the Reformed
Church; and, as a matter of fact, he partially
carried out this intention. He lectured upon
several of the English Puritan preachers, upon
some of the Scottish preachers, and still more fully
upon French preaching, both Roman Catholic and
Protestant. It is specially to be regretted that his
lectures upon the last-mentioned were not written
in a form which will permit publication. His
own tone of mind had perhaps more affinity to the
French than to the German; his students remember with admiration his sagacious insight into the
strength and weakness of Du Moulin, Bossuet,
Pierre Du Bosc, and other French orators; and his
manuscript notes testify to the minute study which
he had made of their sermons.

One other word of explanation should be given
to readers who will expect to find reference to the

influence of Tertullian and Jerome, to those who would fain have had some fuller account from Dr. Ker's pen of Bernard of Clairvaux and John Tauler, and to those who know the direct or indirect influence of Dorner, Harless, and Ahlfeld upon the modern German pulpit. The lectures now printed were supplemented, in conversation-hours, by discussions of men and of epochs that have influenced the history of preaching—discussions which included the above names, with many others. Of these, however, we have no written record.

The references in the foot-notes are as a rule indicated, if not expressly given, in Dr. Ker's manuscript; some of them and some of the dates have been added by the editor for the convenience of students. It should be said that Rothe's *Geschichte der Predigt* (also a posthumous publication) was issued in 1881, after these lectures had been written, and that the references to that valuable work were inserted by Dr. Ker, to mark some coincidences of opinion and even of expression, of which he once spoke to the editor with amused satisfaction.

The special thanks of readers are due to the Rev. James Kidd, B.D., of St. Andrews, for the care with which he has read the proof-sheets, and for other valuable assistance. The index has been prepared by the loving hands of those to whom the editor owes the honourable trust which has been placed in him in the preparation of the volume. It is not easy for one who revered Dr. Ker to judge how far this reproduction of his words will guide and help those to whom he was personally a stranger; but the words themselves are wise and true, with a clear message for our day, and by God's help they will not fail to reach the heart.

A. R. M.

CONTENTS.

CONTENTS.

CONTENTS.

LECTURE I.

WE intend to trace the course of Preaching in the history of the Church, and to turn attention to some of the most remarkable and successful preachers. To-day we may briefly sketch the field of survey, and suggest the advantages of the study.

The work of the preacher may first be looked at as it is related to the Old and the New Testaments, with the view of noting what we may learn from them as to the spirit and the form of preaching, the question of material being meanwhile left out of account. There is then the preaching of the early Church, beginning with the apostles, and going on till the time when Christianity became an acknowledged power in the world of thought

A sketch of the field.

B

Thereafter we have two great branches — the
Eastern Church represented by Origen, Chryso-
stom, and others; and the Western or Latin
Church represented by men like Ambrose and
Augustine.

Then follows the long period of the Middle Ages,
when preaching sank to a great extent under the
weight of ceremonial, or was influenced by the
opposite systems of Scholasticism and Mysticism,
with many bright examples, however, of a clearer
and simpler kind.

The Reformation marks the commencement of
the modern period of preaching, the use of the
principle of individuality separating us from the
old world as by an ocean. We have now, not only
distinct nationalities in preaching, as French,
German, English, Scottish, American, but the
preaching of different Churches—Roman Catholic,
Anglican, Nonconformist; and this last might even
be sub-divided, for the Wesleyan preaching is
different from the Congregationalist, and that again
to some extent from the Presbyterian. There is a
division, also, since the Reformation, into several
epochs; the immediate post-Reformation period—
that of the great doctrinal preachers called in our
country Puritan; the period of moral preach-

ing, of Tillotson and the Moderates; that of the revival, called in Germany, Pietism, and in our country, Evangelicalism; and the various forms which preaching takes in our own time.

It is evident that we have a field which might occupy us for any length of time, and at which we can for the present do little more than glance. We may meantime point out, in advance, the difference of such a study from the study of Church History as usually given. The outward events with which some Church historians deal are often reflected in it; it bears the impress of those varying forms of thought which are known to us as philosophies; the prevailing heresies affect it either in the way of attraction or of repulsion. But besides all this, it leads us into many lines of Christian life which are rarely, if ever, considered in general Church History. I shall mention some of them, and point out certain practical advantages which we may derive from tracing them.

Difference from ordinary Church History.

Advantages to be derived.

As a mere matter of instruction, we cannot take even the slightest view of it without becoming acquainted with the most interesting and important men and events and trains of thought, that have been prominent among the ruling races of mankind since the Christian era began. It is like

General instruction.

sailing down a river, standing in the part of the ship which commands the most characteristic views, and landing to visit the temples, cities, churches, homes of varied races of men that line the banks. It carries us from Jerusalem to Antioch, to Alexandria, to Constantinople, to Rome. We must visit cities on the confines of the great tropical desert, and the lone islands of our own western ocean. The Court of Charlemagne, the forests of Germany, the camp-like settlement of the Anglo-Saxon kingdoms had, nearly at one time, their Alcuin, their Boniface, their Bede. The long period of the middle ages, though brightened by .many an oasis, is, as a whole, a barren desert, till we reach the time when the fountains are unsealed after the Reformation and the waters break out in France, in Germany, in Britain, and in America, parting, like the primitive river of Eden, into four streams to revive the whole face of the earth.

As to distinction of preachers.   In such a survey we meet with what is most distinguished in the Christian Church; for while we have had thinkers such as Melancthon and Pascal and Milton, whose work was done chiefly or entirely by the pen, the great majority of Christian teachers have been men who were drawn irresistibly to use the living voice, and to use it in the great congregation. We have an array of instructors and orators, spread through the ages and over the countries, compared with which the schools of Greece and Rome were but a small handful,—an exceeding great army of men, such as the prophet saw in his vision ; the select and chosen of whom might be compared to the company which John saw in the Apocalypse, standing on Mount Zion with the Great Name written on their foreheads. No one will talk lightly or flippantly of sermons and preachers, who thinks of the thousands upon thousands of men, who, in all the countries of Europe and in all the churches, with the most varied ability, but many of them with the very highest, have devoted themselves to God's work in speaking for Him to their fellow-men. What a different Europe this would have been, poor as in many respects it is, and what a different country ours would have been, but for the seeds of truth and freedom and devotion that, among many weeds, have been sown by these preachers of the Word !

When we consider the character of preaching, and the subjects with which it deals in different periods, it casts the most instructive light upon the *As to state of the Church.*

times, and upon the condition of the Christian
Church. The manners of the old nations of
Europe come before us, when we find—*e.g.*,
Chrysostom and Basil denouncing strongly and
repeatedly the sin of drunkenness, and Augustine
afraid to shut the guilty out of communion, lest he
should lose all influence over so numerous a class.

We thus gain a view of the time which does not
perhaps comfort us, but which keeps us from saying that the "former days were better than these."
If you read Gibbon's or even Mosheim's account of
sects and heresies, you are ready to think that
these old preachers were dry dogmatists, bitter
polemical anathematisers, "blowing about a dust
and noise of creeds." But when you come to their
sermons, and find that with many things alien to
our mode of thought they had such a hatred of
sin, such an ideal of a high and divine life, you see
what slowly raised a new world from the corruption
and ruin of the old. To estimate these men from
Gibbon, would be like estimating our own Churches
from the reports of them in sceptical newspapers.
If you would know their influence on their time,
you must go to their sermons. At the same time,
the faults of the Christian Church and ministry
will come into view, and we may see the inherent

power of the pulpit, that in spite of all faults, it, or rather God's truth, held its ground and conquered. We shall find the sensational school which sought the applause and the clapping of hands which Chrysostom condemned—men contented to beat the drum and draw a crowd. We shall find the mystic allegorisers who discovered wonders of philosophy in abstruse passages, and preferred obscurity to light. We shall find the pedantic and scholastic who turned the great doctrines of the Bible into a wrangling place for logic. The senses, the fancy, the subtlety of dialectics, have in their turn invaded the sphere of preaching, and yet it has recovered and done its work. It has come back to simplicity and power, and by the foolishness of preaching it has pleased God to save them that believe.

Further, in such a survey there is stimulus to be Stimulus. gained from the greatest masters of speech dealing with the greatest of all themes—God, the soul, eternity, sin, Christ, salvation. There is in the highest sense no such roll of orators, and certainly there are no such themes as are presented in the history of Christian preaching. No similar movement in the life of man has ever been effected by the power of speech—so wide, so deep, so continuous. It may fill us with a high and just ambition, with a noble enthusiasm to share in it and to do our best, with God's help, to prove ourselves not unworthy.

Guidance.

There is much to be learned from these men in a directly practical way—from their themes and methods ; from the way in which they addressed themselves to the spirit of their times, sharing and guiding it, or seeking to correct it ; from their sagacity or their fearlessness as reprovers. The greatest of them were all men of their time and yet above their time.

Warning.

We may even learn from their faults, for though we may be smaller men in every way, history will teach us to avoid paths that led them astray. We may learn from the allegorical tendency of Origen, and the excesses of fancy to which it led, to keep to a wise and sober interpretation of Scripture. From the extreme self-inspection of Jonathan Edwards, which led to the morbid analytic preaching of his school, we may learn to give a large attention to the objective doctrines and duties of the Bible—the heart as well as the Bible but the Bible as well as the heart. From the constant moral-essay preaching of the Tillotson school, which ended in a practical ignoring of all that is distinctive in Christianity, we may learn how vitally

important it is to breathe into all duties the life and
the moving power of the person and work of Christ,
to remember that Christianity is a plan, not of
moral teaching, but first of all of redemption and
reconciliation ; birth before life, and life before
work. From the narrowness and the limited view
of the power and range of the Gospel exhibited by
some good men of the Evangelical school of last
century—a narrowness and a limitation which have
filled the ranks of Ritualism and Broad-churchism—
we may learn, while we hold the central truths of
the Cross of Christ, to aim at giving them the widest
application to the lives and ways of men, to show
that Christianity is consistent with every pure taste
and every high position. We may learn to avoid
"the falsehood of extremes." For we shall see that
one excess leads to another, and when an excess
which we deplore manifests itself among men whose
sincerity we admit, we shall consider how we can
meet it, with loyalty to what we believe to be the
truth of God ; not by scolding nor by barren polemics, but by putting that into our preaching for the
want of which, it may be, men are turning aside to
seek satisfaction elsewhere. If some turn to what
is called the Broad School, may it not be because
Evangelical preachers have not been showing how

the Gospel touches all that is human and gives
to common life a tenderness and beauty and
meaning which Broad-church doctrine has not in
itself? If others are turning to confessionals and
spiritual directions and the corporeal presence of
Christ in the sacraments, is it not because we have
not shown clearly and warmly enough the humanity of Christ brought close as a guide and a friend,
always and everywhere? We may have preached
Him as the Son of God in heaven, as the Resurrection and Eternal Hope; we may have pressed the
word, "Believe and thou shalt be saved;" but have
we shown Him to men who are thirsting for a friend,
in the light of His promise, "I will not leave you
comfortless; I will come to you?" So let us study
the preaching of past times that we may add to it
that which was wanting; and while we maintain
the unchanged centre, Jesus Christ, we shall bring
into the circumference a richer and fuller provision,
that, as He himself says, the sheep may go in and
out and find pasture.

Encourage-
ment—

I shall mention now, in closing, one or two
grounds for encouragement, which we may hope
to gain from such a survey.

From the
advance of
preaching.

One comfort is that, as a whole, errors in preaching have tended to correct themselves; that the

ministry of the Word has not been retrograding
in the history of the Church ; that, on the contrary,
its tendency has been onward. I do not mean
that we have now names equal to those great
stars in the firmament—men like Paul, Chrysostom,
Augustine, Luther, Knox, Howe, who subdued
kingdoms, wrought righteousness, stopped the
mouths of lions. These rise rarely, and belong
to all time. Neither do I mean to say that there
are not little retrogressions, and differences in
different places, but that, as a whole, the pulpit
has brought home more of Christian truth to the
circumstances and wants of men, during the last
fifty years, than in any half-century since the beginning of Christianity.

Another ground of comfort is that wherever From its
vital Christian truth has been presented, with any continued
attractiveness.
measure of adaptation to human wants, men have
been found ready to listen. There are men who
preach the Gospel with so little regard for the
circumstances and trials of those around them,
with so little life and warmth, that it has no attrac-
tions. And there are those who deal with circumstances and subjects of passing interest, yet show
so little of the power of Gospel truth that they
only attract the curious, and do not keep them

very long. But where the healing and helping
truth of Christ is brought home to the wounds and
weariness of sinful and suffering human nature,
there will always be a power of attraction in it.
As God has promised, His blessing and His Spirit
attend it. All great revivals, all true advances in
the Church, have come from the simple, earnest
preaching of the Gospel of Christ. Let us never
be allured from this or scoffed out of it. It has
shown itself, age after age, the power of God to
build up the Church, to convince the gainsaying,
and to gather men within the fold of Christ. If we
do not succeed, the fault will not be in the weapon,
but in our way of handling it.

From the
variety of
men required.

And then we may learn this from our survey:
that all kinds of men may be useful as Christian
ministers, provided they are true and earnest and
willing to learn, with ordinary capacity for learning. The preacher must be "apt to teach,"—*i.e.* able
to think, to arrange his thoughts, and to express
them ; but with this, if the heart is right, there
may be the greatest variety in the character of
mind. This is seen in the past, both in sermons
that remain to us and in preaching of which we
only read. Each true Christian minister has had
his place and circle, and he may have still. He

may be a man of genius—there is room for him—
or of the plainest, most realistic understanding.
He may be as learned as the library of Alexandria,
or "a man of one book," provided it be the true
Book. He may be a philosopher of the schools,
or a scholar of common life. He may be original
to the verge of eccentricity, or a traveller in well-
worn paths. Let him only be resolved to make
his gifts the property of his fellow-men in loyal
obedience to his Master. Let his genius be tem-
pered with humility, his originality not worm-eaten
by affectation, his doctrine and duty pervaded by
the living Christ ; and there is work for him. Let
no one covet or grieve at the gift of his neighbour,
but let each diligently cultivate his own. He will
have those who draw to him, because in the wide
variety of the human mind he meets their need ;
and whether his name finds a permanent place in
the records of the Church below or not, he will
receive the approval, Well done, good and faithful
servant.

LECTURE II.

ANCESTRY OF PREACHING IN THE OLD TESTAMENT.

Preaching peculiar to Christianity.

IT may be said that preaching, or regular religious instruction, is peculiar to Christianity. So far as we know the ancient religions, there was nothing in them resembling it. The priests of Egypt and Chaldea and Greece had their mysteries, but they were for the initiated. The philosophers had their schools, but they were for the select. No one thought of going out to instruct the masses in moral and religious truth. The orators addressed the people, but it was on political topics for political ends. When Paul began his work in Athens, the philosophers were surprised, not only at the contents of his message, but at the manner of it. He seemed to be "a setter forth (καταγγελεὺς) of strange gods, because he preached unto them (εὐηγγελίζετο) Jesus and the

14

Resurrection." He proclaimed those truths, making a Gospel of them. This was novel to the Greek mind, and novel to the Greek language.

Among the religions of the present day, preaching is almost as little known. Hindooism cannot be said to have it at all. Buddhism and Mahometanism have had their missions, but they have no regular method of instruction for their adherents; indeed, their preaching, of the early kind at least, has long since ceased. This is scarcely to be wondered at. If you take their sacred books, the Koran for example, you will see how ill adapted they are for continued teaching, how utterly impossible it would be to deal with them as we do with the Bible, and to gather from them texts subjects, and illustrations for the work of preaching. Christianity has this field specially, we may say almost solely, to itself.

But while preaching belongs specially to Christi- Its ancestry.
anity, it has an ancestry which can be traced, and that ancestry is in the Old Testament. Our work to-day is to define what we mean when we say this, to trace the line of descent, to look at the place assigned to the prophetic Word.

When we say that the office of the preacher has an ancestry in the Old Testament, we mean that

the Old Testament had in it the germ and many
features of this office ; that it set apart a special
class of men, as does the Christian Church, to
learn and to declare the will of God to the people.

Prophetic, not priestly. This class was the order not of the priests but of
the prophets. There is one great High Priest ;
but all Christians are priests ; this honour have all
His saints. The prophets indeed are, so far,
represented by all Christians without distinction, as
all should in some way be teachers ; but the work
of teaching, as fulfilled by ministers in the Church of
Christ, follows specially in the line of the prophets.

It is true that in many cases the Hebrew
prophet had some special function. He had a
message direct from God which frequently came
with supernatural knowledge in the power of
prediction. But it was not always so. The
mission of the prophet was often to declare
present truth alone, and the great majority of
those who bore the name were merely instructors
of the people, not foretellers of the future. Taking
God's message as it had been already given, they
unfolded and enforced it. The Greek word,
προφητὴς, though it strictly means "one who
speaks or interprets for another," came to mean
a foreteller, and has thus narrowed the meaning of

the Hebrew נָבִיא, which might as accurately be rendered "the speaker," the man of the word, corresponding to the Greek κῆρυξ. It has sometimes the passive shade of meaning (as though from the *Niphal*, נִבָּא), denoting a man under Divine influence, and so impelled and guided to speak; but sometimes the active shade (as though from the *Hiphil*, הִבִּיע), suggesting one who uses the human faculty. And is not a preacher of Christ, when he uses his human power, still entitled and urged to look for Divine help? Thus, with deduction of the supernatural gift, the prophet of the Old Testament is the ancestor and prototype of the Christian preacher.

Let us then briefly trace the line of this class of religious teachers—the men of the Word of God. The earliest preachers. Of their existence in the earlier part of the Old Testament we find little more than an indication; and this through the New Testament, as when we read of Enoch that he "prophesied," and of Noah that he was a "preacher of righteousness." But this is all. There was no order of men set apart; the nation had not yet been selected in which the Word of God was to be formed for the world.

The patriarchal system is a very beautiful and instructive part of Divine history. It shows us religion in the family, scattered here and there

C

through the ungodly world, and it has for its watchword the saying of Joshua, " As for me and my house, we will serve the Lord." It has also its peculiar revelation, the Theophany, the appearance of God to the individual and the family as a guardian and friend. This corresponds to the appearance of Christ in His human nature among men. Both of them are at the foundation of all the teaching and preaching that follow, but the command to publish the Divine Word has not yet been received. As in the New Testament this comes when Christ goes forth in His Church, so in the Old Testament it comes when the family goes into the nation. Then the prophet—the preacher —appears with a distinct commission.

Moses.   This distinct commission begins with Moses. When he is charged to go to Pharaoh with God's message, he shrinks back because he is not eloquent, and pleads that he cannot speak as he ought. He is met by the response, " See, I have made thee a god to Pharaoh, and Aaron thy brother shall be thy prophet."* Encouraged thereby he fulfils his task, and ultimately holds the office that had been assigned to Aaron. So it often happens ; the man who has most facility at first, falls back if he has

* נָבִיאָ

not the higher tone and spirit, and the man who is slow of speech may be kindled into the highest eloquence. Moses becomes himself a prophet, and there are no words in the Old Testament more full of penetrating power and sublimity than those which he utters. He becomes the guide of Israel, not by his rod only but by his word. He speaks for God to them, and for them to God. But in this Moses is not alone ; there is evidence that he was assisted by a body of prophets or preachers. It could scarcely be otherwise. The Israelites had come out of Egypt ignorant and debased, and they needed instruction about God, and about the mission for which He was preparing them. It was impossible for Moses to do this work alone, and we read that "the Spirit rested upon the seventy elders, so that they prophesied and did not cease." This episode brought out that memorable saying of Moses, "Would God that all the Lord's people were prophets !" Before Moses died, the promise was given that God would raise up for Israel a prophet from among their brethren like unto him. While this promise is perfectly fulfilled only in Christ, there is a long line of prophets indicated—a chain of many links, ending in one link of gold.

It is in every way likely that after Moses there was a continuous class of religious teachers, whose work it was to instruct and warn. We have indications of this in the case of Joshua, in the history of Deborah and Barak, and in the days of solemn assembly, which could not be observed without men being led to speak and listen.

Samuel. It is, however, in the time of Samuel that we find the first great advance in the place and work of the prophets. The circumstances of Israel led to it, and were overruled by God for this very end. The ark, which was the centre of religious worship, was captured and carried away by the Philistines. It fell into temporary oblivion, and the people were in danger of losing their religion and their unity. It was then that Samuel was raised up as a great teacher and reformer, as was most necessary. The ark and the Mosaic ritual were divinely ordained for instruction, but the people had turned them into idols and charms in place of the living God, and gross immorality had invaded their life. And so the ark must be removed, the priesthood set aside for a while, and the nation instructed in spiritual truth. This accounts for Samuel's offering the sacrifice without restraint of place and for his pressing on the people the great truths of obedience and righteousness as the substance of religion. It was a step toward the spirit of the Psalm, "The sacrifices of God are a broken spirit;" and of that saying of Christ, "Neither in this mountain nor yet in Jerusalem shall ye worship the Father."

This is not a violation, as some seem to think, of the unity of the religious worship of the nation. A man was raised by God to restore that unity by giving it spirit and life. The unity of worship around the ark admits the very same exception as the law of the Sabbath,—necessity and mercy.

It is in the time of Samuel that we first read of companies of prophets under a director, of music as forming an accompaniment of their prophecies, and of the Spirit of God falling upon them as in the New Testament Church. But doubtless teaching was the chief part of their duty, and it is at this stage that we find the beginning of that great advance in spirituality of view which appears in the Psalms and later prophets, when ritual was seen to be a lower thing than mercy and truth and righteousness. This was so great a step in the prophetic position that Samuel is spoken of in the ninety-ninth Psalm, as occupying a marked place: "Moses and Aaron among His priests, and Samuel

The Prophetic Schools.

among them that call upon His name." And he
is put in the book of Acts at the head of the
prophet-roll : " Yea, and all the prophets from
Samuel and those that follow after."

The Prophetic office.   We have again a period when the prophetic
office is to some extent hidden. A new power
has risen in the land, that of the king, which brings
danger to religious truth and purity. We read of
Gad the seer and Nathan the prophet, who
reproved David, of Ahijah and Iddo and others ;
but the next notable period is that of Elijah and
Elisha. The kingdom of David is rent in twain ;
In Israel. two tribes follow his dynasty ; the others, moved
by political jealousy and political indifference,
take Jeroboam as their king. It is remarkable that
the first great outbreak of zeal in prophecy and
preaching occurred among the tribes that revolted.
And yet this was natural, for there the need was
greatest, and the Spirit of God raised up the
standard. The history of Elijah and Elisha, the
two witnesses in the kingdom of Israel, is one of
wonderful interest and picturesqueness and beauty
and grandeur. Elijah, Ahab, Jezebel, Carmel,
Horeb, Elisha, Naaman, the widow of Sarepta, the
Shunammite—how we turn to them and read of
them, and find meanings second only to those in

the life of Christ! It strikes us sometimes as strange that no lengthened discourse from this period is preserved. But the words of these men were thunderbolts; they struck, and struck but once; and the place given to Elijah is seen in this, that the forerunner of Christ is named from him, and that he stands beside Moses on the Mount of Transfiguration to represent the prophets. We have abundant evidence that, at this time, the pro-phetic office had become a fixed institution, even among the ten tribes. We hear of "schools of the prophets" at Bethel and Jericho and Gilgal, the very seats of idolatry ; of the place where some of them met becoming too narrow for them ; and of their going forth to form new schools. These seem to have been gatherings of disciples round noted teachers, and, no doubt, the theme of instruc-tion was the character of the worship of Jehovah, as opposed to the Baal-worship against which they met to protest. In some cases they lived together ; in others they had homes and families of their own. Perhaps, if we were to look for a later analogy, we should find it in the "families of Iona," as they called themselves, or the Moravian settlements, or communities of missionaries which form stations like Livingstonia. The position

which they assumed towards the apostate kingly
power reminds us sometimes of the Huguenots of
France after the Revocation of the Edict of Nantes,
or of our own forefathers in the time of Charles II.
and James—confronting kings, and not afraid. It
was by no far-fetched reference that the Camerons
and Cargills among our wild mountains made their
frequent appeals to the Lord God of Elijah.

In Judah. In the kingdom of Judah the work of the
prophet took a somewhat different form. There
were there, no doubt, also teachers and scholars,
and frequent protests against the defection of the
times. But the temple at Jerusalem, the service of
Jehovah there, the line of kingly descent from
David, kept the persecution of the prophets from
becoming as fierce and sanguinary as it was in the
northern kingdom. There was more opportunity
for full speech, and God's message to us comes
through words spoken there which are still preserved. Such were Isaiah and Jeremiah and
Micah. If we learn from the prophets of the
ten tribes to dare and do, to jeopardise our lives
even unto death, we learn from those of the
two tribes how to be kindled with a high and noble
enthusiasm of speech, to ask from God the tongue
of the learned, and to speak the word in season

With some points of difference, it is like the distinction between Scotland and England in the dark days of the Stuart reign. The hand of persecution did not fall so heavily in the south, and England had its Howe and Baxter and Bunyan, who, when they could not speak, could write though it were in the prison. But our forefathers were among those who "wandered in deserts and on mountains;" they had a short passage from the prison to the scaffold, and their history is that of their devotion to the death. If we had then the fewer prophets, we had the greater martyrs.

There is one period of prophetic work to which we can refer only briefly, though it is of great importance. It is that of the prophets of the Captivity—Ezekiel and Daniel, and of the return—Haggai, Zechariah, and Malachi. These men had a double duty ; first, to be watchers over the remnant, and to keep it steadfast as the world's religious hope ; and, next, to represent in some measure to the outside world the great light which was yet to visit it. They were what may be called the " missionary prophets," and after Isaiah, who towers above all, there are none who so distinctly bring out the design of God for the whole race of man, or so prepare the heart of Jew

During the Captivity.

and Gentile for the coming of Christ. If we find throughout the world at the time of our Saviour little bands of Jews and proselytes to whom the apostles first addressed themselves, and who became hearths for the sacred fire, we owe it through God's guidance to the men who lifted the thoughts and hopes of the chosen people above the natural limits of their land and race into the atmosphere of those grand truths which express the needs and meet the wants of all mankind.

After the Return. This closes the line of divinely inspired teachers whom we call, in the highest sense, prophets. But, as we have already said, the word prophet has a far wider meaning, as applied to all teachers of religious truth. In this sense we find men in the time of Jehoshaphat and Josiah reading and explaining the Word of God, and not less in the time of Ezra and Nehemiah. These were evidently epochs of great religious revival and reformation under what we call "the ordinary teaching of the Word." Such teaching continued down to the time of our Lord, with many a turn of the tide, but exciting desires and giving knowledge which made the world more ready for Him and for the Gospel.

If the survey we have taken be at all a just one, then the prophetic office grew in importance all through the Old Testament till it took the leading place. You will not understand me as depreciating the history or the divinely appointed symbolism. The prophet accepts these as the basis of all his teaching, but more and more does he penetrate to the heart of them, show the symbol to be nothing without its inner meaning, and turn away to the great reality, to Christ before and to God above. Moses, Isaiah, Christ—the law, the prophets, the Son of God—that is the ascending scale, and then the Son of God becomes the centre of the law and the prophets, and sends us forth again as His messengers of truth and grace.

If we follow this ascending scale, we shall be guarded against several errors.

The teaching of this survey as to—

Some critics tell us that the more minute development of Jewish ritual was superimposed long after the time of David; that Judaism was simpler in its elements as it came from Moses, but became more detailed and elaborate in its later history. We could understand this if it were a merely human growth; for it would resemble the addition of ceremonialism to the simplicity of the New Testament by the Romish Church. But if the Old Testament be, as we believe, a Divine education, then to put the law in its full form after the

(1) Course of Jewish history

prophets, is to misapprehend and invert the whole
course of Jewish history.   The mission of the
prophets was to pass from form to substance,
from symbol to reality, from ritual to righteousness and truth.   God's path is from the dark to
the clear and ever clearer, shining more and more
unto the perfect day.

(2) The place   We shall also be warned against giving ritual
of preaching. or symbolism a higher place than preaching in the
Christian Church.   Even under the Old Testament,
the whole course of progress was towards presenting
Divine truth in its simplicity and power by bringing it close to the understanding.   God gradually
sets aside the mere form, and it is not for us to
reimpose it.

(3) The mater-   We may also learn something as to the matter
ials for preach- of our preaching.   In some respects the work of
ing. the Old Testament prophets was very different
from ours, and yet in many respects it was the
same, since they too had to instruct the people.
We find that their teaching was occupied with
three great spheres.   (*a*) It laid its basis in the past,
in the facts of a Divine history—what God had
done in His great interpositions.   Nothing moves
men like this.   He who does not care for the
past is doomed to mental and spiritual poverty.

(*b*) Further, they faithfully brought the past to bear on the present—present sin, present duty ; without this the past is dead. (*c*) And still more they pointed to the future, for without the future the present cannot be understood ; unless we know the end how can we know the way ?

Now the Christian preacher has still these three spheres. He has *their* past, but a greater added to it in the history of Christ and of what God has done through Him. Yet this will be dead—mere orthodox doctrine, unless you bring it to bear on present life, on the wants and duties that are here and now. And you have also a future to point to, a greater future, when Christ shall return to make all things new. Whatever may be said about the magnanimity of thinking only of the present life, and the grand unselfishness of letting the future alone, we must take our teaching from the apostle's maxim, " If in this life only we have hope in Christ, we are of all men most miserable," and from Christ's saying, " I will see you again, and your heart shall rejoice." I could not believe in a Christ who excited desires which He could not satisfy. I should as soon think of taking the pole-star from the sky, and the haven from the voyage, to make the sailor safe and happy. Men may call it magnanimity to

be willing to die and think no more of God, but it is
the magnanimity of indifference.   Fill your preaching with the past, the present, and the future, and let .
Him to whom prophets looked beautify them all.

(4) The spirit of   Lastly, acquaintance with them and with their
our preaching. words will serve to enkindle our spirit and ennoble
our life.   To enkindle our spirit, let us study the
apostles not less, but the prophets more.   The
greatest preachers have risen by their inspiration—
the deep spirituality of the Psalms, the majesty of
Isaiah, the tender pathos of Jeremiah, the dusky
grandeur of Ezekiel, and the twelve Lesser Prophets,
if we can call them less, who shine with a lustre each
his own.   And to ennoble our life, we may well
follow them.   There has seldom been a time when
we more needed their singleness of purpose, their
steadfastness, their courage, their trust in the living
God, who is the God of truth and right.   When we
look at the materialistic Baal-worship, at the sensu-
alism of the Phœnician Ashtaroth, with its gilded
corruptions, its hatred of appeals to conscience and
righteousness, we seem brought face to face with
real dangers of the present day—materialism, the
worship of pleasure more or less refined, a religion
that shall not stir the conscience nor command the
life, a charge of puritanism or fanaticism against

those who are earnest in any moral or spiritual purpose. Do we not have it in too much of our literature, our press, our society talk? It is the same old battle between the world and the living God, and we may learn from these men how to bear ourselves. Often it must have seemed to them as if all were going to ruin, as if God Himself had gone up and left them to fight the battle alone. But they stood firm, and they have gained the day. Ahab and Jezebel and the abomination of the Zidonians—where are they beside those men whose names are among the cloud of witnesses, and shine out through the troubled skies as a guide and hope to us? Science is good, and literature, and art, and beauty, but separate them from conscience and God and eternal life, and they will lower the world to the abyss into which the Baals and Ashtaroths have long since gone down. If there be any power under God to save the world, it is a living Church with faithful ministers who shall fearlessly witness for the living God. Let us thank Him that we have many true men in all departments of life and thought, but the ministers of God must show the courage of these old prophets, if they are to share in the joy of the victory which shall surely come, though it may not come through us.

LECTURE III.

THE EARLIEST CHRISTIAN PREACHING.

THE earliest Christian preaching, as we all know, is found in the New Testament, but the preaching to be found there is very different from that which prevails among us—I mean in shape and form. Even the Sermon on the Mount, the longest sermon in the New Testament, is not meant to serve us for a model of construction. If

The preaching of the New Testament.

the New Testament had given us sermons elaborately and artistically framed like the orations of Demosthenes and Cicero, it would not have been so suitable for the work of the Christian ministry. In instructing men in physical science one does not go to the product as it is wrought up into artificial shapes, but as it is seen in nature—gold in the ore, not in the finest vase that workmanship can form. The object of the New Testament is to give us religious truth *in situ*, in the original field, and then to leave successive generations to put it into all the shapes that are needed for the wants of men. Had the Bible given us truth wrought out into all the fitting forms, it would have required to be a very different book as to size—a book which would not have met the daily necessities of the great body of men ; and then, with those fixed forms, it would have led us into uniformity and stagnation. Therefore the Bible, and specially the New Testament, gives *primordia*, first materials and principles and guiding lines, and sets us forth to the work of preaching in a more free and natural way, with the fresh movement of our own minds, and the help of God's Spirit.

Still, we may gain from the New Testament, not only materials, but definite suggestions of the highest value ; and in search for these we shall to-day briefly consider the preaching of Christ and His apostles, and then, leaving the New Testament, glance at the preaching of the early Christian Church.

With regard to the preaching of Christ, we can name only a few points.

The great work of Christ during His life was Christ's preaching. His testimony about Himself is, that Preaching He came " to bear witness to the truth." The works

D

which He performed in healing men were simply
preaching put into visible and palpable form. His
miracles are parables clothed in acts. But the
spoken word is His great power in life. And this
is natural. The word, language, is the highest outcome of human nature, that by which man understands himself, holds fellowship with other men,
and even communes with God. So Christ, throughout His life, was above all things a preacher.
Nicodemus spoke the truth when he said, "no man
can do these miracles that thou doest except God
be with him;" but Peter had reached higher
ground when he said, "Lord, to whom shall we
go? Thou hast the words of eternal life."

Its aim.   Is there, then, nothing greater than Christ's
preaching? Yes, certainly, there is Christ himself,
Christ in His own person, living, dying, rising, and
becoming the mediator between man and God.
Accordingly, His own preaching constantly leads
us to Himself: "Come unto Me, all ye that
labour;" "I am the good Shepherd;" "I, if I be
lifted up from the earth, will draw all men unto
Me;" "I am the Resurrection and the Life." This
would be egotism in any one else than Christ; but
for Him to refrain from it would be to be untrue
to His mission. The sun enlightens by shining,

and Christ saves by showing Himself. Here, then, are two things to remember: preaching is the great Christian work, and in preaching we have to preach Christ.

When we come to the characteristics of Christ's preaching, we name these as among them. *Its character istics.*

There is *great simplicity and yet there is a never-fathomed depth.* The words and figures are within the comprehension of the most unlettered, and even of children ; while the thoughtful student feels that he cannot exhaust them. If we aimed at this way of preaching, we should suit every capacity.

There is *great variety and yet there is one constant aim.* His illustrations are as wide as nature and as human life, but they all bear on God and our relation to Him. This combination reminds us of the two-fold plan of the apostle, who "determined not to know anything save Jesus Christ and Him crucified," yet "was made all things to all men."

There is *great sympathy and yet great faithfulness.* He may justly be said to "speak the truth in love ;" piercing to the conscience, bringing it into the presence of the holy law and character of God, and yet appealing so tenderly to the heart. This is, indeed, the meeting together of righteousness

and mercy. If we could unite these characteristics, how powerful we should be as preachers!

Different
spheres of
Christ's
Preaching.

Then we may learn something from the different
spheres of Christ's preaching.

(1.) There is what may be called His stated
preaching. We read again and again that He
taught in the synagogue; "as His custom was He
went into the synagogue on the Sabbath day."
An example is given us of His method. He
read the Scripture, explained it, and applied
it to the audience: "This day is this Scripture
fulfilled in your ears." This corresponds to our
regular work among those who know the Bible;
and we learn from it what we have to do,—to take
the Bible in its meaning, above all about Christ,
and bring it to bear on the hearers.

(2.) Another sphere was his occasional preaching,—on the mountains, by the sea shore, in the
city, wherever men gathered round Him. In this
He seems to have spent the greater part of His
ministry, and though such work falls more rarely
to us, His method in it is instructive, specially for
the Christian missionary. To begin without a
text, from something in God's world, or man's life,
that arrests the hearers at the time, is the best
way to approach an outside multitude; and any

one who wishes to do this should try to make himself acquainted with nature and life in all their variety, and to learn how to express their spiritual significance. They are adapted to such use. Nature is a parable, and we find God to be the subject of it when we learn the handwriting. The sooth-sayers and astrologers cannot read it, but it is ours to find out the hidden interpretation. It would give even our ordinary preaching great freshness and interest, if we could bring the voice of the days and seasons into the pulpit. Christ meant to teach all preachers this; to make us speak as men who in one sense or another have not only God's Word but God's world in view.

(3.) The third sphere of Christ's preaching was to the individual, when he spoke to single persons, who touched Him or were touched by Him in the house and by the way. This should still be included in our work, when we visit Christian families and in the intercourse of life. It may seem like a paradox to say that we shall learn here not to preach at all. Notice how Christ does. He drops a saying, sometimes little more than a word—"Go and sin no more," "Oh, thou of little faith," "One thing is needful;" and He sends them away with this, to think of it and to preach about it to themselves. See that you follow His example. You can preach to men gathered together, but when you have a person, do not preach, do not lecture him, whether young or old; but be a friend, saying no more than the " word in season ": by your very silence you will show that Christ has been your teacher.

The Preaching of the apostles.   We come now to the preaching of the apostles. We have no complete report of any one sermon. The longest, perhaps, is that of Peter's sermon on the Day of Pentecost, but it is evidently only a summary, for we read at the end that " with many other words did he testify and exhort."   But when we look at the book of Acts and the epistles as a whole, we learn some general truths.

They had two kinds of preaching.   The one was " missionary," for bringing men to a knowledge of Christ ; the other was " ministerial," for building them up in the faith and in the practice of it. The first of these we have in the book of Acts ; the second we have in the epistles.

Missionary.   In their missionary sermons, whether to Jews or to Gentiles, their chief aim seems to have been to make men acquainted first with the person and history of Christ. This is the foundation of all Christian knowledge and preaching. God's way of saving the world is by an interposition in time,

through the life and death of a person, through the
Son of God becoming the son of man, and so making
men again the sons of God. It is for this reason
that the gospels go before the epistles, and the
order suggests a valuable lesson for missionaries
either at home or abroad. Give the life, doings,
death, resurrection of Christ as clearly and warmly
as you can, and with all that variety which the
gospels put in your power. To point to Christ as
He walks and say, " Behold the Lamb of God ! " is
an appeal which reaches men even without argument. No doubt we must tell something of the
meaning of His life, but at first the life itself
should have the foremost place. I think that
even in Home Mission work, and in our ordinary
preaching, this should be borne in mind. There
are always children, there are always half-instructed
people for whom views of the Gospel history are
the very best of all preaching, and these may be
given in a way that will make them profitable to
the most advanced intelligence. Therefore preach
a great deal from the gospels.

But the apostles had another kind of preaching, Ministerial
which followed their missionary labours. We have
little of this in the book of Acts, only a glimpse
in Paul's address to the elders of Ephesus; but it is

fully represented by the epistles. These are really examples of the kind of teaching that must often have been given orally to Christians who were more advanced in knowledge ; and it is a great testimony to the new intelligence that had been called out among the slaves and freedmen of

Its character. Rome, that they could have such letters read and such sermons preached to them. You may be sure that Paul measured his audience ; think then of the natural powers of reasoning, of the spiritual insight, of the lofty and sanctified imagination that would be needed to follow the first eight chapters of the Letter to the Romans.

Preaching should be doctrinal. There are some who say that we should not enter into such subjects as these in Christian preaching, that we should keep simply to the history of Christ and not meddle with doctrine. The life of Christ, they say, is sufficient in itself without these mysterious and metaphysical deductions from it.

Doctrine in the gospels. But if you consider the gospels by themselves, you will see that they could never be understood withwithout some doctrine—*i.e.*, instruction about their meaning. When Christ says, "Dost thou believe on the Son of God?" the hearer naturally asks, "Who is He, Lord?" Christ Himself presses the question—"Whom say ye that I am?" The answer given is doctrine. He tells them the meaning of His death, that it is "a ransom for many;" and He promises the Spirit of truth to guide them into all truth, to testify of Him, to take of the things that are His, and show them unto them. This, which is the teaching of the epistles, is thus implied in Christ's own plan.

Now, when we look at the epistles, one or two How presented in the epistles. things may guide us in dealing with Christian doctrine, so as to make it intelligible and interesting.

First, all their teaching starts from and returns to Christ. I need not prove this; you can verify it for yourselves. His life and death and resurrection penetrate everywhere, and are the roots of Christian faith and hope and practice. They are the river of life, by the side of which trees grow and blossom and fructify. If you can connect doctrine in this way with Christ Himself, it will be clear and fresh to everyone.

Further, they preach doctrine with an eye to the lives of men. It is varied according to the different churches, their circumstances, their faults, their temptations. The Romans, the Corinthians, the Galatians, the Hebrews, have their practical differ-

ences dealt with, and this holds not only in the
case of the churches, but in that of individuals.
Our preaching should be so adapted — close,
discriminating, individual, without being personal.
This, also, will give interest to doctrine.

Notice, again, how each writer or preacher has
his own bent, and yet the preaching is all the
while Christian.   Christ Himself has all the
elements ; the different preachers take their parts.
Of. the Sermon on the Mount, the practical side is
reproduced by James ; the warm, vehement appeal,
which is found in the address to the multitudes, is
taken up by Peter, both in the Acts and his
epistles ;   the teaching about redemption   and
the ransom is specially the work of Paul ; and
the spiritual insight belongs to John.   Christ and
Christ crucified are in all of them, but each has his
own manner.   We, too, should be true to our own
view, provided we are making Christ and His Cross
our centre.   So the breadth of preaching comes
out, and every true Christian minister secures his
sphere.

Lastly, we learn that we must study and think
if we are ever to preach well.   This is made
clear specially in the Pastoral Epistles, which are
indeed the Homiletics of the New Testament, and

deserve the minute attention of every minister. If there is any enthusiast who thinks he will be able to preach by trusting simply to the inspiration of the Spirit, or any genius who thinks it will come to him by intuition, or any sluggard who is waiting for something to occur, he may be undeceived by reading these letters of the great preacher Paul. The preacher may expect Divine help, but only in the use of all proper means. He is to stir up the gift that is in him; to give himself to reading and to meditation; to be nourished in the words of faith and sound doctrine; to make himself acquainted ever more with the Holy Scriptures, though he has learned them from a child; to distinguish all the relationships of life so that he may touch them with discretion; and in all things to study to show himself approved unto God—"a workman that needeth not to be ashamed, rightly dividing the word of truth." So good preachers were made at first under apostolic guidance, and so good preachers must be made to the end of the world. *Oratio, meditatio, tentatio.*

We shall now glance at the preaching of the early Church immediately after the time of the apostles. The period may be said to extend to the time of Origen, who was born in the year 185

The Post-Apostolic Church.

A.D., and with whom a new epoch in preaching commenced. Our information about the preaching of this period is somewhat scanty. It was a busy time; the disciples spread the knowledge of the Gospel, organised communities, met persecution; but they left few written records. The best account of Christian worship, and of the part preaching takes, is given by Justin Martyr, who was put to death at Rome in 165 A.D. It is our chief authority :—

The form of worship.

"On the day which is called Sunday, all the Christians inhabiting the towns or country assemble in the same place. The memorials (ἀπομνημονεύματα) of the apostles and the writings of the prophets are read as time permits. When the reader has finished, the president of the assembly delivers an exhortation and charges his hearers to imitate those holy examples. Then we all rise together and offer up prayers. After the prayer, bread is brought forward, and wine and water; the president then in his turn presents prayers and praises to God, according to his ability (ὅση δύναμις αὐτῷ), and the people express their assent by saying, 'Amen.' The Eucharist is distributed, and every one partakes of it, while the deacons carry a share to those who are absent. Those who possess worldly goods bring a free-will offering in proportion to their means. The offerings are collected and placed in the hands of the president, who, by this means, supplies the needs of the orphans and widows, of those who are in want through sickness or other causes, of those who are in prison, and of sojourners who are strangers. In a word, he is the helper of the needy" (Justin, Apol. i. 87-8).

Without entering into a minute consideration of this interesting passage, we may note these points. The meeting together on Sunday, elsewhere called the Lord's Day (κυριακὴ), is now established throughout the Christian Church. The disciples have a central place of worship where they all convene, if it can contain them. In some places they have several; in Rome, *e.g.*, at an early period, above forty. This place of meeting was called κυριακόν, the Lord's House, an adjective, the origin of our words Kirk or Church.* The name of the Lord is given both to the House and to the Day— in Latin *Dominicum* or *Dominica,* whence the French word *Dimanche.* The procuring of a separate meeting-place was gradual. At first they met in the synagogue, and they remained there if the

---

* Not from κυρίου οἶκυς, as has often been said.

people became Christian. If not, they adjourned
to some convenient place—to a large house of some
adherent, or to a hall, as "the school of one
Tyrannus." Then they began to erect places
of worship. These were constructed not on the
model of the Jewish Temple, which had separate
courts, nor of pagan temples such as the Pan-
theon, but like the Basilica or Court of Justice,
and hence early Christian churches are called
Basilicas. The form is an oblong, with a raised
place at one end occupied by the judge, and
in the Christian buildings by the president or
bishop or presiding minister, who in Justin's time
was the preacher. Before him was the lector,
whose duty it was to read the Scripture, and who
is still found in the French Protestant Church, as
he was in our early Scottish Church. His descend-
ant is the precentor or clerk. Next was a space
occupied by the Presbyterion or body of Presbyters;
then the company of the faithful, and farthest out
the non-Christian hearers. Justin's account of the
service is probably an abridged one, but we can see
that the sermon occupied a prominent place. It
was founded on the portion read by the lector, and
had two features—an explanation of the passage,
and an exhortation based upon it. It was partly

exegetical and partly hortatory. That the minister studied it beforehand, appears from the special praise bestowed by early writers upon men who were known to have preached on certain occasions without opportunity for preparation.*

The preaching, so far as we can judge from what Character of remains of it, was far beneath the epistles of the Preaching. New Testament in spiritual grasp, and very different from sermons of the present day. Of the teaching of the Apostolic Fathers, as they are called, and of their immediate successors, little remains to us. What we have is of a very simple kind—good, pious exhortation, without much force of thought or breadth of vision, and without any effort at artistic presentation. The light of inspiration has faded, and the human mind has not yet applied itself in its full power to God's revelation. They know that they have a great treasure in the field, but they have not yet explored the veins of gold, nor begun to smelt the ore in the crucible of reflection and to mould it into forms of beauty. It was, besides, a time of heavy · persecution, and the preaching was of the kind

* Eusebius (vi. 36) relates that it was not till Origen was sixty years of age that he allowed shorthand writers to report his lectures.

that such times require, calling men in few stern
words to a watchful course. In this and in other
ways, it was no doubt suited to the times and to
the audience, which could not be so Christianly
intelligent as that to which Paul addressed his
letters. A mixed audience, lower in intelligence
and tone, had pressed into the Church; and the
Christian thought of the time seems to have been
put not so much into sermons as into books, as we
find in many parts of Germany in our day. There
was a stage of this kind of preaching in Scotland,
though it came much later.*

Change in
Christian life.

During the latter part of this period, however,
the preaching altered greatly. Next to the Cata-
combs, perhaps the most interesting walk in Rome
for the student of Christian history is through the
gallery of the Lateran Museum, which contains
the early sepulchral monuments of the Christians.
One whole gallery is devoted to inscriptions and
emblems and sarcophagi, chronologically arranged.
At first they are very simply and rudely executed,
apparently in haste and fear, and often by the
hands of the poor and illiterate. The orthography
and syntax would have brought a sneer to the lips
of a Ciceronian or a . Platonist, though not perhaps

* *Cf.* Note A on page 53.

to the lips of Cicero and Plato, for through the rude forms the great hope is struggling to find expression—the hope which the Tusculan Questioner and Phædo would have rejoiced to trace. We have the simple words, " He departed to God," " My dear child fell asleep in Christ," with a lamb or a dove or a palm branch rudely etched above ; the years, the days, the very hours of a child numbered up, as if life had now received a new significance. But as we pass along the gallery we can read the gradual triumph of the Gospel. The style becomes correct ; the rude etchings blossom out into beauty ; the richly sculptured tombs carry us back to the classic times ; only, instead of Bacchus and the Satyrs—" Let us eat and drink, for to-morrow we die "—we have the resurrection of Lazarus, the feeding of the multitude, the appearance in the storm—" It is I, be not afraid."

A similar change shows itself in the preaching of the Church. For the simple-hearted Apostolic Fathers, with their persecuted flocks, we have men of learning and culture who addressed thousands of Greek and Roman citizens in the great basilicas, some of which still remain—that of Ambrose at Milan, St. Sophia at Constantinople, and some think the Mosque of Omar at Jerusalem. This

Development of Preaching.

E

is a new thing in the world's history. On the Areopagus and in the Forum thousands of men had assembled to listen to eloquent speech, but it was only of civil and secular things—nothing else would attract the masses. There had also been discussions on the gods and their nature, the soul and its essence, the supreme good and law ; but these had been among the few, in the groves of Academus or on the brow of the Alban Hill— "Others apart sat on a hill retired." But to find the multitudes eagerly listening to those questions, awake to the divine, the eternal, the burden of possessing an immortal soul—this was something new ; this could only come from the Great Preacher, His life, His death, His risen power. It was the fulfilment of His own word, " I, if I be lifted up from the earth, will draw all men unto Me."

Two centres of Preaching. In this period there were two great centres of preaching power—the one in the Eastern or Greek Church, represented by Origen, Basil, and, above all, Chrysostom ; the other in the Western or Latin Church, represented by Jerome, Ambrose, and Augustine. Of these, the most worthy of the attention of the preacher are Augustine and Chrysostom, and Chrysostom more that Augustine. Augustine was the greater man and divine,

Chrysostom the greater preacher. No one can read of the effect of his preaching in Constantinople without feeling that he was a mighty power. "As well want the sun from the sky, as want Chrysostom from our city," was the cry when he was banished; and yet he was constantly preaching to the conscience. The most accessible account of Augustine's idea of preaching is his own *De Doctrina Christiana*, especially the fourth book. The student who judges by modern standards will find indeed much imperfection. The form of the sermon has not been reached; it is rather a discursive lecture on a part of the Bible, with wide digressions. The treatise is also imperfect in doctrinal statements. Augustine is distinct on the broad questions of sin and grace, and powerful on the practical conscience. The life, the death, the resurrection of Christ, the Divine and human, are always prominent; but the ring of Luther, the jubilee trumpet of the Reformers, is not well heard. The interpretation of the Bible is not infrequently fanciful and far-fetched, though Augustine and Chrysostom are in this more sober than most of their predecessors. Exegesis was not the gift of that age. But they have a freshness and loftiness of thought, a vigour and brevity of expression, a

high conception of the grandeur of Christian truth
in its bearing on life, from which the preacher may
always receive inspiration.   They preached, moreover, to their own generation and to the conscience
of their hearers ; and, lastly, though they knew the
Greek philosophy well, and had benefited by the
training of its schools, they did not drag it into
their preaching.   They felt that they had found
a far higher Master, and they preached Christ.

Note A, see page 48.

In the Advocates' Library of this city (Edinburgh) you will find an old volume which contains the "Instructiones Sancti Columbani"—not of Columba, but a later disciple of his school, who visited France and Switzerland and the north of Italy, and preached both in Latin and in the vernacular. The "Instructiones" are generally brief, giving probably little more than the line pursued, and are headed in this way :—

Instructio VII. De caecitate hominis qui neglecto spiritu inservit corpori ; he begins with this strong apostrophe, O te caecam insaniam, O te caecam foveam, humanam voluntatem, quae accepta celas et data non reddis.

Instructio VIII. Quod ad coelestem patriam, viae praesentis finem festinandum sit.

Instructio IX. De Extremo Iudicio.

„ XI. De Dilectione Dei et proximi.

There is not much of what we should call profound or fresh thinking, but it is very earnest, very practical, and close up to the condition of the hearers ; and it must have sounded fresh enough to the ears of those wild Scots and Picts who, not long before, had been practising barbarities upon poor provincials whose wailing cries have come down to us.

LECTURE IV.

ORIENTAL CHURCH PREACHING

WE spoke last day of the character of preaching in the Christian Church down to the year 200. It was of a simple and natural kind, not aiming at what is called oratory, but rather pious exhortation founded upon the portion of Scripture read in the assembly of Christians. It might be compared to the addresses given at the ordinary prayer-meeting, and was no doubt adapted to the time when Christians were gathered together in small companies, exposed to persecution or newly escaped from it. It has no lesson for us in regard to art, but teaches much in regard to earnestness and adaptation to circumstances.

Character of the period.

The next period in preaching may be taken as extending from 200 to 600 A.D. The reason for selecting 600 is that about that time, the time of Gregory the Great, Bishop of Rome, we are at the

54

commencement of the middle age, when preaching undergoes a change, and declines till it almost disappears. You will understand that this is a gradual process. The decline can be traced before 600, and it is not at its lowest till long after that date ; but 600 is a marked epoch.

The period is a very long and important one, filled with great events and great contests, apologetical and polemical, with histories of councils, and of great men in all the fields of Christian thought ; but it is not with these that we have to do. Our concern is with the character of preaching, and with what illustrates it. We can, of course, only select a few preachers of the greatest name and influence, as typical of the time.

The Church of this period falls into halves— Contrast occasioned by geography, or, more properly speak- between Eastern and ing, by race—the Eastern and the Western Western Churches. Even during the unbroken unity of Churches. the Roman Empire, there were two influences at work. Though Greece was conquered, its language, its literature, its philosophy, remained and modified the thinking of the conquerors.* This influence was often of a very subtle and

* *Cf.* Horace, Epistles II. i. 156. Graecia capta ferum victorem cepit.

speculative kind, and became even more so from its proximity to the great mystical systems of the East,—the religions of Zoroaster and Mani, not to speak of others still more oriental. But with all this modification the mind of the West retained its own bias. It was more practical and humanistic. The East tended to ascend from the human to the Divine, the West to descend from the Divine to the human.

The greatest impulse to the separation of the Churches was given when Constantine transferred 330 A.D. the seat of empire from Rome to Constantinople. The jealousy of feeling widened till it led to the final breach which continues to this day. The histories of those two Churches have been very different. The Eastern began with wonderful brilliancy, but it was ere long clouded, and it has never returned to its first promise. The Western seemed at first likely to be engulfed and to disappear amidst the irruptions of the heathen hordes of the north. But its missionary zeal subdued these hordes and made them the greatest elements of its strength. It is through them, above all, in Europe and America and our far-off colonies that present history is fulfilling ancient prophecy, and giving to Christ the promise of the world's possession. Out of the eater has come forth meat, and out of the strong has come forth sweetness.

When Pilate wrote the inscription on the cross, it was in three languages—in Hebrew, in Greek, and in Latin. The word of God passed from the Hebrew and became more living in the Greek; from the Greek to a wider life in the Latin or great West; may we not expect that the life will return again and restore what has fallen, that it will revive the East and bring in Israel? The history of the human race is one of fall and recovery, and it would seem as if this were also to be the history of the Church. "And so shall they fear the name of the Lord from the west, and His glory from the rising of the sun."

We shall to-day confine ourselves to the preaching of the Eastern Church in its early period. After the year 200 A.D., there was a marked change in the character of preaching. It left its simple, unadorned form, and took to itself the helps of knowledge and rhetoric. The causes of this were various, and, so to say, inevitable. *Change in the Preaching of the Eastern Church. Causes.*

(1.) First, there was the great increase in the number of Christians. In spite of all the forces of *Increased numbers.*

persecution, and all the reproaches cast upon
Christianity, as they are indicated by the brief
descriptions of Pliny and Tacitus, and as they
come out more fully in Celsus and Porphyry, it was
taking possession of the cities and, ultimately,
of the country. The reason lay in the insuffi-
ciency of polytheism, and of the philosophies, to
satisfy the intellectual and moral want of the time.
There was a great void, and there were deep
desires which heathenism could not meet. There
was, besides, the life of the first Christians, which
overcame all calumny, so pure and loving and
self-sacrificing and steadfast to the death. And
I have no doubt that the preaching, simple as it
was, did its work. It brought before those who
stole in to hear it a new world and a new power—
the love of God in Christ and life eternal. But
its success involved a change in its character.
You cannot speak to a thousand people as you
can to a hundred. When a preacher has a
large basilica, and a sea of up-turned faces, he
must, in spite of himself, use some of the methods
of oratory.

Change in
the audiences.
(2.) Another cause of the change was the character of the new audiences. I remarked upon the
evidence of this in the Lateran inscriptions, which

are, at first, of a very unlettered or indeed illiterate kind, but begin, as time advances, to imitate the old classical sarcophagi, with different emblems. Partly, Christianity was raising its adherents through the character which it gave them; and partly, the upper classes gradually became Christian, till Constantine acknowledged Christianity as the state religion.* 323 A.D This change in the character of the audience affected the preaching by calling for adaptation to a different class of hearers. It became more cultured, and also, perhaps, less spiritual.

(3.) Preaching was also affected by the new The new races that were now receiving and dealing with races. Christian truth. God has made of one blood all nations of men, and the Gospel is adapted to the common needs of human nature; but each race has its peculiar character of mind. The Semitic has more of the intuitional—of direct vision; the Aryan, or Indo-European, more of reflection, of criticism, of philosophy. Although this contrast is frequently exaggerated, there is essential truth in it. The Gospel was now entering among the great races of the West—Greek and Roman, Teutonic and

* Some think it might have been better had he contented himself with the full toleration which he gave it eleven years before.

Celtic, somewhat as a clear ray from the sun
enters the atmosphere of the world to be reflected
and also refracted ; and refracted it was, in reason
and fancy and imagination, and all those forms of
human thought that are so wonderfully interesting
to the student of history. This was, no doubt,
part of a providential plan, that men might reach
the hidden meanings and far-reaching applications
which are laid up in the Gospel of Christ. It
showed itself, also, in the change which took place
in preaching, when it came more fully into the
possession of this new race.

We shall now proceed to mention the more
remarkable schools, and some of the preachers of
this period. There were two schools pre-eminent,—
Alexandria in Egypt, and Antioch in Syria.

The School of Alexandria. In the school of Alexandria, the first great name
that meets us—the greatest of the school indeed
—is that of Origen. Alexandria was at this
time one of the most remarkable cities in the
world. It was the meeting-place of the world's
commerce, where the East poured its treasures into
the lap of the West, and received in return, as it
still does, the products of industry. It was also
the meeting-place of ideas. The Greek philosophy
encountered the mystical and pantheistic creations

of the East, and soared into the speculations of
Gnosticism and Neo-Platonism, like the Alhambra
in Spain, and the Kremlin in Russia—gorgeous
and gigantic elaborations of fancy, where the
dreamy waves of the East break on the more
solid shores of Europe, and rise in showers of
sun-tinted spray.

Origen was born in the year 185 A.D., a time
when the advance of Christianity was calling forth
bitter persecution, both from the populace and from
the government. His father died as a martyr, and
it was with great difficulty that Origen could be prevented from offering himself also to death, yielding
to the spirit of the time. He learned more wisdom
afterwards, but he never abated in his fidelity and
zeal to the cause of Christ. He spent a life of
seventy years in continuous labour—lying down to
sleep among his books, and waking after brief
repose to study. He travelled, studying by the
way, to all parts of the known world, in quest of
learning—to Greece, to Rome, to Jerusalem and
the East. During the Decian persecutions, he was
imprisoned and tortured, and, after a history which
would make a strange romance, he died—worn
out with work and suffering—at Tyre, where his
tomb was long afterwards shown.

Origen, 185-254 A.D.

The character of his genius. There can be no doubt that Origen's mind, despite strange aberrations, was one of the greatest that have appeared in the history of Christianity. When he was a child he was taught by his father to read and commit daily to memory portions of the Bible; and the strange searching questions which he asked filled those who heard them with a kind of fear. As he grew up, this bold spirit of inquiry continued to manifest itself. He sought to master all the learning of his time, sacred and secular, but he handled it in the freest manner. He was a critic, a polemist, an apologist, a natural philosopher, a metaphysician, a speculator in theology and theosophy; but withal he was a sincere and devoted Christian, amid strange fancies, loving Jesus Christ as the Son of God with a single-hearted love. This is not the time to examine the system or rather the systems of theology which he propounded, touching the Trinity, the doctrine of sin, the Atonement, the intermediate state, and the final condition of souls and of the universe; but it may be said that many of the theories thrown out in later times are only fragments of his teaching. His mind had in it something of Plato, something of Jacob Böhme, something of Schelling; but still his heart was with Christ.

It is necessary to say this, in order that we may His place in the development of Preaching. understand his place in the history of preaching. Origen has been called the father of Christian preaching; yet he rarely wrote or delivered sermons, and he was never what would be termed a great preacher. I shall try briefly to explain how he stood related to the office and helped its progress. When he began his course, numbers of the heathen of the middle and higher ranks, as well as of the lower, were passing over to Christianity. They needed instruction, and cate-chetics became the most important part of the work of the Church. During most of his life, Origen devoted himself to imparting a knowledge of Christianity through the explanation of the Bible. Men and women gathered round him till his classes became little congregations, and his instructions took the form of lectures which reviewed the greater part of the Bible. So he became the founder of the popular exegesis or lecture, which deals with the Scripture on a sus-tained system of interpretation. Further, the kind of interpretation adopted by him sprang from the necessity of the time. The condition of the new converts required a higher kind of teaching than had sufficed for the first simple-minded Christians,

and led to the application of learning and philosophy and criticism to the interpretation of the
Bible.

His Mysticism. There was still another circumstance. In the
early Church the bare Jewish element largely
prevailed, and it induced a love of the letter, a
narrowing of the sphere of Christianity, a lowering
even of the nature of Christ, which would have
brought back a kind of modified Judaism. Its
common name was Ebionitism, and its successor
was the Arian system. To oppose this interpretation of the letter, Origen dwelt on the interpretation of the spirit, and found mysteries of knowledge—indeed a whole system of the universe—in
the sentences and words of the Bible. By this he
has become the father of all the mystics and mystical interpreters, who carry their fancies to the
Bible, and find in its words, and even in its
silence, endless allegories. On the one side, the
Bible is turned into hard clay in which nothing can
grow ; on the other, it is sublimated into a cloud
which takes the shape of the onlooker's fancy.

The School of We may pass to the other great school of the
Antioch.   Eastern Church, that of Antioch.

Antioch, in Syria, where the disciples were first
called Christians, was a great and noble city—so it

is named by Cicero—standing in a beautiful position on the river Orontes, noted then for its commerce, its wealth, and its intelligence, and noted
long afterwards for its varying fortunes in the wars
of Crusader and Saracen. Very early it became
decidedly Christian, and was the seat of several
famous bishops. The distinction of its school
from that of Alexandria was that it applied the
practical reason rather than philosophy or speculation to the interpretation of the Bible. It was,
therefore, more moderate in its treatment both
of the Bible and of Christian doctrine, accepting
those views of the nature of the Trinity, the
person of Christ, and the uses of the Bible, which
in the course of ages have prevailed, It differed
also in this, that while the teaching of Alexandria
was more for the learned, that of Antioch was
more for the people, and was, therefore, more
oratorical.

The great man of Antioch was John—in after Chrysostom,
ages Chrysostomus, "of the golden-mouth." He 347-407 A.D.
was born at Antioch in 347, and died in 407 A.D.
He was brought up in a Christian family, like
Augustine, by a devoted Christian mother ; though,
unlike him, he never wandered. He was trained
with great care in the learning of his day, and in

F

the schools of rhetoric. At one time he thought of
devoting himself to the Forum and to law, but
deep religious impression led him to give his great
abilities to the ministry of the Church. He studied
theology for three years under Meletius, Bishop of
Antioch, and for six years at a later period in the
silence of a monastery among the mountains. He
commenced his work of preaching when not much
under forty, being ordained as a presbyter in
386 A.D., so that he had only twenty years to do
his work and to acquire the name that has been
his ever since.

He had scarcely begun his work in Antioch
when he rose at once to the summit of his fame.
The crowds that thronged to listen to him were
immense, and he had to repress, by rebuke, the
applause which followed his eloquent appeals. He
was called to Constantinople (æt. 50), to take the
place of bishop and patriarch, and the great church
of St. Sophia was crowded with all classes, sometimes for days in succession. He denounced with
fearless honesty the vices of the clergy, the people,
and the court. He was banished by a faction of
the bishops and courtiers, but recalled in com-
pliance with the urgent demand of the people. *

* See page 51.

Through the persistent machinations of his enemies, and the hatred of the Empress Eudoxia, he was again banished in 404 A.D., and died in exile near Comana, on the bleak shores of the Euxine. Thirty-one years afterwards his body was brought back and buried amid the tears of the multitude.

It is evident from these few facts that the discourse of Chrysostom was of a different kind from that of Origen. It had not so much of teaching but more of preaching; less statement of truth or endeavour after it, more appeal to the feelings, the fancy, and the conscience. In this power he would seem to have been unrivalled. His appeals to the feelings held men enchained in interest, his brilliant declamation drew rapturous applause, and the pungency of his addresses to the conscience is attested by his repeated banishment. He was evidently a preacher who had in him the spirit of Stephen and Paul, and was willing to make men enemies by daring to tell them the truth. It is his first and highest praise that, with such power and popularity, he thought so little of them, compared with fidelity to his Master. He wrote a treatise on the Priesthood, Περὶ Ἱεροσύνης, the earliest surviving discussion of Homiletics. Although imperfect as

His preaching.

Its boldness.

compared with Augustine's, it is strong on this side, that the first duty of the preacher is to deliver God's message, to look for His approbation, and to think nothing of man's applause.   If the Eastern empire could have been saved from its corruptions, we can conceive of no more fitting instrument than Chrysostom.   *Si Pergama dextra defendi possent, etiam hac defensa fuissent.*   But it trampled him down, as Judaism did Stephen, to its ruin.

Its rhetoric.   The next excellence in Chrysostom was his great power of enlisting the feelings and exciting the imagination.   This largely came from his natural sympathy with what is pure and noble—an elevation of soul that gave him wings—but also partly from the careful culture of his oratorical powers which made him the first and perhaps the greatest master of pulpit rhetoric.   Yet his strength was the source of failings.   It often betrayed him into false glitter, forced antithesis, occasionally into hollow and affected pomp.   The Roman Catholic Church has set him up as a spotless model.   He was constantly before the eyes of ecclesiastical orators of the reign of Louis XIV., in his eloquence, if not in his honest truth-speaking.   Luther, on the other hand, calls him the "gilder," not the golden; but the truth lies between; indeed, when we think of his deep sincerity, it lies on the side of gold rather than gilding.

The weakest side of Chrysostom is the want of Its defect. Scriptural instruction in his sermons or homilies. He takes a portion of the Bible, says something about it, and then leaves it for digressions which, though interesting and eloquent, fail to bring out the depth and power of the Word of God in its bearing on the heart and conscience. This, again, was the fault of the time and school, rather than of the man. As Origen was led astray by philosophy, Chrysostom was led astray by art; and the best preaching would be that true treatment of the Word of God to which Origen pointed, with that application of it to the nature of man at which, after all, Chrysostom was sincerely aiming. The Christian Church has been slow in learning to preach, if she has learned yet.

There is still one man of the Eastern Church of Ephrem Syrus, whom something should be said, as typical of 308-373 A.D. Orientalism in its monastic and imaginative form: Ephrem the Syrian, called in the East Mor Ephrem—my lord Ephrem. If he belongs to any school it is to that of Antioch, but he has a place by himself. He was born after 306 and died in 373 A.D., and thus comes in time between Origen

and Chrysostom.   He belonged to the Syrian—*i.e.*,
Semitic race, and he is still regarded with reverence throughout the Christian East.   He is the
prophet of the Maronite Church, and his writings,
which have been translated into Armenian, are held
in the highest veneration.   They are very voluminous,* including poetry in the form of hymns, prose
in the form of commentaries, and homilies, some of
which are mid-way between poetry and prose, being
composed in a kind of rhythmical swing, resembling
the old ballads without the rhyme.   Ephrem was
born in a heathen family,† but he early became a
Christian, embraced the life of a hermit, which was
coming into favour in that troubled land and time,
retired to a cave near the city of Nisibis, on the
frontier of Persia, composed his works in that
solitude, and came forth to deliver or chant the
strange homilies that still remain.   At Edessa,
which was latterly the centre of his influence, he
had a hard battle to maintain against heathens,
heretics, and prevalent vices, and his homilies are

* Sozomen (Eccl. Hist. III. 16) says that Ephrem wrote
three million lines.

† This is the account given in the *Acta,* prefixed to the
Roman edition of his works, although it differs from the
statement made in his own *Confessions* (Opp. Gr. I.
129).

of a very practical kind.* Sometimes they are paraphrases of Scripture narratives, in a bold, dramatic style, that must have deeply affected such an audience. They remind one of the more elevated passages of Zachary Boyd, and still more of the Gospel paraphrases of the Saxon monk, Cædmon of Streaneshalch, of whom you will find a short account in Dr. Eadie's English Bible—the first versions, or rather paraphrases, of the Bible in our mother tongue. Ephrem does not seem to have known Hebrew or Greek,† and his knowledge of Scripture was from the old Peshito or Syriac version, to the elucidation of which his works are a great help. Unfortunately, I have none of his works near, and could make little of them if I had ; but I shall translate a few lines from Bassler's " Collection of Old Christian Poetry." It is on the appearance of the star to the wise men :—

---

* It was at Edessa that he adopted the plan of meeting the fatalistic heresies of the Gnostic Bardesan by composing popular and orthodox hymns.

† This point is discussed in the *Dictionary of Christian Biography.* One may also refer to Roediger's account of him in Herzog. Some of his homilies and hymns have been translated into English by the Rev. J. B. Morris and by the Rev. H. Burgess.

Suddenly shines a clear star in Heaven,
Strange and sparkling, smaller than the Sun,
But greater than he when its secret is known.
The star of the East shot forth its rays
To the land of darkness where men were groping,
And showed them the way to the soul's true light.
They offered their gold and received life eternal :
They worshipped and they went.
Two heralds had the Son of God,
The one in the height, the other here below ;
The bright star sang of Him in Heaven,
And John preached upon the earth ;
The heavenly guide showed majesty Divine,
The earthly showed Him made like to man.

We are far enough away from the cave on the
Persian frontier, and our time requires a different
kind of preaching; but it is something to know
that we belong to the same Church, and that the
Gospel, in a purer form, is finding its way back to
these Churches of the East.

LECTURE V.

WE propose to-day to consider the condition of preaching in the later Oriental Church, the causes of its decline, and its present prospects. We have looked at the two early schools, Alexandria and Antioch, with their two great figures, Origen and Chrysostom. Let us return to these and follow their course. We have seen that the characteristic of Origen was the mystic-allegorical. This marked his interpretation of the Bible. He looked on the letter as the shell, the inner sense as the kernel ; and he set himself to reach its meaning chiefly through the imagination. Scripture became the storehouse of cosmogonies, philosophies, and eschatologies, *prima, media, et ultima,* which had also, however, their application to human life. But knowledge rather than life is the aim of Origen, and he is the father of all the dreamers and system-makers.

73

Origen.   He had one of the most active minds that have appeared in the world. The first part of his life was spent in constant learning, the later part in learning and teaching. He taught for hours every day. His lectures on the Bible, from Genesis to Luke, were taken down by shorthand writers, chiefly ladies, and it is to them that we are most indebted for our knowledge of his teaching. One hundred and ninety-six of his homilies, chiefly on the Old Testament, have in this way been preserved. They witness to his wonderful learning, his fancy, his original genius, and must have excited a great commotion in the Christian thought of the time. A painful picture of the turbid after-currents is given by Kingsley in his *Hypatia*, but it should be said that in Origen himself the movement had a moral earnestness and a charity which it too often lost among those who followed.

When Origen died, the school divided itself, as generally happens, into a " left " and a " right." The "left" developed his method of allegorising and theorising, until Christianity passed into clouds and ether not unlike some forms of modern Hegelianism. The " right " took up the study of Scripture in a more sober spirit than Origen, and produced some great theologians and preachers. To this

side belonged the celebrated Athanasius. Some Athanasius,
few homilies of his remain, but compared with 296-373 A.D.
his other writings, they give an imperfect view
of him. Great controversialists are not always
great preachers. There were others of the
school of Origen much more important in this
respect.

The three greatest are nearly of the same age The Clover-
and of the same country, called the *Clover-leaf* of leaf of Cappadocia.
Cappadocia. They are Basil the Great, Gregory
of Nyssa, his brother, and Gregory Nazianzen, his
chosen friend.

Basil the Great, who died as Bishop of Cæsarea, Basil the
has left the highest name as a preacher, and was Great,
329-379 A.D.
compared by his contemporaries to Moses, Elijah,
and Paul. One of his chief productions in preaching remains to us—the *Hexaemeron*, Sermons on
the Six Days of the Creation, which describe the
animals with lively fancy, and present lessons for
human life, with reflections on the goodness and
wisdom of God. His brother, Gregory of Nyssa, Gregory of
has less mental power with a tendency to mysti- Nyssa,
335-395 A.D.
cism ; and Gregory Nazianzen, his friend, has less Gregory
imaginative power, with oratorical flights that rise Nazianzen,
325-390 A.D.
at times into the falsetto. In all of them the
influence of Origen is discernible in a kind of

cosmic rather than human handling, but this is more temperate in them than in their master.

Chrysostom. The other school, that of Antioch, produced the one great preacher of whom we have already spoken, John Chrysostom. He was a man, as we have said, of great honesty and zeal, admired and beloved by the people, feared by princes, envied by many of his fellows on account of his popularity, and disliked by them because of his secluded life and reserved manner. The people do not feel this fault ; fellow-ministers do. If a popular preacher is to be liked by his brethren, he must be very frank and human.

It should be said that what remains of Chrysostom cannot give us a full idea of his power. This is in a degree true of all men who have produced the most remarkable effect. They had the individuality, the fire of electric power, which no writings can reproduce. A sermon of Whitfield, say, or Chalmers, lies like a meteoric stone compared with the flash of the meteor. Chrysostom's sermons have come down to us chiefly through reporters ; and, preaching as he did almost daily, he had little time to correct and restore their proportion and point. Nevertheless they reveal to us his fearless moral earnestness, his power to interest hearers, his elevation of thought. When one reads or hears the sermons of a great preacher, it is not so much by the form as by the inspiration that one receives benefit, though no doubt the form intensifies the inspiration.

The greatest of the school of Antioch, after Chrysostom, is perhaps Theodoret, Bishop of Cyrus, in Asia Minor. He also owed much to a pious mother. He is noted in the controversies of the time, being a defender of the views of the Antioch School, and an opponent of the theory that two natures mingled in the person of Christ. The Divine, he said, took the nature of the human, but was not changed into the human. So he denied that the Divine could be said to be crucified or even born, though he yielded to the spirit of the time in giving to Mary in a modified sense the title Θεοτόκος, out of which sprang Mariolatry. His style as a preacher is simple and clear, but he tends to be too minute, and loses himself in detail till he reaches triviality. This is often a difficulty in preaching—to be graphic, without being small and shallow and becoming like the river Euphrates, smitten in the seven streams till men can go over dry-shod.

The last preacher of the Eastern Church whom we shall name is John of Damascus. We select

Theodoret, died 457 A.D

John of Damascus, died 759 A.D.

him because he marks an epoch. He was born at
Damascus, and lived at the court of the Arabian
Caliph, true to his religion. He is greatly praised
for his smooth and fluent speech, and is called
Chrysorrheus, the gold-flowing. In his preaching we
trace for the first time the influence of the Mahometan power, which has now seized a central city in
Syria. It is notable that many of John's sermons
are directed to the praise of the Virgin. He gives
an account of her birth and early life, of the minutest
incidents of her history, of her death, and her
assumption, with the most unquestioning credulity.

Defect of   The defect of the preaching of both schools
both Schools. has now fully appeared. It may be described in
one word as want of Scripturalness. Antioch had
less of this defect at first than Alexandria, but erelong no great difference could be discerned. A
portion of Scripture was taken to head the discourse, but it was not dealt with in the way of
reasonable interpretation and application to doctrine and life. There was a lack of instruction in
the great truths of the Gospel, and of the quickening that springs from them. This developed two
tendencies which have frequently reappeared from
the same cause. The one is towards the preaching
of nature and morality on a mere theistic basis, which

in our day would be called Broad-churchism ; the other is the laudation of saints and martyrs and ecclesiastical seasons, which in our day would be called High-churchism. These go on often hand in hand or by reaction, till the ecclesiastical gains the mastery, and Christianity hardens into a stiff clay crust. No doubt many Christians remained with a true life in the midst of all the coldness, and preachers could not take the Bible and the great facts of Christianity in any way for a theme without doing good ; but the good was neutralised and weakened by great defects and aberrations.

It is not our part to trace the history of the Eastern Church or Churches—of the Orthodox Greek with its own patriarch, the Russo-Greek with the Czar at its head, the Maronite, Armenian, Nestorian, and Coptic. It is enough to say that a great torpor has benumbed the preaching of this church for centuries. No great name stirring the hearts of the masses, and shining out to lands beyond, has appeared for more than a thousand years.* The Latin Church has had its Alcuins and Bedes, its Anselms and Bernards, its Fénélons and Bossuets ; the Protestant Churches have given to God's ordinance of preaching a place and a

The decline of Eastern Preaching.

* See Dorner's Hist. I. 18.

power unknown since the days of the apostles ; but in the East there have been no such men, no such movements. What is the reason of this? Are we to look for no change? We shall attempt to answer this question.

Causes. The reasons for the decline of preaching in the Eastern Church, and for that decline of the Church itself which always accompanies this, may be ranged under two heads—things within the Church, and events outside.

Polemical strife. 1. Within the Church there was fierce polemical strife. The first great controversies between Christians were in the East, and they were carried on with peculiar bitterness. I need only remind you of some names—Athanasius, Arius, Nestorius, Eutyches, Macedonius—and of the factions and fightings which took place around the most solemn questions that can be proposed to the thought of man. It was impossible but that such contests should have a hardening and petrifying effect ; and the first decline of Christianity began amid those furious polemics. Men could fight with less harm, as they did in the West, about Pelagianism and Augustinianism, about faith and works, and free-will and predestination, than they could about the person of Christ, the nature of the Holy Spirit, and the most sacred mysteries of the Christian faith. This brought them near to crucifying the Son of God afresh, and putting Him to an open shame.

It is right that the faith delivered to the saints should be defended, and, so far, these conflicts were unavoidable in the face of error; but if the conflict is to end in good, it must be conducted with some measure of charity. Otherwise, though orthodoxy be maintained, Christianity will suffer, for Christianity is orthodoxy *plus* charity. When the Apostle says, "Hold fast the form of sound words," he adds, "in faith and love which is in Christ Jesus."

If you ask here, how their polemics came to be so bitter, we answer,—so far, from the general spirit of the time, but specially from their ideas of the constitution of the Church. The political system of one great empire had led to the thought of a great external Church, with visible unity and an earthly head. To belong to this Church was to be within the pale of safety, and to be outside was to be lost. *Extra ecclesiam nulla salus.* This idea of outward unity to be maintained at any cost was asserted with persecuting violence both in the East and the West, and it spread even into the churches of the Reformation. But when men

The idea of external unity.

G

came to see that the unity of the true Church is
spiritual and invisible, that those who hold various
views in separate communities may yet constitute
the real Church of Christ, the chief reason for
pushing polemics to physical force and for excom-
municating others from the body of Christ disappears.   We may organise ourselves separately for
the sake of more harmonious worship and action ;
but we need not thereby unchristianise and un-
church one another, and so destroy that higher unity
which comes of charity, and of the exchange of
Christian service as far as this is possible.   Those
are chargeable with schism who exalt their outward unity into a denial of the Christianity of
those who are not within it.   And we may say
that those also are guilty of schism who persist in
remaining in a community when they have
abandoned its principles.   It is in the interests of
love, as well as of truth, that we should have
separate communities, co-operating in a catholic
spirit with one another.   This is "the unity of the
Spirit in the bond of peace."

Thus the idea of an imperial Christianity, like
that of Orbis Romanus, embittered those factions
and fightings.   We can trace its growth in the edicts
of the emperors of the East and the wars that

followed. It prevailed, no doubt, in the West with similar effects ; but through the weakness of the Popes it was later in asserting itself, and through the arrival of the Reformation it had a speedier antidote. This, then, was one great cause of the decline of life and of preaching in the East ; for life affects preaching, as preaching affects life.

Another cause of decay, closely connected with Dogmatism. this, was that the doctrines of Christianity were made into dogmas. This comes about in times of conflict, unless there be great charity and a high Christian life, and these were wanting in the Church of that day. If you ask the difference between a doctrine and a dogma, I should say it is this: a doctrine is a truth held for its practical value, a dogma is a truth held merely for its place in the creed. The dogma is *ut credam,* the doctrine is *ut vivam. E.g.,* the belief in the Trinity is a mere dogma if it is only the recitation of the Athanasian Creed, although that is good in its place, if you keep away the subtle distinctions and the anathemas ; but the dogma rises into a precious doctrine when we appropriate the promise, " I will pray the Father, and He shall give you another Comforter, that He may abide

with you for ever." Now, when a church passes
from doctrine to hard barren dogma, one of
two things happens—either there comes the torpor
of spiritual death, an ossification that penetrates
to the very heart ; or, if there be intellectual movement left, there comes a recoil, not merely from
dogma but from doctrine, and men pass under the
reign of rationalism ; they denounce the formalis-
ing of spiritual truth in any way, and give up
the hard shell of dogmatism for the formless gas
of negativism. The first of these has prevailed
in the East ; for a time it affected the West also,
until there the Reformation came to give dogma
the life of doctrine.

Ecclesiastic-
ism.

There is still another cause common to both
East and West, but prevailing first, and most
strongly, in the East. When the great truths of
Christianity became dead dogmas, and men ceased
to have a living interest in them, there sprang up
an abnormal brood of subjects which became
matter of study and preaching, but hindered
instead of helping the Christian life. There were
the questions of the merits of saints and martyrs,
and orations on these took the place of Christian
preaching. There were the practices of asceticism ;
the exact time of the keeping of Easter ; the

forms of the Tonsure; the question of the difference between adoring an image and a picture; the
number of days and weeks for fasting; the forms
of genuflection; and all the blind, creeping things
that spring up when life goes and corruption comes.
Good men, and even great men, occupied themselves with these themes in that age of littleness
and decay. So the shadows fell East and West,
but in God's providence the West has had an
earlier dawn.

2. We come now to a cause of decline in the Failure of
Eastern Church which lay in outside events. There missionary
spirit in the
was a marked difference between the ways in East.
which the West and the East met the wants of
heathen masses. In the West, the Goths, the
Vandals, and the Franks were more open at the
time to Christianity; while the Church there had
more life to labour and preach, her corruption not
having as yet sunk so deep. There is probably
truth in both explanations. The Western races
were then more susceptible, and the Church
had more of a living missionary spirit; thus
these races, when converted, became a source of
new strength and life. We cannot tell how much
we owe to men like Ninian and Columba and
Boniface, who went out into the deep dark around

In times of decay and failing faith, the zeal of the missionary brings in new tides of life.

But in the East it was otherwise. The hordes of barbarous races that came rolling in—Saracens, Turks, and Tartars—were, by temperament or circumstances, less susceptible of Christian influence; and the Eastern Empire had to breast the first rush of that terrible series of waves. But worse than this, Christianity had become so corrupt and effete that it could do little or nothing to win them for the Gospel. If there had been a living active Church, Mahometanism would either never have arisen, or would have been limited in its sphere. The stern, simple Monotheism of Mahomet came in as a recoil from the idolatrous saint-worship of Eastern Christianity; and the corrupting luxury and weak, unmanly asceticism of people and priests went down like a barrier of sand before the fanatic sweep of the Saracen armies. But worse than the Saracens were the Turks who followed. The Saracens gave the Turks the fierce bigotry of their religion without communicating to them the civilisation which they then had, and the stolid weight of Turkish despotism has lain like a curse upon the East ever since. The struggle of Christianity has been to live, and the wonder is that it has survived. It has survived under the Turks, but in a state of torpor alternating with torture ; and under the Czar, in a state of torpor which has had no alternative, through that protecting pressure and jealous super-intendence which is often as hurtful as persecution.

And yet, since it cannot but be for some end in God's providence that sixty millions of professing Christians are still preserved in those lands of the East, let us briefly consider what are the prospects of Christianity and, with Christianity, of preaching in the land of Origen and Chrysostom.

The prospect of the East.

There is no doubt that both civil and religious liberty are making their way through those countries in the midst of, and often in spite of, man's struggles to repress them. The day of the conquering Saracen and Turk is far in the past, and it would be impossible to repeat what took place little more than fifty years ago, when the Patriarch of Constantinople, his clergy, and 30,000 Christians were massacred in cold blood. The religion of Mahomet is shewing signs of a fatal decay, fatal because it is connected with its first principles,—not like that of Eastern Christianity, with a departure from them. These principles are a sensual paradise, degraded womanhood, and the

Turkey.

fusion of the religious and the political in such a way that the fall of the political is the fall of the religious. It is not with it as with Christianity, which can live without pope, king, or emperor. The Caliphate of the Sultan, the spiritual chieftainship of the Mussulmans, decays and dies with his secular power. Life may survive for a while in the extremities, but the head is wounded to death. Christianity, in its most extreme State Church form, in its most Erastian conjunctions, is not thus vulnerable.

Russia.　　If we turn to Russia, again, where the majority of Eastern Christians are to be found, we can see a great change imminent. The only way in which society can be maintained in that country is by the granting of constitutional government; and, with this, religious liberty must enter. It is impossible for us to say what the results will be, but almost any change in religion will be for the better. From what we know of the sects in Russia, there is life waiting to break forth. Those Eastern lands have a deep spirit of devotion, which takes abnormal and superstitious shapes under repression, but which, with the Bible and clear Christian teaching, may, and we believe will, come out with a power we have never yet seen.

There are two methods by which the West is Western influences—even now seeking to influence the East. The one By Church is that of the Church union, in which the union. hierarchies are negotiating, as they have often negotiated to no purpose before, to bring the Anglican and Greek Churches together. This is a movement of priests without the people, and history tells us that such movements never succeed. If a system of hierarchies and of ritualism has reduced Eastern Christianity to its present level, we need not expect that the reassertion of those influences will elevate it. When liberty and light come, in the natural course of things, there will be a reaction to the other and older side,—to the life and light of the great Eastern dawn. The people will desire not more ritualism, but less.

The second way of approaching them has given By missions. us proof of this. Those who come in contact with Russians of the more educated class speak of the desire which they have for simple Gospel truth; and the little churches, planted chiefly by American missionaries, in Asia Minor and Egypt, among Armenians and Copts, tell of a fuel there ready for the kindling. We live in great times. As Jean Paul has said, "The times are great if the men are not." But God will send us the men,—

in the West men of power to shake us from our
apathy, and in the East men with Chrysostom's
eloquence, but in happier days. Meanwhile let us
not be moved away from the hope of the Gospel, or
from the simplicity of Scriptural truth, the loss of
which has brought about such long decay, and the
recovery of which has given us all that we possess.
We spoke the other day of the history of Israel
and Judah, as applicable to the history of Scotland
and England; but on a larger scale we may apply
it to the East and West. The East has been
trodden, like Israel, under the feet of invading
hordes, and led into a long captivity; while the
West, like Judah, has had its great prophets of the
Word of God, its preachers, and its teachers.
But though there are long circuits in Divine
Providence, they have a destined end, and the
times seem to point to a union of these far-divided
branches of the Church of God. "In His day
Judah shall be saved, and Israel shall dwell
safely: and this is His name whereby He shall
be called, The Lord our Righteousness"—this,
this the name that must guide preaching if it is to
be strong against rationalism and ecclesiasticism,
the one name under Heaven given among men
whereby we must be saved!

LECTURE VI.

WE have spoken of the preaching of the Eastern Church in the time of its fullest blossom; of its decline; and of the reasons why there has been no revival until now, when we see promise both in political events and in internal tokens.

We come to the Western Church, and we take The two the period from 200 to 430 A.D. By the Eastern Churches distinguished Church we understand generally, that which began by language. to develop itself through the Greek language; by the Western, that which employed the Latin. In both Churches there were exceptions. In the East there was preaching in the Syriac, the Armenian, the Coptic; in the West, in the Celtic and Germanic tongues; but Greek and Latin were the great central languages; the greatest preachers spoke in them, and by far the largest amount of

91

homiletic literature has come to us through these channels. The gift of tongues at Pentecost was a prophecy that fulfilled itself slowly in the history of the Church.

The era of preaching later in the West.

There is a question that presents itself whenever we turn to consider the preaching of the West—viz., why did the great era of preaching come later than in the East?

Reasons.

I shall try briefly to answer this. One reason was that Christianity was later in reaching the West with full power. Almost all the epistles of the New Testament were written to Eastern or Greek-speaking churches. There is indeed only one epistle to a Western church, the Epistle to the Romans, and it is in Greek, no doubt because so many early converts used that language. This is an indication of what took place in the early history of Christianity. It found its way westward with wonderful power, but somewhat slowly, and this naturally affected the development of preaching.

Another reason connected with this was that the schools of learning in the East were sooner brought under Christian influence, and made available for the training of Christian preachers. We have already referred to Alexandria and

Antioch, but the chief cities of Greece and Asia Minor had similar institutions. There were, no doubt, also in the West many such schools,—at Rome, at Carthage, at Marseilles, and elsewhere ; but, partly because these had a strong Greek infusion, and were therefore not suited to those who had to speak to Latin audiences, and partly because they retained longer the non-Christian spirit, they were not so soon engaged in training a cultivated Christian ministry.

There was still a third reason belonging to the same class. The great documents of Christianity, the New Testament and the Septuagint, were in Greek, and it was only by degrees that they found their way into Western tongues, through the Vulgate and the Moesogothic. To the great West the language of the Bible was for a considerable time foreign and unknown. This affected also the early Christian literature. Little was written to develop the intelligence of a Christian public inclined to listen to a higher style of preaching, and it is from an intelligent Christian public that a high class of Christian preachers is produced. All this naturally took place later in the West than it did in the East. I do not mean that there was no Christian teaching or preaching, but it

continued longer on the simple basis of the first
two centuries, and resembled somewhat that which
we seek to carry on through native catechists and
preachers in India and China. It is after Christianity has laid hold of the masses, and has possession
of schools and of a native Christian literature, that
great preachers arise.

The era ot preaching longer in the West.

    This may be a fitting place to glance at the
kindred questions, why the line of great preachers
was not cut off in the West as it was in the East,
and why those two different states of Christendom
present so striking a contrast at this day in regard
to the influence of preaching, and in regard to the
consequent activity of Christian life? You will
understand that I do not mean to ignore the
Providence of God, and the quickening power of
His Holy Spirit, but I speak of causes which we

Reasons.

are able to trace. I mentioned as one reason for
the decay of spiritual life, and therefore of
preaching among Eastern Christians, the bitter
polemical struggles in which they became involved.
Conflict was inevitable, but the spirit in which it
was carried on, about the most solemn truths that
relate to the nature and person of Christ, had a
hardening effect which was seen in the dead state
that followed the Athanasian and Nestorian

controversies. This is a lesson for us in our preaching. The West got the benefit of this struggle without paying the full cost, for though it had its Arian controversies, they were not as a whole marked by the same factious spirit, and left large room for the preaching of a simple and practical Christianity. The questions agitated in the West, about original sin and free-will and grace, were bitter ‚enough, but passion when stirred by such topics is less hurtful to the spiritual nature.

The next great cause why the West has not suffered the same eclipse in its preaching and spiritual power—and I must repeat that those two always go together—was the providence of history. It is right that we should recognise God's hand in these things. There were two great battles, to speak of no more, on which, so far as we can see, the fate of all Christian Europe depended. The first was on the field of Châlons in the north of 451 A.D. France, when Attila and his Huns were defeated by the Roman General Aetius, but chiefly through the aid of the Gallic and German peoples.*

* Gibbon (chap. 35) says that the exaggerations of Idatius and Isidore, who reckon the slain at 300,000, justify the historian's remark, that whole generations may be swept away in a single hour by the madness of kings.

Jornandes, the Gothic historian, gives the number slain at 162,000, which is not thought by modern historians to be an exaggeration, for it was a battle of continents. The popular mind was so impressed by the bloody pertinacity, that a weird story rose of the spirits of the slain fighting for three days in the air over the field of battle, and Kaulbach has made it the subject of his great fresco painting of the Hunnen-Schlacht, at Berlin. The 732 A.D. second battle was at Tours, where Charles Martel, who gained his name from that fight, defeated the Saracens under Abdalrahman.* The Mussulman power had conquered all the north of Africa, had advanced through Spain like a nation in movement, and the question seemed to be,—Will Europe for the time be Mahometan or Christian? The battle lasted seven days, and it is said that fully 300,000 Saracens were left on the field. It saved Europe from the fate of Asia Minor and the East.† I do not say that, even if these battles had

---

* *Cf.* Gibbon, chap. 52, and Milman's *Latin Christianity*, Book IV. chap. 9.

† A victorious line of march, says Gibbon, had been prolonged above a thousand miles from the Rock of Gibraltar to the banks of the Loire; the repetition of an equal space would have carried the Saracens to the confines of Poland and the Highlands of Scotland. . . . The Arabian

been lost, Christianity would have perished ; for, apart from the direct movement of God's hand, there is a moral power in Christianity which insures its victory in the end. Frederick the Great's saying that "victory always goes to the strongest battalion," is frequently untrue in the immediate issue, and always in the final result. The victory goes in the end to the strongest moral force, and this is one proof that there is a God. But those battles insured for Europe a quicker religious development, and saved it from the long winter through which Eastern Christianity has passed. They did for Europe what Joshua did for the old prophets and teachers ; what Wallace and Bruce and John Knox did for Scotland. They gave a field, and guarded the unfolding life from being trodden down by barbarous hordes. *Te Deum Laudamus*, has often been desecrated on battle-fields, but I think we might have joined in it on the fields of Châlons and Tours.

The third influence that has made the West different from the East in the history of preaching is the Reformation. I shall, meantime, do little

fleet might have sailed without a naval combat into the mouth of the Thames. Perhaps the interpretation of the Koran would now be taught in the schools of Oxford.

H

more than name it.   It was intimately connected
with the events of which we have been speaking,
having its roots in the far past; but it was also
the inspiring breath of God, and it has made
preaching within the Roman Catholic Church, and
still more outside it, the chief Christianising power
of modern civilisation.   Thereafter, whether men
took the side of the Reformation or not, it was
necessary that they should preach ; and evermore,
in these days, the Church that cannot and will not
preach, and preach well, must go down.   The
Eastern Church has not yet had her Reformation.
Let us pray that the dayspring from on high
may soon visit her, to give light to them that sit
in darkness.

Western
Preaching.

Having traced some causes of the differences
between East and West, we shall now return to
the course of preaching in the West, selecting the
three most important names.

Cyprian,
200-258 A.D.

The first is that of Cyprian, Bishop of Carthage.
He was born, probably near Carthage, of heathen
parents; became a Christian; and, after a bishopric
of thirteen years, suffered martyrdom with great
courage.   He had a short but very active time
of work, being occupied in the keenest ecclesiastical and doctrinal discussions.   He adopted

what we should call " High Church" principles
in the matter of the Church, and in his view
of the Sacraments; opposing the power of the
presbyters and people on the one side, and
the authority of the bishops of Rome on the
other. His life is specially significant, therefore,
for Church history. We have, however, to form
an opinion of him as a preacher at second-hand,
for it is doubtful if any of his sermons survive;
but we have some of his work akin to sermons, and
we have references to him by Augustine, in his
Doctrina Christiana, and by Lactantius. Augustine quotes him, and praises him highly; Lactantius
says of him, " One man stood forth chief and
illustrious, since he had acquired great glory
from his profession as an orator, and he wrote
many admirable things of his own kind. He had
a ready, copious, and pleasant faculty, and that
clearness which is the greatest excellence in a
discourse, so that it would be difficult to say
whether he was more ornate in stating, or ready
in illustrating, or powerful in persuading."* The
significance of Cyprian in the history of preaching, His signifi-
is that he was the first, or one of the first, who cance in the
history of
preaching.

* Lactantius *De Iustitia,* V. I. *Cf.* Augustine's *Sermons,*
312-4.

introduced oratory into the preaching of the
Western Church.* This was owing to his previous training as a secular orator, and also to his
natural temperament, which was of an ardent kind.
It is noteworthy that we owe to Africa the first
marked step in the preaching of both Eastern and
Western Churches. The faults of Cyprian are that
he falls into Origen's allegorising style in explaining
Scripture, and that he shews a one-sided extreme-
ness which belonged to his fiery character. But
he had a true idea of what preaching should be,
as will be seen by a short quotation from one of his
letters: "In courts of law, in platform speeches,
the resources of eloquence are at the disposal of
voluble ambition, but when the voice is raised
about our Lord and God, its pure sincerity aims at
conviction, not by the strength of eloquence, but
by realities. In a word, lay hold not of what
is elegant, but of what is powerful; not of
things that are coloured by polished speaking, so
as to allure a popular audience, but of things that
have the simplicity of unadorned truth, and set
forth the Divine compassion."†

---

* He is said to have edited a phraseological dictionary of
Cicero for the use of Christian preachers.
† Cyprian *ad Donatum*, chap. ii.

The second name we take is a remarkable one— Ambrose, that of Ambrose, Bishop of Milan, born probably 340-397 A D at Trèves, in Gaul. The story of his life gives a curious picture of the time. His father was " Prefect of the Gauls," and the young Ambrose was destined for a civil career. The quarrel between the orthodox and the Arian parties was running high at Milan after the death of one of the bishops (Auxentius), and Ambrose, then thirty-four, was sent to still it. His wisdom and decision were such that the people raised the cry, "he shall be our bishop," and, after vain attempts at refusal, Ambrose yielded. He had received no religious training, he could scarcely be called a professing Christian, and the whole procedure shows how Paganism and Christianity were blended within the Church. But Ambrose was a sincere man, and with all his might he strove to qualify himself for his office. He began to study the Bible, and took for his masters Origen, Athanasius, and the Cappadocian Clover-leaf, especially Basil. It is not our part here to tell how he became a great prince and power in the Church, through the assertion of its independence as against the civil authority ; how his anti-Erastianism, long before the time of Erastus, has been celebrated in painting and speech; and how he has made famous the old Basilica at Milan, from the door of which he repelled the emperor. These are for Church As a preacher. history. As to his preaching, it shows such defects as we might expect from what has been said. Augustine, who was bound to him by ties of deep reverence and affection, praises him beyond measure.* It is the custom also of Roman Catholic historians to speak of his sermons as spotless models, but they are of comparatively little value for us, either in their contents or in their form. They are marred by the deep defect of the Origen school—endless and lawless allegorising. *E.g.*, he has twenty-two sermons on the 119th Psalm. In the division into sections of eight verses, he finds mysteries of the unity and purity of the Christian life, because the eighth day was the day of purification; and then he finds mystical meanings in every letter. But with all this, there are many sweet wells and green spots of true religion, with a tendency to the practical which often carries him from the school of Alexandria to that of Antioch. The two chief merits of Ambrose are—that he gave us church music, and that he helped to give us Augustine.

* See his *Confessions*. Book IX.

Augustine, Bishop of Hippo, in Africa, his Augustine,
native land, was born at Tagaste. Augustine is 354-430 A.D
the greatest figure in the Christian Church from
its origin to the Reformation, and his life and
work deserve the study of every minister. Their
chief features are well known—his early youth and
the influence of his mother, Monica—his fall
through sensual passion into sin and unbelief—his
recovery through the influence of Ambrose, and
the voice that sent him to the Bible (first of all to
Romans xiii. 13)—his subsequent life of thought
and toil and battle. These are best described in his
own book of *Confessions*, which must be ranked
beside the *De Imitatione Christi*, Pascal's *Pensées*,
and Bunyan's *Pilgrim's Progress*, among the great
classics of the Universal Church.

Augustine rendered more important service to
preaching than any other before the time of the
Reformation. He has left 394 sermons, and the
notices of him tell of his power as a preacher. At
meetings of bishops the sermon was always assigned
to him. His preaching was brief, as befitted
the impatient, fiery Africans whom he addressed,
but it was pregnant, and often called forth that
applause which was a feature of the time, and not
the best. Yet he was not free from the faults of

his age. He did not escape the spirit of allegorising, though he had less of it than many others,
and he shared that ascetic and superstitious
tendency which deepened in following centuries.
It is possible for both Romanists and Protestants
to appeal to him, though, as I think, he was much
more of a Protestant than of a Romanist. The
spirit of Paul flowed through him to Luther and
Calvin, to Pascal and Arnauld and the Jansenists,
to Baxter and Howe, and to our own Secession
fathers and Chalmers. They were all of one spirit
and one Church.

His place in
the develop-
ment of
preaching.
The merits of Augustine, so far as the development of preaching is concerned, were very great—
(1.) There was his strong adhesion to the Word of
God, which, with all his wanderings into allegory,
he grasped in the breadth and depth of its meaning.
(2.) There was the emphatic impulse which he
gave to instruction in truth and to impression
through it, as opposed to the arts of the mere
orator. (3.) There was an apprehension of the
great antithesis of sin and grace, of man's fall
and the redemption through Christ, which must
always be the central theme of preaching, and
round which it may circle with infinite variety.
(4.) There was the intense moral earnestness and

deep spiritual insight by which he searched the
hidden man of the heart, as from his own self-
knowledge. These points suggest the broad
lessons we have to learn from Augustine as a
preacher.

But more important as a study for us is his own His idea of
idea of preaching, as given in the *De Doctrina* preaching.
Christiana. While Chrysostom's treatise on the
Sacred Office contains some excellent thoughts as
to the motives that should govern the preacher's
mission, Augustine's work is really the first Manual
for Preachers that was written in the Christian
Church. As such it deserves careful reading, and,
though we now have many works more fitted to
our time, there is no one of us who may not derive
guidance and stimulus from it. It shows the
wonderful genius of the man, that he should be so
far in advance of his own age and even of later
ages, and that in many things he should come close
to our own. The work consists of four books ; the
first three are occupied with the method of discovering matter for preaching, *modus inveniendi quae
intelligenda sunt ;* the fourth and last, with the mode
of setting it forth, *modus proferendi quae intellecta
sunt.* In the third book, however, he also discusses
such points as, how the pronunciation of one who

reads the Bible in public may affect the interpretation of it by the hearer.

Its substance and form.

In dealing with "the discovery of truth," he gives directions for the searching of Scripture, and discusses both the substance of the truth and the forms through which we have to reach it—words and symbols. Here he virtually lays down the Protestant principle, that all preaching is to be founded on the Word of God; the sound rule of interpretation that we must pay regard to the unity of Scripture,—*i.e.*, the "analogy of faith;" and the obligation to use such human means as language, history, and logic, in dependence on God's help. In the fourth book, on "setting it forth," he gives illustrations from Scripture itself, and from Ambrose and Cyprian. He applies to Cicero for rules of speech, but draws the distinction between *sapientia*, the divine wisdom, and *eloquentia*, the best human expression. *Sapientia* without *eloquentia* will do good; *eloquentia* without *sapientia* will do no good, and will often do harm; but the union of *sapientia* with *eloquentia* must be our ideal. He closes by showing that the life and earnestness of the preacher himself are the greatest and the hidden power.*

* *Habet autem ut obedienter audiatur quantacunque gran ditate dictionis maius pondus vita docentis:* chap. xxvii.

It should be said that the fourth book was not written at the same time as the others, but nearer the close of his life, so that it shews us the result of his own experience as a preacher. Here are some headings of the pages :—The duty of a Christian teacher—Wisdom of more importance than eloquence to the Christian orator—The sacred writers unite eloquence with wisdom—The cultivation of perspicuity of style—The aim of the orator is to teach, to delight, and to move*—The spirit of the hearer must be stirred—The Church teacher should pray before his sermon—Human direction not to be despised, though God makes the true teacher—The Christian teacher must use different styles on different occasions—Examples of various styles drawn from Scripture and from teachers of the Church.

One meets with such thoughts as these : " If a man desire to speak not only with wisdom, but also with eloquence (and assuredly he will prove of greater service if he can do both), I should rather send him to read and hear and practise himself in imitating eloquent men, than advise him to spend time with the masters of rhetoric, but only if his

Some of his sayings.

---

* He quotes loosely the maxim of Cicero—*Est igitur eloquens qui ita dicet ut probet, ut delectet, ut flectat.*

models are wise as well as eloquent." "It is especially necessary for the man who is bound to speak wisely, even what he cannot say eloquently, to retain in memory the words of Scripture ; for the more he discerns the poverty of his own words, the richer ought he to be in the words of the Bible, that he may prove his own statements from them, and that, though defective in what is his own, he may so far gain power by the testimony of the great." "As soon as the speaker has ascertained that what he says is understood, he ought either to bring his address to a close or to pass on to other topics." "A true teacher prefers to please by matter rather than by words ; nor should he think that a thing is well said except in proportion to its truth ; the teacher should be the master not the servant of his words, lest, as the apostle says, the Cross of Christ should be made of none effect." *

And thus he concludes : "This book has extended to a greater length than I expected or desired, but the reader or hearer who finds pleasure in it will not think it long. He who thinks it long, yet is anxious to know its contents, may read

* *De Doctrina Christiana*, Book IV., chaps. v., x., xxviii. ; the first of these quotations is abbreviated.

it in parts. He who does not care to be acquainted with it should not complain of its length. I, however, give thanks to God that, with what little ability I possess, I have in these four books striven to depict not the sort of man I am myself (for my defects are very many), but the sort of man he ought to be who desires to labour in sound—*i.e.*, in Christian doctrine, not for his own profit only, but for that of others also."

This was the tide-mark of Homiletics for many a day, and I commend it to your reading.

LECTURE VII.

WESTERN CHURCH PREACHING—MIDDLE AGES.

IN this lecture, the last of the Session, we must cover a very long period—from the death of Augustine to the Reformation.

Division of period. It may be divided into two, from the death of Augustine to the time of Charlemagne, and from the time of Charlemagne to the Reformation.

First section, 430-800 A.D. In the earlier half of the period, the three chief figures are Leo the Great, Gregory the Great, and Bede. Leo the Great was Bishop of Rome, Leo the Great, 395-461 A.D. or Pope, as he was now frequently called, for twenty-one years. He is the first Pope of whom we have any Homiletic remains, and he has left ninety-six sermons. The style of his sermons is His preaching. peculiar. They are generally very brief, they sometimes have no text, and they aim at a kind of antithetic smartness, which must have pleased the ear, but which to us seems puerile, and is often gained at the expense of justness of thought and clearness

110

of ,statement. In the choice of topics, too, his sermons are much beneath those of Chrysostom and Augustine. They are occupied with ecclesiastical days, saints' festivals, the dignity of the Virgin, the merit of alms-giving and fasting, and the pains of purgatory. A new class of .materials takes the place of the practical appeals of Chrysostom, and the deep experience of Augustine.*

Gregory the Great stands much higher. He was a man who had all the learning of his time, but was none the less entangled in its faults. His early life was first devoted to study, and then to the severe duties of the cloister. When raised to the Popedom, he befriended the monastic orders† and sent them out on their missions of preaching. There still stands in the Gregorian Way, between the *Via Sacra* and the *Via Appia*, the church from which it is said he sent out that Augustine who became the apostle of the Anglo-Saxons, and whose follower, Wilfrith, came into collision with the Culdees of Iona at Whitby. You recollect the story—how he

Gregory the Great, 540-604 A.D.

---

* Milman (Book II. chap. iv.) estimates Leo's sermons more highly.

† In him, says Milman (Book III. chap. vii.), monasticism ascended the Papal throne.

saw some fair-haired captives in the Forum, and
learned that they were called Angli.

"*Angli?* yes, angels indeed. From what province?"

"*Deira.*"

"Yes, *de Dei ira* they must be saved. And their
King?"

"*Aella.*"

"Alleluia must be sung in his dominions."

His relations to preaching.　Gregory attached much importance to preaching.
His constitution had been weakened through fasting and austerity, and he had sometimes to give the
sermons he composed to others to read. But he
made great exertions to deliver them himself, as the
sermon, he says, has most effect when given by
the person whose it is. Gregory has left a book
on preaching, far inferior to that of Augustine, but
so highly esteemed that it was translated into the
Frankish, the Anglo-Saxon, the Greek, and other
tongues.* It is not so much on Homiletics as on
Pastoral Theology, or rather cases of conscience,

---

* *Liber Regulae Pastoralis;* it is in four parts, and is addressed to a certain Bishop John. Leander of Seville circulated it in Spain. Mauricius had it translated into Greek.
Several Gallic synods appointed it to be read by all bishops.
Hincmar of Rheims, in the 9th century, says that a copy of it
was always delivered to bishops at their ordination.

showing how to deal with different ages and states of mind according to the ideas of that time. His own sermons, of which many remain, are superior to those of Leo, as they keep closer to Scripture and seek to give a practical application of it. But the exegesis is often of the most extravagant kind, not merely three but seven senses being found in the passage, one within the other—historical, moral, spiritual, mystical, analogic, anagogic, and so on. He deals with such questions as, Why the angel at the grave of Christ sat on the right hand, and What is the significance of the 153 fishes that Peter caught. His style, however, is natural and popular.

Reference has already been made to the preach- Bede, ing of the descendants of Columba,* which seems $^{673\text{-}735}$ A. D. to have been on the whole more Scriptural and practical than that which prevailed elsewhere, and I may here speak of Bede whom we are accustomed to term the Venerable. If you are a day or two in Newcastle, you will find two places of antiquarian interest. Besides the remains of the famous Wall of Hadrian, of which a worthy Presbyterian elder has published the best account, there is the Church of Ceolfrith, in Jarrow, where Bede lived,

* See pages 48 and 53.

read, wrote, and died.   He was perhaps the most
learned man of his time—a good Latin and Greek
scholar; a geographer and an historian, as far as
geography and history could then go ; a musician
and a poet. His great work is an Ecclesiastical History of Britain, which gives us the fullest and most
faithful view which we have of the early condition of
our country, for he was a painstaking and thoroughly
His sermons. trustworthy man.   His sermons, of which we are to
speak, are in Latin, and were, therefore, probably
meant for the clergy.   He preached and wrote
poetry in Anglo-Saxon, but unfortunately nothing
of this is left.   The sermons are brief homilies,
giving a simple commentary on a portion of
Scripture.   Their lessons are sometimes very good,
although over and over again the allegorising
spirit of the time comes in and spoils them.   But
there is this peculiarity in Bede, that he often introduces his subject by a description of the place
and the time, and thus vivifies the passage; while
everywhere the genuine sincerity and piety of the
speaker are apparent.*

General char-   On the whole, however, the times are evil for
acter of
preaching of   * Palmer in Herzog, s.v. *Predigt*, ascribes to Bede the in-
this epoch.
troduction of the novelty of arranging his sermons according
to the seasons of the ecclesiastical year.

preaching. The manner of Origen carries the day; while the roots of the Middle Ages are in the ground, and already show signs of growth. Credulity and affectation carry us as far from the good taste of the classical age as from the spiritual insight and divine wisdom of the New Testament. It rouses a curious sense of contrast to read one of these sermons after one of the epistles of Paul, or a chapter of the gospels.

We come now to the second section of the period, Second section. 800-1517 A.D.

The year 800 is a remarkable one. Charlemagne —Carolus Magnus—was the greatest warrior and organiser between Cæsar and Napoleon, and in some respects a more enlightened and less selfish man than either. He was born probably at Aix la Chapelle, where he lies buried. His life was one of incessant war against the Huns in the East, the Saracens in the South, and the Saxons in the North. The last of these he compelled by force to renounce heathenism, and was therefore called *Armatus Saxoniae Apostolus*, the armed apostle of Saxony. His kingdom extended from Hungary to the German Ocean, and from the Elbe to the Pyrenees. He carried his arms into Italy, subdued the Lombards, then a formidable power, and estab-

Charlemagne, 742-814 A.D.

lished the temporal dominion of the Pope, which has continued down to our time. When he was worshipping in St. Peter's church, Pope Leo III. suddenly, though no doubt by agreement, put a gold crown on his head and saluted him, " Carolus Augustus Imperator ! " This was in 800 A.D., and marks the beginning of the Holy Roman Empire, the cause of innumerable wars, for it expressed the idea that there could be only one empire in the world, as there could be only one Church. Charlemagne and the Pope were lords of all, bodies and souls, and they helped one another in their government. It is well to remember the year 800, and to reflect how far we are from it with our ideas of nationality on the one side, and of conscience on the other.

His efforts on behalf of preaching.

The name of this great monarch, who figures so frequently in the romances of chivalry with Roland and Oliver and the twelve Paladines, seems far removed from the subject of preaching. But Charlemagne concerned himself with all the interests of his subjects. He attended to commerce, to agriculture, to education, and to the Church. After Constantine, he was the chief champion of State-churchism. He held church councils at Rheims, Tours, Châlons, and other places, at which there was much discussion about preaching. Charles saw its great power as an educator and civiliser of the people, and he required the bishops to give themselves to the work of instruction. They were ordered to study the Catholic creed and the Lord's Prayer, that they might understand them and be able to explain them to the people. When the bishops were absent, portions of the Bible and of the writings of the Fathers were to be read to congregations. That this might be carried out, Paul Warnefrid, called Paulus Diaconus, was commanded to make a collection of " the best flowers out of the beautiful meadows of the Fathers, that those who were unable to preach might read them." This collection, which was called the *Homiliarium,* was the beginning of those books of homilies which became afterwards so famous. The homilies were arranged according to the festivals and seasons of the year, and as the passage for the day was called a Pericope or section, this gave rise to the Pericopic system of preaching, which prevails still on the Continent in many Protestant churches, and which leads English clergymen to select the text from the lesson for the day. Each homily began : *Post illa verba textus,* " after these words of the text ; " whence these homilies came to be named

Postils, a term which, with the verb *postillare*, to preach, often occurs in mediæval Latin,* and is still in use.

Injurious result of them.   This attempt of Charlemagne was well meant, and it is quite likely. that it did some good at first, but it led to harm. The clergy and the bishops came to depend on the *Homiliarium* and its Postils, instead of thinking out the subject for themselves, and all that was necessary was to be able to read, not to preach, and to read a language which they often understood imperfectly. They became therefore more and more indolent and ignorant, and incompetent to give instruction either publicly or privately.

A corresponding effect was produced upon the people. Few of them understood the homilies, which were in Latin,† and those who did understand them came to regard them, when they returned again and again, as parts of a piece of mechanism, and not

---

* The principal authorities with regard to the *Homiliarium* are quoted by Gieseler, Part II., chap. iii., sec. 10.

† Efforts were repeatedly made to prevent this. Thus the third council of Tours held in 813 A.D., expressly enjoins— *ut easdem homilias quisque aperte transferre studeat in rusticam linguam Latinam aut Theotiscam, quo facilius cuncti possint intelligere quae dicuntur.* Capit, Turon iv., 17. Hincmar of Rheims insists that parish priests should be able to expound the Athanasian creed in the vernacular.

as the living words of living men. They generally
left the church when the homily began, and we find
orders from time to time to compel them to remain.
"To read a homily," "as dry as a homily," became
proverbial expressions. The mass and other ceremonies which appealed to the senses gained the
upper hand, while instruction and intelligence
among the common people died out. Thus the
darkness deepened till about the year 1200.

I have heard some people among ourselves say
that it would be well if many ministers, instead of
giving us their own sermons, would make selec-
tions from those of other men, and read them
to us; and then, with good music, we could
enjoy the service. This system was tried more
than a thousand years ago, and it produced an
ignorant ministry and a careless people. Those
who would persuade you to anything like this,
would rob you of your power. Whenever a
thing becomes easy, it is thought to be of little
worth, and such a plan would soon bring the
ministry into contempt. People would buy their
own sermon-books, and read them at home, if they
read them at all. What is needed in the pulpit is
living Christian men who give their own thoughts
and feelings to the people, and the people soon

His mistake instructive.

discover from the very manner of the preacher
whether he does so or not. The same rule applies
to periodicals of the Homilist and Expositor type.
If they help us to think for ourselves and put us
on the track, they are good, giving us stimulus
and guidance which no man should be above
accepting. But if they take the place of our
own thinking, they are very evil. All that you
get from them should be incorporated with your
own mind and heart, and brought out in your
own way.

Light in the   We are not to think, however, that the light of
darkness.
Christian truth was entirely veiled in the preaching
of those times. Although the sermons were chiefly
about the Virgin and the saints, and relics and
legends, and dry etymologies ; yet in the midst of
them there was warning against vice and inculcation
of Christian virtue, which gathered in some way
round the name of Christ. And outside the Papal
Church, or half outside, there are tokens of a current of a purer kind in the valleys of the Alps,
both on the French and the Italian side, among
the Bohemian mountains, and, it may be, in some
of the secret places of our own land. Sometimes
it was in the heart of a bishop such as Claude of
Turin, sometimes under the cowl of a monk or the

coat of a peasant.* There is a river in Spain called
the Guadalquivir, which disappears underground,
and comes up again after some miles, but ever
and again it has openings where it visits the daylight for an interval to show that it is flowing on.
The Spaniards call these *los ojos del Guadalquivir*,
the eyes of the Guadalquivir. The spiritual Church
of Christ has such eyes in the dark ages, looking
up even at midnight to the stars.

It is about the year 1200 that the dawn begins, The dawn.
when we see and hear preaching again, and, as
Milton says, "the bird of morning begins to sing."

Some of the causes of this movement towards Causes.
light and life may be mentioned.

The clergy came to be better instructed, and Better instruc-
more able to deal with the old stores of learning, clergy.
and with the Bible, first in the Vulgate, then in
Greek and Hebrew. Very curiously this was due
to contact with the Saracens, who at that time
were admirers of the Greek literature, especially of
Aristotle. From them we got our beginnings of
algebra, of chemistry, and of astronomy ; in which

---

* This is one of our answers to those who ask : "Where
was your Church before Luther?" It was where the Christian Church was before Christ—mixed up with ceremonial
elements ; when He lifted up the standard it went one
way, and the men of ceremonies another

sciences a number of their terms survive. They also gave a stimulus to theology. Then there came direct contact with the East through the Crusades. Constantinople was still in the hands of a Greek-speaking population, and a taste for Greek arose, leading to the foundation of universities—Bologna and Paris among the first. There was a general stirring of thought which raised up men more fitted to teach.*

Use of the vernacular.

The next cause was, a general attempt to speak to the people in their own mother-tongue. There had been such attempts before. Columba addressed the Picts of Inverness in the Celtic; St. Gall learned the Franconian, that he might preach to the Franks round Lake Constance; Bede used the Anglo-Saxon as well as the Latin; Alfred had homilies on sacred history rendered into the Anglo-Saxon; and similarly in the rest of Europe. In the commotions of the time, however, the confusion of tongues was great; disorder and irregularity prevailed. It was the time of Babel, and Pentecost had not fully come. But about 1200, the present languages of Western Europe began to take shape, and to be the medium of communication between teachers and taught. There were

* See Note B on page 131.

two great branches : the *Lingua Rustica Latina,* in the south, became the mother of the Italian, French, Spanish, Portuguese, and Romance tongues, all drawing more or less from the old Latin of the common people ; in the north, the *Lingua Theotisca* became the mother of the German, Dutch, English, and Scoto-Saxon. Lays, *minnelieder,* were chanted ; poems were made ; and great writers by-and-by arose, notably Dante in Italy. Preaching in the vernacular became more frequent ; the peaks were appearing above the long flood ; the dove with the olive leaf was moving over the waters around the ark of promise ; and in time the ark would open and a new world begin.

We who believe that the God of history is the Lord Jesus Christ should recognise these movements, and try to see how they are connected with His cause. He makes an opportunity, and when He gives the command, " Go, stand and speak in the temple," there are men ready to fulfil it. But besides this gradual movement, we cannot doubt that there was a direct impulse from God's own presence. Those who watch the currents of history in their higher aspect must recognise epochs when, without secondary causes, or above them, there are

God in history

tides of great revival, as when God at first, over
the waste and emptiness of chaos, said, " Let there
be light," and there was light. It is not through fate
or accident, but through the Divine plan, that we
hear the trumpet-call of the Gospel waxing louder
and louder like that of Sinai, till men begin to stir
and wake. I thank God that I believe in this, for it
comforts me in times of reaction and decay, or
what seem so to us. " They have seen Thy goings,
O God, even the goings of my God, my King, in
the sanctuary."   Such a time was this—slow at
first, but ever growing.

Different
forms of
revival.

The lowest period in the life of Christianity, and
therefore in preaching, was from 800 to 1200 A.D.
Thereafter it began to rise, though with many
fluctuations, and we shall glance at the different
forms which the revival took in preparation for the
Reformation.

The Scholas-
tics.

Thomas
Aquinas,
1225-1274.

There is first the Scholastic type of preaching,
of which the most eminent example is Thomas
Aquinas. He is the great master of the Domini-
cans, the most celebrated order in the Roman
Catholic Church. He was born at Aquino, in
Italy, of a noble family; was a student and
teacher in the most celebrated universities in
Europe; and is the standard theologian of the

Roman Catholic Church, recommended by the present Pope as the best antidote to the scepticism of the age. His great work is the *Summa Theologiæ*, in which he seeks to reconcile theology, as he understood it, with the philosophy of Aristotle. The preaching founded on it addresses itself to the intellect rather than to the heart or conscience, and to the intellect of the Schools rather than to common intelligence and reason. It often introduces questions of the most fanciful kind, and abounds in divisions and sub-divisions, and in the most subtle distinctions. And yet it is from this, simplified and purified, that we have learned to apply method to our preaching as well as to many other things.

The second school of preachers was the order of The Mystics. the Mystics. They were very numerous, and held different positions. Within the Roman Catholic Church was the celebrated Bernard of Clairvaux, the Bernard, preacher of the Second Crusade, and author of the died 1153. hymn, *Salve caput cruentatum.* There were other Mystics whose object was to serve not so much the Church as Christianity, and who were therefore under suspicion. The most famous, though not the earliest, of these was John Tauler of Strasburg, Tauler, a great favourite with Luther, who filled the im- 1290-1361.

mense cathedral with crowds, and preached the Gospel fervently when the black death raged in 1348. He had the same effect on Luther as the mystic William Law, the author of *A Serious Call*, had on John Wesley, filling him with a hazy warmth, and preparing him for that clear view of the Gospel which he afterwards gained.* Both of these men preached in the vernacular ; Bernard in the Romance, then forming itself into a language that is now dying before our eyes, and Tauler in German. Tauler professes that he will quote little Latin and prove everything from Scripture.

If the Scholastics were light without heat, the Mystics were heat without light. You may gain a very good view of them from Vaughan's *Hours with the Mystics*, or in a popular way from *Theologia Germanica* (translated by Miss Winkworth), a book by an unknown mystic, which also Luther much admired at an early period of his life. The Mystics did good service, as preachers of feeling who spoke to the conscience and spirit, though

* Tauler, who was strongly influenced by Nicolas von Basel, a Waldense, preached with wonderful power on behalf of the oppressed, and against the avarice and luxury of clergy and laity, not sparing even the Pope.

in a darkling way. Their sermons want form
and clearness of arrangement, dealing greatly in
iteration.*

Allied to this, there grew up a popular school, The popular
with much of the Mystical in its character school.
though clearer in form and presentation, and with
more direct hold of Christian truth than the
Scholastics. They resembled Latimer of the
English Reformation more than Luther—*i.e.*, they
dealt more with duty than with doctrine, and
yet we feel that doctrine is underneath. They
are entirely Christian, and set little importance
on rites and ceremonies.

The most eminent representative of this school Berthold,
was Berthold of Regensburg or Ratisbon, a died 1272.
number of whose sermons still remain. He has a
Bunyan-like power of using quaint similitudes,
and can still be read with interest for his parables
and comparisons. No church could hold the multitudes that flocked to hear him, and he preached
in the market-places and fields to thousands,
reckoned by the fifty or the hundred—vague
numbers, but telling of the immense popularity

* Herder says that "he who has read two of Tauler's
sermons has read all." *Cf.* Milman's *Latin Christianity.*
Book XIV. chap. vii.

of the man, and of the growing desire to listen to Christian truth when presented plainly in the mother-tongue.

Some of these men were all but outside of the Roman Church, and entirely so were others of whom we have glimpses among the mountains of Dauphiny and Piedmont, and also in Bohemia.

Character-
istics.

Their preaching had a tone which has never been heard in the Eastern Church. Whether from the trials through which the Western world had passed, or from the influence of new races, there arose a sense of the imperfection of life, and yet of its grandeur, a feeling of the mystery of existence, and a bending of the heart reverently before it, which we do not find either in the speculation of Origen or in the eloquence of Chrysostom. This perception of an infinite ideal of the soul above the finished completeness of the human intelligence, became in religion the entrance of the heart and spirit within the range of deeper and higher questions than can be settled by the common understanding, or by the ordinary laws of ethics.

The rise of the
modern feel-
ing.

Thus, as we advance, the word " reform " is heard, first with reference to manner, and then with reference to doctrine. There is an element of earnestness and pathos, deeper and more searching than anything in the old patristic preaching, revealing that more sensitive openness to the world's imperfection and its mysteries which distinguishes romanticism from classicism. It was all there in the Bible—in the Psalms, in the New Testament, in the life and death of Christ; but it becomes the possession of the people only when the Bible touches the hearts of the northern races. There spring up the Gothic architecture, which is mysticism put into stone, and the *Divina Comedia*, and the hymns of Thomas of Celano and Bernard of Cluny, and the *Imitation of Christ*, and all the products of feeling that make the modern world so distinct from the full, rounded, self-inclosed life of the classics.

This one feature is enough to disprove the position of Professor Havet, who seeks to shew that the present form of Christianity is to be traced to the Greek mind. We owe the Greek mind very much in regard to form and expression; but the formative spirit and the contents lie far beyond, by Siloa's brook that flowed fast by the oracle of God, and the receptive spirit lies more in the blood of the northern races, which has given us this element of mysticism. Yet there was still wanting the clearness of expression which was necessary to make

Havet's theory.

K

Christianity once more the religion of preaching, as it had been in the days of Augustine and Chrysostom, only now in a still richer and clearer and higher way.

Harbingers of the new era. There were harbingers of the new era, men who united warmth with clearness—the great chancellor, John Gerson, in France, a man of noble spirit who turned from the cares of State to teach little children ; John Wycliffe in England ; John Huss in Bohemia ; Savonarola in Italy. All these were men of immense popular power; and what distinguishes most of them is a new view of the questions of sin and redemption—an approximation to the doctrine of Luther and the Reformers, and an evident advance on the preaching of even the greatest of the Fathers. We can see, like Columbus when he was approaching America, that a new world is at hand by the fresh leaves and fruits that are drifting on the current.

NOTE B, see page 122.

UNIVERSITIES IN THE 13TH CENTURY.

At the suppression of convents in 1803, there was found in the Abbey of Benedict-beuren a MS. of the 13th century, previously unknown. It is now at Munich, called *Codex Buranus*, and M. de Boernstein has published from it *Carmina Burana Selecta.* They are in German and Latin. M. Laistner has translated some from the Latin, and published them under the name *Golias.* Many of the songs are so gross that they have to be excluded. The whole codex is a curious picture of the student life of the time.

In the 12th and 13th centuries a number of German convents had flourishing schools with monks for teachers, Fulda, Reichenau, St. Gall, Hirschau, Benedict-beuren, &c., In France there were Paris, Rheims, Laon, &c. The students travelled from school to school, and had important privileges in journey and residence. As long as the monks were moral, order and discipline were maintained ; but when they fell into license, the schools fell into disorder and all sorts of excesses. The songs belong to that period (Minnegesang). The scholars of Paris were accused of playing dice on the altars, and were forbidden by edict to commit murder, brigandage, and house-breaking when journeying. In France, in Germany, in England, they went in troops that were formidable, and gave up study altogether for a wandering libertinage. Most of them were theological, and became a scourge to the lower clergy and convents on whom they lived, many adopting their profession merely that they might live a life of idleness and vice. The banks of the Rhine, which were called " The Highway of the Priests," swarmed with them. The Synod of Passau (1248) and the Council of Salzburg (1291) issued decrees against them, and

after the foundation of lay universities there was an improvement for a time. These students called themselves Goliards
or Golias, from the Goliath of the Bible, who was canonised
in jest. (From this probably the boy's rhyme "Here come
I, Goloshau—Goloshau is my name," the picture of a brag-
gadocio ; the modern tramp is the feeble type of the race
of *clerici vagi.*) The movement broke out again in the 15th
and 16th centuries among the lay universities, and great
numbers, Poles, Bohemians, &c., travelled as low comedians
and jugglers under the guise of students. The songs were
in all the European tongues, with the Latin, and spread
thus from land to land. The *Gaudeamus, Crambambuli,*
&c., of the Studenten-Lieder are purified relics. Spain is
the only country where this usage survives in any measure,
and at a carnival in Paris in 1878, the *Estadiantana* of
Spain made a sensation.—See *Revue Suisse,* February, 1880.

LECTURE VIII.

PREACHING IMMEDIATELY BEFORE THE REFORMATION.*

IN order to understand the effect of the Reformation on the history of preaching, we must
look a little more closely into the state of things
that immediately preceded it.

The change that took place in the thought and Importance of
Reformation
period.
life of Europe at the Reformation is one of the
most remarkable in the history of the world. We
are accustomed to speak of the present epoch as
more important than any previous one, and, no
doubt, it is a period of wonderful activity in every
department of knowledge ; but, if you look at
the state of things before and after the Reformation, you will see that there was then a revolution far surpassing that of our own time, striking

---

* This Lecture and those which follow were addressed to
students, only half of whom had heard Lectures I.-VII.

as it is.   Indeed, the only other that will compare
with it for importance is that which occurred at the
Christian Era.

Revival of
learning.

You have to think how the revival of learning
brought Europe face to face with the old world of
Greece and Rome which had previously been
buried except to a few, and by these few had
been imperfectly known.   The capture of Constantinople by the Turks in 1453 had sent numbers of Greeks, even nobles and princes, over the
Western world, who taught their language and
literature in Italy, France, and England.   The old
classic authors were sought out, annotated, and
commented on, and some of the greatest scholars
in classic literature appeared.   The Bible began
to be read and studied in the original, and the
laws of hermeneutics and exegesis were applied to
it with unprecedented accuracy.

Inventions
and dis-
coveries.

The various discoveries of the time made knowledge the property of many.   The invention of
paper and of printing multiplied books, and put it
in the power of vast multitudes to study them.
Never before in the world's history had there been
so many readers and thinkers.

The invention of gunpowder had its influence.   It
introduced science into war, and secured Europe

against inroads of barbarism like those which had destroyed the ancient civilisation. It gave a sense of leisure for study such as a man feels who knows that the policeman is patrolling the bounds, compared with one who has to watch every sound for house-breakers' footsteps. If you consider what it cost Europe to repel Huns, Tartars, Saracens, and Turks, you will see that even our bloated armaments, bad as they are, are not so disturbing as were the terrors of the Middle Ages. Now, for the first time, burghers and peasants, formerly forced to follow some feudal lord with spear and hauberk to foreign lands, could cultivate their fields and their minds.

' The physical discoveries of the time stimulated men's thoughts. A new world was added to the old by Columbus ; the way to India and China was made accessible by Vasco di Gama ; the heavens were penetrated by Copernicus and Kepler ; and men's minds were open and sensitive to the new and strange.

The national languages of Europe were now National formed and made fit for being vehicles of instruc-languages. tion to all the people. Italian, French, German, and English took their shapes about this time, and learning was brought to the poor man's door.

These few words will serve to indicate the importance of the period at which the Reformation was born, and of the influences which were around the Bible, when Luther brought it from his cell at Erfurt. So it was that, when the Lord gave the word, the company of them that published it was very great.

"Then," as Milton says, "was the sacred Bible sought out of the dusty corners where profane falsehood and neglect had thrown it, the schools opened, divine and human learning raked out of the embers of forgotten tongues, the princes and cities trooping apace to the new-erected banner of salvation ; the martyrs, with the unresistible might of weakness, shaking the powers of darkness, and scorning the fiery rage of the old red dragon."

Preaching prior to the Reformation ;

We shall be better able to understand the change that came upon preaching, if we look at its condition immediately before this great upheaval.

non-existent as a Church institution ;

It may be said that for several centuries preaching, as a recognised institution of the Christian Church, had been non-existent. Bishops who preached were rare exceptions. As a rule they were occupied in contests for power and honour, many of them being feudal lords who

headed their vassals clad in armour, while not a
few of them led lives of shameless and uncon-
cealed immorality. You have but to read such a
book as Ranke's *Lives of the Popes* to see this.
Better that these men did not try to preach even
if they were able. It would have been to add
scandal and hypocrisy to sin. Scotland was then
as bad as the rest of Europe—in some respects
worse. You may remember the anecdote of the
bishop who came to head a fray in the High Street
of Edinburgh with armour beneath his gown ;
protesting eagerly about something, he struck his
breast till the coat of mail rattled. " Be my
conscience ! " he said. " My lord," said one of the
bystanders, "your conscience is not guid, for I hear
it clattering." When George Wishart was preaching in Ayr, Dunbar, Bishop of Glasgow, who had
never before preached, took possession of the pulpit
to exclude the reformer, but all he could say was,
" They say we sold prieche. Quhy not ? Better
late thryve nor never thryve. Haud us still for your
bishope, and we sall provide better the next time."

Among the secular clergy, *i.e.*, the clergy who
had charge of parishes, things were much the same
as among the bishops. Their chief work was
performing the offices of the Church, reading the

mass, and giving absolution.   David Lyndsay says
in regard to them—

"War nocht the precheing of the begging freris,
Tint war the faith amang the seculeris."

owing to
state of the
Church. It could not well be otherwise when these places
were put up openly for sale, or bestowed on strolling
bards and players, and on creatures of the courtiers
and bishops.   The people came to lose faith in the
secular or parish clergy, and the churches were in
a large measure deserted, or frequented only on
certain festival days when the more solemn rites
were performed.   The Romish churches were worse
attended in these "ages of faith," as they have been
called, than they are now when Protestantism has
given a stimulus to Popery.   Those who say that
the union of Christian Churches would bring the
lapsed masses to the church may have some
reason if they mean a true, living, and loving
union ; but if they mean merely the uniformity
of the Churches, they are utterly wrong.   There
were never more " lapsed masses " in Europe than
when there was the greatest uniformity, never
more ignorance and vice and immorality.   What
is wanted in Churches is life—spiritual life ; union,
if you will, but only with living unity, the unity of
the Spirit.   The army that is to conquer the world

is not to be a collection of dead bones, such as the prophet saw in his vision, but a force of living men.

There were, however, in the ages before the Reformation, organisations for preaching. There were the monks of different Orders. When the secular clergy became so corrupt and indolent that religion seemed likely to die, an attempt was made to reform the Church from within, a reformation of the Church from without having indeed scarcely been thought of. The monkish orders sprang up for this work. They were called friars, brothers, or "regulars," being bound by the "regula," or rule of their order ; and this distinguished them from the secular clergy, who had parishes and benefices connected with them. Among them the most numerous were the Franciscans or Grey Friars, founded by St. Francis d'Assisi, and the Dominicans or Black Friars, founded by Dominic, or Domingo, a Spaniard. These two orders had great variety among themselves, but the Dominicans carried off the palm as preachers. It was to them that the famous Thomas Aquinas belonged. They were known also as the Jacobines, and gave name to the famous Jacobin party in the French Revolution, because their sittings were held in the Jacobine or Dominican monastery—a curious

The rise of preaching Orders.

irony, the Romish order giving name to the reddest republicans.

Their success. At first these Orders did good. They were founded by zealous men who, with all their errors, wished to serve their time faithfully. They had their centre in some abbey where they observed their rules of devotion, and from which they issued to preach and to teach the people, after special training for this purpose. They had such zeal and gained such influence that often the parish churches were given over to them, along with the revenues. *E.g.*, Holyrood Abbey had the charge of Corstorphine and Liberton and various places round Edinburgh. This produced great enmity between them and the parish clergy.

Their corruption. But, with time, the preaching Orders became as bad as the parish clergy, or worse. Their monasteries increased in wealth, and became seats of immorality. Their preaching power declined. They either entered into the region of polemics, or became lazy, and yielded to the temptation of easy popularity. Thus the Dominicans were the fathers of the Inquisition, and much of their preaching was bitter denunciation of the growing heresies of the time—Albigenses, Waldenses, Bohemian Brethren, and Lollards. They held up the cross in one hand, and applied the faggot with the other; and their preaching was as fiery and fierce as their conduct. In this they were consistent. Others set themselves to please the people with legends and amusing stories. The time of Easter was the great season for this, when it was supposed that people needed amusement after their fast; and so "a paschal laugh," *risus paschalis*, became a proverb for the greatest merriment. The Carnival, which has now fallen into the hands of the mob, and of which it is getting ashamed, was then a Church ordinance. There were exceptions to all this—men who deplored it, and protested, and preached in a very different way; but I speak of what was the prevailing practice in Europe before the Reformation.

But we must give some account of the sermons that were in use; for sermons were preached, and collections of them remain to us, besides the records preserved by literary men like Stephanus and Erasmus and Ulrich von Hütten. They may be said to have been of four kinds.* Different types of sermons.

---

* A succinct account of those preachers will be found in Rothe's *Geschichte der Predigt*, section 81; specimens of their sermons are given by Lentz in his *Geschichte der christlichen Homiletik*, vol. I., part iii.

Ready-made.　　1. There were those who read the sermons that came ready made to hand. The *Homiliarium* of Charlemagne, to which I have already referred, was within reach, and sometimes the king or bishop, if he were a more than ordinarily zealous man, enjoined the use of it. It was followed and varied by a number of collections bearing such titles as *Gesta Romanorum*—a curious name to give to a homily-book—which led to a facetious parody that has given origin to our word "jest." Another was called *Lumen Animae,* light of the soul ; and another *Dormi Secure,* sleep at ease, intended to assure a man of his Sabbath night's rest. Some of these, and especially the earlier, were more Scriptural, and consisted of a comment on some part of the gospels or epistles, too generally of a fantastic and allegorical type. The evil of this method, as we have seen, was that it destroyed the native power of the preacher, and the sermons, being in Latin, were unintelligible to a great mass of the hearers.

Scholastic.　　2. On the other hand, the more learned preached sermons of a Scholastic type, full of plays upon words and ridiculous conceits. Erasmus gives an account of one which he heard from an old theologian who "looked so wise that you thought

Duns Scotus had come to life again." He took
the word "Jesus" as his text, and showed
what wonders it contained. 1. It is declined in
three cases, Jesus, Jesum, Jesu ; wherein we have
manifestly an image of the Trinity. Then, the
first of these ends in *s*, the second in *m*, the
third in *u* ; which is a deep mystery, *summum,
medium, ultimum.* Further, if Jesus is divided
into two equal portions, *s* is left in the middle,
which in the Hebrew is ש, sin, and this in the
language of the Scots (*Scotorum opinor lingua*)
signifies *peccatum ;* it is thus implied that Jesus
takes away the sin of the world.

The custom of those preachers was to have an
introduction, which they called *praeambulum*, as far
from the text as possible, so as to keep the hearers
in suspense, and make them say, *Quo nunc se
proripit ille ?* Where is the man rushing to now ?

Stephanus tells of similar preachers who dealt
with such questions as these :—Whether God could
sin if He chose ; whether He could know what He
did not know ; whether Christ would have been
crucified if Judas had not betrayed Him ; and
so on.

3. A third class of preachers, found chiefly, Legendary
as already indicated, among the monastic orders,

related stories about saints and legends of the most trifling and irreverent kind.

4. Others again amused their hearers with ridiculous anecdotes, and acted the part of comedians and jesters. In this the parish clergy showed as much skill as the friars. Their extravagances would be almost incredible, if we had not the authority of grave and trustworthy writers who give the names and parts of the sermons of some of the preachers. Maillard, Menot, and Barletta were noted in this department.

While such preachers made it their sole aim to gain a laugh or to excite empty wonder at their learned nonsense, men like Tauler and Berthold and Wycliffe were gathering round them those who had become conscious of their spiritual needs. Unfortunately the Papal Court of the time was afraid of the earnestness of the true preachers, and put itself on the side of the triflers or story-tellers. And so the Reformation came.

Survival of those types.

It was necessary to give some idea of this state of things, that you may understand what the Reformers had to do, and that you may have some idea of the change that took place. And yet, I am afraid that this kind of preaching has not wholly passed away. It is true that we do not have it in the same gross and palpable forms ; but we have its counterparts.

We have the men who patch up sermons out of old Homiliaria, worth as little as if they were given in the Latin tongue—dull and dead, never passing beyond the ears of the people. We have the Scholastics—men who deal with subjects that have no connection with life and practice, who ring the changes on syllogism and premiss and entity and etymological profundities, while " the hungry sheep look up, and are not fed." We have not perhaps, in Scotland at least, the old-legend-man, but in his room we have the modern question-of-the-day handler. What says so and so on some political or social topic—and the newspaper gets it to rehearse, advised of it by the careful author or some admiring friend. And we have the sensational advertiser and religious jester, as far as decency will now permit.

Let me only hope that you will take a different way ; that you will speak to men, feeling that they have souls, and knowing that you have a message from God to them ; and that you will make it your endeavour to declare simply, faithfully, and earnestly the word of

L

eternal life. If religion is to be preserved, if we are to be delivered from reaction to a dead ceremonialism, and from stumbling forward into an empty paganism, it must be by living preachers, and the preaching of Life.

LECTURE IX.

CHRISTIANITY has shown that it possesses Christiar the power of public speech in a special oratory. and unprecedented degree. In Greece and Rome we have distinguished orators—Demosthenes and Cicero are transcendent names—and the power of speech was placed by such rhetoricians as Aristotle and Quintilian at the summit of all the arts ; yet it is only when Christianity enters the world that we see its highest achievements. If the value of speech may after all be best measured by its effects, then no other sphere in which language has been employed can be compared with Christian preaching ; for, by what the apostle calls its "foolishness," it has produced unparalleled results. We have but to think how it evoked the cry, " Men and brethren, what shall

we do?" and how the apostles met that cry,
drawing both Jews and Gentiles to the Gospel.
Here lay the true apostolical succession : "The
things which thou hast heard of me, the same
commit thou to faithful men who shall be able to
teach others also." There never has been such
a company of men as followed in the history
of the early Church—men like Origen and Chrysostom and Ambrose and Augustine, on whose
lips thousands hung. No doubt they gained their
power over their fellow-men from the new truths
which had been disclosed, but God's blessing was
shown in the burning eloquence with which they
proclaimed them ; for when His Spirit converts
men, He puts earnestness into their heart and lips,
and conveys the word "from heart to heart."

Protestantism   But it may be said, also, that Protestantism,
the religion of as compared with Romanism, is the religion of
public speech.
public speech. The early fire of Christianity
died away, and its heat survived only in a blind
devotion choked up and covered with the ashes
of ceremonial. There are great preachers in
the Middle Ages ; but they are rare, and they
have their power in spite of the system, not in
consequence of it. Many of them scarcely belong
to the Romish Church, Tauler, Wycliffe, Jerome

of Prague, Huss, and Savonarola—the Reformers before the Reformation.

It is with the Reformers that the new era of preaching begins, an era greater even than that of the early Church, if we except the apostles. The Roman Catholic Church, and especially the French part of it, has since then produced great preachers, but their advent was the result of Protestantism. They did not appear until the quickening power of the Reformation was felt within the Romish Church. Leaving this, however, for the present, we shall speak specially of the preaching of the Reformation, beginning with Germany and with Luther.

The Reformation a new era in preaching.

We shall not consider Luther's general work, which was enormous—a volume large or small on an average every fortnight of his active life. We shall speak of him as a preacher, and explain his views on preaching. Preaching was the centre and spring of his power ; by preaching he moved Germany and then Europe, till he shook the Papal throne. Melancthon was a scholar and theologian, Calvin was a theologian and an exegete, Cranmer was a religious statesman ; Luther was great in all those respects, but still greater as a preacher. In this, he and John Knox had much in common ;

Luther, 1483-1546.

Knox also being statesman and educationist but principally preacher.

Luther's reluctance to preach.

It is remarkable that Luther was at first unwilling to preach. Like Moses, he did not recognise his work. He distrusted himself, or he had not yet the impelling fire of Jeremiah and Paul: "It was as a fire within me;" "Woe is unto me if I preach not." It was at the command of his superior, under the vow of obedience, that he first preached in the refectory or dining-room of the cloister at Erfurt, and afterwards in the little cloister church of Wittenberg.* But when he once began, the spirit of preaching grew upon him, and at the request of the town's-people, he agreed to preach in the town church of Wittenberg, which afterwards became so famous, and in which he lies buried side by side with Melancthon. This was about the middle of 1515, two years before his rupture with the Romish Church. Some of his

His earlier sermons.

sermons of this period were composed in Latin, and for the learned, discussing the nature of the Eternal Word and His relation to God the Father, with references to the Schoolmen. He has not a definite idea of the Scripture doctrines, nor of

* The room was thirty feet long and twenty feet broad.

what preaching should be. But he is growing. He preaches more frequently, sometimes four sermons a-day, in German, and on practical subjects : on the Ten Commandments, the Lord's Prayer, Repentance, the True Life. He presses the importance of the Bible and of Christ, but he has not yet gained a clear view of Christ's Cross and its meaning, nor of justification without the works of the law. He has glimpses; he sees rivulets of the river of life, but has not reached the stream and fountain-head.

The preaching of Luther soon excited move- Their power. ment. Wittenberg on the Elbe, the university of Gesenius and Tholuck and Julius Müller, was the chief seat of learning in the north of Germany,* and students as well as town's-men flocked to hear him. They felt the newness and boldness of his style and even of his doctrine. His sermons did not treat of ceremonies and fasts, but addressed the moral and spiritual nature of his hearers with unmistakable meaning and directness. He was taking aim at the heart, with arrows which reached their mark ; and men love this in preachers. But in the midst of the

* The University of Wittenberg was transferred to Halle in 1815.

attraction there was repulsion and opposition. There were Scribes and Pharisees—the ceremonialists and legalists; there were also Sadducees—the worldlings and secularists. Yet Luther went on, and the body of the people were with him.

His matured preaching.

Then came the breach with the Papal system through his opposition to indulgences, and this led him to the simplicity of the Gospel, and to the central truth of his preaching—justification by faith.* He now found firm footing, and his preaching gained a power which roused all Germany and shook the souls of men. There had been nothing like it since the day of Pentecost. On his way to Worms, to meet the Diet, he could not escape from the crowds. At Erfurt where he had commenced in the little refectory, the great church was so crowded that they feared it would fall. At Zwickau, the marketplace was thronged by 25,000 eager listeners, and Luther had to preach to them from the window.

---

* "When I was young," he says, "and especially before I was acquainted with theology, I dealt largely in allegories, and tropes, and a quantity of idle craft; but now I have let all that slip, and my best craft is to give the Scripture, with its plain meaning; for the plain meaning is learning and life."

When the Reformation was finally established, regular pastors were placed at Wittenberg, the well-known Bugenhagen and others. Luther had pressing work—the care of the Church and all the controversies, the training of preachers, translating the Bible, writing pamphlets and volumes, giving counsel to princes and people; but nothing could keep him from preaching, at home and wherever he went, on Sabbath-days and during the week. He continued to preach all his lifelong, though broken in health—in this, too, like Knox—and so enfeebled that he often fainted from exhaustion. But to the end he retained his wonderful power. The last time he ascended the pulpit was on February 14th, 1546, a few days before he died.

We shall now briefly explain Luther's idea His view of of preaching.* After the revival of learning, two preaching. treatises on the subject appeared, both in Latin, and both by humanists or classical scholars— Reuchlin† and Erasmus;‡ but Luther's views, although not presented in definite shape and only

---

* The passages in Luther's writings which bear upon his views of preaching are carefully collected by Nebe in his *Geschichte der Predigt.*

† *De Arte Prædicandi*, 1504.

‡ *Ecclesiastes, s. Concionator Evangelicus*, 1534.

scattered through his letters and his *Table-talk*, are more valuable than theirs, as being given by a man who had deep experience and who dealt not only with form but with matter.

Its import-ance.

Luther holds that preaching is the most important part of public worship, and agrees therein with Paul, who sets it above mere outward ordinances—Christ sent him "not to baptise, but to preach the Gospel." He gives to preaching a place even above the written Word. This may startle us at first, but Luther is speaking not of the authority of the Bible but of the ordinary use of it, and he means no more than our Shorter Catechism, that God "maketh the reading, *and especially* the preaching of the Word, a means of convincing and converting sinners." By "the preaching" is meant the Word of God passing through the heart of the living witness, and carried home to the heart of the hearer. It is the Church of Christ, with the aid of the Holy Spirit, using the Word of Christ. "The Spirit and the bride say, Come."

Its basis.

He says that, while preaching "rises above the Bible," and gives it life and application, it must always be rooted in the Bible, and go back to it for its authority. The best preacher is the man who is best acquainted with the Bible, who has it not only in his memory but in his mind, who understands its true meaning, and can handle it with effect.

But to understand it, is not merely to know the words and the grammar, and to reach the literal meaning, though all this has its place and use ; it is to enter into its real meaning and to feel its living power as imparted by the Spirit of Christ. " He shall receive of Mine, and shall show it unto you."

What, then, is the great subject of preach- Its subject ing ? " It is," says Luther, " the glory of God in Jesus Christ. We preach always Him, the true God and man who died for our sins, and rose again for our justification. This may seem a limited and monotonous subject, likely to be soon exhausted, but we are never at the end of it. We preachers are like young children who are learning to speak, and can use only half-words and quarter-words." And then he gives the excellent counsel that each one should speak as he feels, and try to feel more, in order to speak better. " If you wish to preach, go to God and say : ' Dear God, I wish to preach to Thy glory, to speak of Thee, to praise Thee, and to show forth

Thy name, though I cannot do so as I would.' Do
not look to Philip, to me, or to any learned man,
but be sure that you are best taught when you
speak of God in the pulpit. I have never
troubled myself with fears about not preaching
well, but I have often been troubled and terrified,
that I must stand in God's presence and speak
of His great majesty and glorious nature. Therefore, only be strong and pray."*

If this be so, it is easy to judge of sermons.
How do they deal with Christ? If He is absent, or if they make little of Him, they are
poor. "Better," he says, "that sermons and
pulpits were burned to ashes, as they deserve
to be, than that they should betray poor souls
to their ruin."

The form of
the sermon.

As to the form of the sermon, Luther recommends the use of a text; but every text,
even a single verse, has many things in it, and
may lead many ways. The preacher, then,

* This reminds us of the story of John Welsh, who
preached before the famous university of Saumur, with as
much ease as if he had been in a Scottish village, and was
asked by Boyd how he could venture it; he replied that he
was so filled with the dread of God that he had learned to
have no apprehension of man at all. This is misapplied by
some forward preachers, who neither fear God nor regard man.

while he may use other parts, should seize fast hold of the main thought and keep a firm grasp of it. He cannot speak on everything ; men who try to do so never reach the end. In his quaint way he compares them to a maid-servant going to market, who wastes her time in talking with this one and that one on the road, and arrives too late. We should impress the leading thought, and send away the people saying, " the sermon was on such and such a point." He makes little of the beginning or the close of the sermon, of fine introductions or brilliant perorations. It is the main body of it that should be considered ; and in this the preacher has two things to do—to instruct and to impress ; he must be *dialecticus* and *rhetor*—tell his hearers some things for the understanding, and give them some things for the heart and conscience. Teaching and exhortation—these are the two parts of a sermon. One man may give more of the one, another man more of the. other ; but every preacher should aim at something of both.

In regard to style, Luther is never weary of insisting on the necessity for clearness and simplicity. Everything in regard to division and expression ends in this—Have the people understood

Its style.

me? Can they carry this away in order to apply it? We must call white white, and black black, and speak in a way that every one can comprehend. Children and servants and old men and women come to our church to hear what will do their souls good, and we are not to hunt for big Greek and Latin words and spin long involved sentences, but to speak home to them in their own tongue. How careful was our Lord Christ to speak simply of the vine and its branches, of sheep and lambs, of trees and fields, of wheat and tares; and how anxious He was to make His meaning plain! There are no more important rules than these two—to preach the great saving truths of the Bible, and to preach them clearly and simply. To preach clearly and simply is a great art.

Luther's own preaching. Of Luther's own preaching it is difficult to form a proper idea from what is left to us. We have a great mass of sermons, or lectures as we should call them; but he wrote none or very few of them; they were taken down by others, and sent out without his being able even to look at them. There were what are called his House-postils— lectures on portions of Scripture to his family, friends, and neighbours who filled a large room. These are like our week-evening lectures, evidently

poured forth out of his fulness at the time. There
were also his public discourses, in the Church, at
home, and wherever he went, which were delivered
much in the same way, only after more careful preparation. It was his habit, when he had chosen a
text or a subject, to meditate upon it, to arrange
his thoughts, jotting them down perhaps in outline
with his leading illustrations, and then to throw
his heart into the theme. He did not see the
sermon till it had been taken down and printed,
and frequently he did not see it even then. Indeed, he was so occupied with the preaching of
other sermons, with the duties of the Church, the
university, the Protestant community, and with the
incessant consultation and correspondence which
these involved, that when a sermon was once
delivered, all thought of it was gone.

He almost always took for his subject a por- His theme.
tion of Scripture, and a considerable portion, most
frequently from the gospels or epistles. This resulted from the system of Pericopes,* which prescribed a "section" for every season, and required
the preacher to deal with it. It had the disadvant-
age that, since the same section returned year after
year, the preacher was driven either to repeat him-

* See page 117.

self and land in monotony, or to exercise a fatal
ingenuity in finding new and sometimes forced
meanings. It had the advantage of letting the
people know the subject beforehand, and of presenting large and important passages so as to
increase their acquaintance with the Word of God.
With a view to this result every minister who
cares to have an intelligent congregation should
adopt some "pericopic" system, reserving freedom
for occasional divergence from it.

Central truth
seized.

The next thing to be remarked in Luther is his
skill in seizing the central truth in his subject or
text. He does this by a kind of instinct, and
throws all his strength into its enforcement, that
the people may carry away one leading thought.
His treatment is two-fold, moral and spiritual—
i.e., he deals directly with duty, and also with the
inner nature, which is the spring of duty; sometimes with the one, sometimes with the other, but
generally with both. He was far from holding
the bare, superficial idea of duty, as a number
of external acts unconnected with the inner life;
and on the other hand he was equally far from
the idea that religion consists in meditation or
conviction without reference to the regulation of
conduct and character. Duty founded on doctrine,

works springing from faith, the fruits from the root
—these were Luther's constant points.

There were two extravagances of these which Extremes
Luther often reproved ; the one was the running avoided and reproved.
of duty into outward ceremony and ritualism—the
idea of the Romish church ; the other was the
running of the spiritual into the mystical and the
morbid—the idea of the mystics, which led to an
unnatural interpretation of Scripture in the manner
of Origen, and took shape in modern Sweden-
borgianism. Both ceremonialism and forced
mysticism were abhorrent to Luther's strong,
practical mind. In giving instruction and enforcing
duty, he made direct appeal first to Scripture and
then to healthy reason ; and he was at the furthest
remove from the petty profundities and misty
nothings that are based on fancies and covered
with vague, sounding phrases.

Next, while this was the matter of Luther's Manner of
teaching, his manner of expressing it was expression.
singularly clear, direct, and forcible. He aimed
at this constantly, and he reached it sometimes
by what we should esteem roughness and want of
taste. But we are to remember the age in which
he lived and the work he had to do. He had to
wield a sledge-hammer, and a sledge-hammer

M

cannot always measure its touch like a graver's
tool. It is a question whether we should not
wield the hammer sometimes even now. Luther
chose the simplest and most telling words, he
seized and sought out figures drawn from things
that could be seen and felt, he employed parables
and proverbs, he frequently took one of Æsop's
fables and put a Christian meaning into it; in
short, he used every means to make people listen
and comprehend and feel, without condescending to
trick or sensationalism.* He was, beyond almost
any other, the preacher of the people, and would
have been a Bunyan had he possessed more of
the dramatic and poetic gifts, and had the prison
in the Wartburg given as much leisure as the
prison on the bridge at Bedford. But, though
primarily a preacher to the people, Luther could

* "When I preach I regard neither doctors nor magistrates,
of whom there are in this church about forty; but I have
an eye to the multitude of young people, children, and
servants, of whom there are more than two thousand. Will
the rest hear me? The doors are open unto them: they
may begone. I see that the ambition of preachers grows
and increases, and this will do the utmost mischief in the
Church. . . . When they come to me, to Melancthon, to
Dr. Pomer, &c., let them show how learned they be; they
shall be well put to their trumps. But to sprinkle their
sermons with Hebrew, Greek, and Latin savours merely of
show, according with neither time nor place."

speak to all classes. Indeed, his presentation of truth, while simple, clear, and graphic, was so broad and deep in addressing the wants of men as to reach the wise and noble and learned. This is the perfection of preaching. It is a vulgar mistake to think that there is one way of speaking to the rich and another way of speaking to the poor. Yet, on fitting occasion, Luther could vary his mode. He could preach to children and write hymns for them ; he could thunder among strong, passionate hearts, and write his *Ein feste Burg ;* and, when it was needed, he could quote Homer and Aristotle, as Paul quoted the Greek poets on Mars' Hill. He could become, like Paul, all things to all men.*

There was this, lastly, about Luther's preaching, which also makes him like Paul, that he had one over-mastering thought, and that thought was Christ. At all times his central idea was " Christ our righteousness, that He may be Christ our strength and sanctification." Without this his varied gifts would have left little trace, but this made him, in God's hand, the instrument of the most wonderful awakening of the Church since the

The controlling though:.

* A sketch of one of his Homilies will be found on page 166.

days of the apostles, the greatest preacher of his
own or of later times, at least the one to whom God
has assigned the greatest work. We may find other
preachers greater than Luther in their own departments. He has not the majesty of Howe, the
spiritual fervour of Baxter, the searching spiritual
insight of Jonathan Edwards, the ideal beauty of
Vinet, the concentrated rush of Chalmers ; but, for
his own work, Luther was the man chosen of God,
and the Church of Christ bears the mark of his
personality as of none other since the canon of
Scripture was closed.

If you wish to have a good view of Luther as a
teacher in the house, and of his singular gift of
retailing wisdom, read his *Tischreden*—his Table-
talk. If you want to know the doctrine he
preached, read his standard Commentary, that on
the Galatians. If you wish to see his character
cleared, read the vindication of him by Julius Hare
—a noble book.

Lessons for preachers. Luther is above our reach in almost everything, but there are many things which, as
preachers, we all can learn from him: to be laying up stores of knowledge on all subjects, especially by the study of human nature ; to seek a
thorough acquaintance with the Bible, the book of

the preacher, the sword that nothing can with
stand ; to have sympathy with men and a single
desire to do them good ; to aim at a clear, natural,
direct style of speech ; and to grasp the grand
doctrine of justification by faith, and hold it up as
the standard of the Church of Christ, and the
source of comfort and strength and holiness in
the Christian life.

NOTE C, see page 163

SKETCH OF ONE OF LUTHER'S HOMILIES.

Luke xiv. 16-24—The Marriage Feast.

He begins without any introduction by saying that in the gospel for the day two points are notable. The first is, how gracious and merciful God is in wishing that everyone should be saved. He causes a great feast to be made, and invites the Jews first, because they had the promise of the woman's seed, the Lord Christ, &c. The second is, the frightful ingratitude of the Jews in refusing to receive such grace. From this he proceeds to show what the spiritual blessings are which the feast typifies, and how it came about that the Jews would not have them. When speaking of their excuses, he turns round on the errors of the monks and Anabaptists, who would not have marriage and property. To have oxen and fields and families, is not in itself an evil, nor is there any holiness in dispensing with them. Holiness is to be gained, first, by coming to the feast and sharing in it ; and, next, by patiently discharging worldly business, whatever it may be, and attending to it honestly. For this is God's command, and He will graciously give His blessing to it. So much for the Jews and for the first part of the gospel of to-day.

The next part applies to us heathen (Gentiles), showing how we have been compelled to attend the feast. God, through this gospel, condemns and casts away all merit and work-righteousness as serving nothing to salvation, and points to His Son alone, that we may put our confidence in Him, believing that for His sake God will forgive our sins and save us. When our hearts hear this truth they are alarmed, and lose their confidence in their good works and merits, and hang humbly on the Lord Jesus, and desire, through His merit and death and resurrection, the grace of God and the forgiveness of our sins. So it is that we are compelled to attend this feast.

We should not, then, think of our earthly goods more than of the Gospel, but take warning from the punishment of the Jews, for our hearts are as weak and bad as theirs were. . . . Remember, again, that, when we take the Gospel, we are not to forsake our family or our business. ' If thou desirest to be a Christian, thou art not to leave thy place and trade and calling, nor to alter it, so far as it is honest and good. Keep by it ; be diligent to support, with God's help and with honour, thy wife and child and household, and, if thou doest this in the fear of God, He will help thee with His blessing. . . . Yet be sure thou dost not forget the feast or despise it ; seek first the kingdom of God and His righteousness, for so shalt thou make certain that God will both bless thee for time and save thee for eternity. He will give His blessing to thy work and care, and will bestow salvation on thee for Christ's sake.' The sermon ends with a short prayer.

This is a fair specimen of his house-postils, which were very simple, not seeking out plans or words or skilful transitions, but going straight to the substance and speaking to the times

THE PERIOD FROM LUTHER TO SPENER.

Period of
decline of
preaching.

THIS is a long period ; for Luther died in 1546, and Spener was born in 1635, so that it was more than a hundred years from Luther's death till the time of Spener's full activity. But the character of the preaching during this period may be dealt with in one survey. Although it had its

Causes.

changes and varieties, it was, on the whole, a period of decline, and we shall look to-day at some of the causes of the decline.

National and
political
disquiet.

1. The first of these was national and political disquiet. During Luther's lifetime insurrections had broken out ; and one of them, the Peasants' War, known also as the War of the Anabaptists, had brought special discredit on the Reformation, and wasted a great part of the west of Germany. It was a kind of communistic rebellion, and was suppressed with difficulty. In the very year of

168

Luther's death, Charles V., urged by the court of
Rome, made a determined effort to suppress the
religious freedom of the Protestants, and sanguinary battles were fought between him and the Saxon
princes. At last the emperor, Ferdinand II., fana-
ticised by the Jesuits, began in 1618 the terrible
Thirty Years' War. First, Bohemia, with its Reformation, was trampled under foot, and then the
war was carried by the savage Tilly and the formidable Wallenstein into the heart of Germany. Denmark and afterwards Sweden were called in by the
Protestants to their help. Gustavus Adolphus fell
in victory at Lützen in 1632, but the war went on,
and when it was closed in 1648, by the Peace of
Westphalia, a great part of Germany was left a
desert. The peasants had given up the cultivation
of their fields ; the inhabitants of captured towns
had been massacred in cold blood ; three hundred Protestant ministers had been slaughtered ;
and in many districts it took more than a century
to remove the marks of the struggle. Religious
liberty was secured in some parts of Germany ;
in others, especially within the Austrian dominion,
Protestantism was crushed ; thus Germany was
divided into two camps.

The effect upon religion and, as a consequence,

upon preaching can be understood. The Protestants had to fight for their freedom ; and although
to some extent they secured it, the passions that
were roused were not favourable to the studies of
ministers or to the edification of the people. The
wonder, indeed, is that religion survived.

Doctrinal disputes.

2. There was another kind of war that told un-
favourably on preaching—the war of doctrine.
There was first the polemic of Protestant with
Romanist. The Reformed church had to justify
itself to its own adherents ; and all the preachers of
the time, not only in Germany but in France,
England, and Scotland, were occupied with the
Romish controversy. There were, besides, the
controversies between the Protestant churches.
Very early the Reformation divided itself into two
great parts—the Lutheran, to which the name
Protestant first belonged, and the Reformed, which
followed Zwingle and Calvin. Both of these
found a footing in Germany ; the Lutheran chiefly
in the north, the Reformed along the Rhine.
Their controversies are now well-nigh laid, but
then they were very keen and long. The precise
import of the Sacraments, of Justification, of Sufficient Grace, &c., was debated in every possible
form, and absorbed the attention of most of the

prominent preachers. Out of those controversies arose another, about peace and union. Calixtus, professor at Helmstädt, and one of the most distinguished divines of the day, seeing the evil of those divisions, proposed terms of concession by which the contending churches might be brought together.* He was attacked for the proposal, and for the heresy of holding that there could be open questions in such a case. His chief antagonist was Calovius, professor at Königsberg, a man of ability and great learning, but of the most combative and dogmatic spirit. This controversy, known as that of Syncretism, filled all Germany, and raged for years. Its effects on the minds of preachers and of people were of a very hurtful kind.

3. There arose out of this still another evil, that Dogmatism. of hard dogmatism in matters of faith. The truths of the Gospel were considered in their relation not to heart and conscience, but to the logical reason. The aim of Christian teaching was not so much that they should be felt in their saving and re-

---

* Calixtus suggested the concurrence of the first five centuries (*consensus quinquesecularis*) as a common basis for all the churches, maintaining that the diversities which have since arisen are secondary.

generating power, as that they should be held in an
orthodox creed, and defended to the utmost edge
and article. Thus religion hardened into a crust;
and the doctrines of religion, instead of being like
the bones and vertebræ of a man, covered by the
muscles and flesh and skin, yet giving strength,
solidity, and form to his structure, came to resemble those hard surface shells which shelter
feeble and molluscous creatures. Appeal was now
made to the authority of Luther and Calvin, rather
than to the Bible; and these great reformers
would have been as much surprised and pained
had they seen the use made of their names, as
Peter would be if he came back to find how the
Romish church regards him. Let it be understood, also, that those were days of gigantic industry
in learning—in philology, in antiquities, in writing
commentaries, above all in framing theological
systems; and this not only in Germany, but
throughout Protestant Christendom. It was the
age of the great French Huguenot divines, of the
English Puritans, of those Scottish theologians
whose names and works are enumerated by Dr.
Walker of Carnwath, and of the Dutch theologians
of the Federal School, Cocceius and Witsius. These
men did great work for their time in settling the

basements of Christian belief, and their writings are
mines of thought and learning for those who can
use them. But they are not models for preachers,
and the evil was that they were so used. The
preaching which resulted became in many cases of
a Scholastic kind, dry and hard and formal, full
of endless disputes. One well-known volume of
sermons, for example, preached in 1658, by Jacob
Andreä of Esslingen, is divided into four parts,
for the four quarters of the year ; the first against
the Papists, the second against the Zwinglians, the
third against the Schwenkfeldians, who were the
mystics and perfectionists of that time, and the
fourth against the Anabaptists. When such heresies had all been dealt with, preachers turned to
the early Christian age, and in their sermons the
Patripassians, the Nestorians, and the Valentinians
rose and fought again like the dead at Châlons.

There were men, however, who were conscious Efforts to
of the evil of all this, and of its bewildering and correct this
tendency—
deadening effect on the people ; and various
attempts were made by them to remedy it.

The first of these was the issue of works on the By variety in
best manner of preaching. There were as yet no method ;
lectures on homiletics or pastoral theology in any
of the universities ; but books were issued by

scholars and divines. Scarcely any work on homiletics worthy of the name had been published since the *De Doctrina Christiana* of Augustine. In the very beginning of the Reformation, Erasmus issued an elaborate treatise in four books, *Ecclesiastes*, or the Preacher, which was, however, of a scholastic character; Luther gave valuable hints in his *Table-talk;* and Melancthon, in his *Loci Communes*, suggested from the Bible topics for preaching, which served a useful purpose in the way of guidance.* But the man who did most

Hyperius, died 1564.

in this direction was Andreas Hyperius of Marburg, who may be called the father of the later Reformation preaching. He was too little appreciated in his time, but his merits are being now acknowledged, and his homiletic treatise, *De Formandis Concionibus Sacris*, which deals with the discovery of texts, the finding of materials, and the form of the sermon, has in it the foresight of genius. Had he been taken as a guide, the preaching of his country would have escaped many errors and a long decline. But he was followed by a number of men who either neglected his principles or pushed them to an extreme. The chief

* *Cf.* page 153; see Rothe's *Geschichte der Predigt,* section 88.

of these was Andreas Pancratius. This Pancratius often receives the credit of being the inventor of the synthetic mode of preaching, which was called after him the *Pancration.* It was, however, in use long before, as it could not but be, only he brought it more fully into notice. You are aware that there are two recognised methods of dividing sermons, the textual, or analytical, following the contents of the text, and the topical, or synthetical, selecting one or more points, generally one, from which the preacher branches forth. The earliest preaching was, as we have seen, of the textual kind, in the extended form of a Scriptural lecture, but there was always a tendency to pass from this to the synthetical or topical. Now, however, there were found out endless methods which were discussed in special treatises. As many as twenty-five are reckoned up in the Scholastic style—*methodus paraphrastica simplex, methodus paraphrastica mixta, methodus zetetica,* &c. There were also methods named after the different universities, the *Wittenberg method,* the *Jena method;* and methods were imported from other countries, the *English method,* the *Dutch method;* books being published with these titles as commendations. Exact rules were laid down for the treatment of texts; sometimes three introductions, *special, more special, most special,* were recommended, with five different kinds of applications. Nature was sacrificed to art ; texts were stretched out on the rack, and dealt with, not according to their contents or the wants of the people, but according to the method of some particular homilete or university. The formalism of the dogmatic theology of the time thus found its way into the manner of preaching, and the attempt to improve sermons by such means only made them worse.

By variety in subject.

Reform was attempted in another way, not so much by dealing with the form of sermons, as by varying the choice of subjects and matter. There were such men as Spangenberg who set themselves to comment on books of the Bible, and they no doubt did good. But the fashion of the time, which was for minuteness and word-hunting, led commentators into microscopic minutiæ, till they became wearisome to the last degree, while they overlooked the great moral and spiritual truths, and forgot the wants of the people. It was the old tithing of mint and anise and cummin, to the neglect of the weightier matters of the law. Others again gave discourses on the hymns of Luther and the other great German hymn-writers, approaching the old Scottish custom of prefacing the psalms that were sung by an explanation ; and this served a very good purpose, for people had come to sing without intelligence, if they sang at all. But as a substitute for preaching it failed, for it left the breadth and depth of God's Word out of sight. There were others who made it their chief aim to avoid doctrine, since dry dogmatics had done so much harm. If they were of a fanciful temperament, they took some emblem,—a rose, or a lily, or honey, and pursued it through all forms of allegory, ending in nothing. If they were of a practical turn, they took a proverb, not always a Bible proverb, and applied it to some phase of social life. There were sermons on the dressing of the hair, tobacco smoking, and so forth. Scarcely one of the subjects chosen by our sensational advertising preachers had not its prototype more than two hundred years ago in Germany.

But we are not to suppose that these things give us a full view of the state of things in Germany during this period. There were men who not only felt the evil, but saw where it lay, and sought the true remedy. There was Valentin Andreä, of Stuttgart, whom Spener wished he could recall

The true remedy.

V. Andreä, 1586-1654.

N

from the dead, and whom Herder has called "a rose among thorns." He was a living preacher, and also a poet, who satirised in verse the formalists and scholastics of his time. There was

Scriver, 1629-1693.

Christian Scriver, a man devout beyond most, whose works are still read by pious people in Germany, and whose "emblems" have something of the curious quaintness of old Francis Quarles. But the chief, and in some respect the master, of

J. Arndt, 1555-1621,

this school was John Arndt. For preaching and popular edification he is the foremost figure between Luther and Spener, and has, more than any other of that time, the characteristics of our Puritans—of men like Baxter and Rutherford and Bunyan, though without Bunyan's genius. His principal book, *Das wahre Christenthum*, "The true Christianity," which has lately been republished by Stier with some of Scriver's writings, was long a classic in Germany, and has gone through more editions on the Continent than any other book of devotion except *The Imitation of Christ.* It circulated even in Roman Catholic countries, with some changes and without the author's name. His avowed aim in writing it was (1) to draw the minds of students and preachers away from combative and scholastic theology ; (2) to lead good

Christians from a formal to a fruit-bearing faith ;
(3) to bring them from the mere science and
theory of Christianity to the enjoyment and the
practice of it ; (4) to show the meaning of a
Christian life as indicated by the apostle's words,
" I live, yet not I, but Christ liveth in me."

While seeing the evils of the hard dogmatism of
his time, Arndt did not cast aside doctrine, but
rather sought to quicken it with life, and to preach
to the heart as well as to the head. He was, like
Luther, a lover of John Tauler, and he was attacked
at the time as a mystic and an enthusiast, but
his defence was that when he was thirsty he would
rather go to a troubled spring than to a dry well.
While the sermons of the dry dogmatisers and the
trifling moralisers are forgotten or quoted only as
curiosities, Arndt is still a source of life in Germany ; and when the Gospel of Christ revives in
that land, the hearts of the children will turn to
him as one of the best fathers of the Lutheran
church.

Arndt was followed by two noted men of the The Gerhards.
name of Gerhard, cousins ; the one, John Gerhard,
the greatest theologian of his time, who owed his
warmth to Arndt ; the other, Paul Gerhard, a
great hymn-writer, whose sacred songs have done

much to ke :p alive religious feeling in Germany.
Indeed Arndt had scholars in many districts
who struggled for a while to preserve Christian
warmth ; but the. spirit of the time was too
strong for them, and they could not resist its
chilling forces.*

The teaching   The survey of this period, however, is fitted to
of this period. be useful to us. It may teach us never to despair
of the revival of religion in any country. For
a whole century after the death of the leaders
of the Reformation, Germany was in a state of
spiritual hardness and coldness of the most dis-
tressing kind. The warmth and life were chiefly
in polemical passion. Witnesses for the better
kind of Christianity were rare, and they were subjected to bitter attacks as enthusiasts. Yet a
genuine revival came in the course of the seventeenth century, and we shall hope that another
and a more lasting one will dispel the rationalism
of the present day.

In regard to preaching, we may learn not to
give ourselves much to polemics. Mere orthodoxy is nothing without life. A man may hold
all the articles of the creed, and preach them
regularly and in close harmony, without producing

* See Nebe's *Geschichte der Predigt,* vol. II., page 97.

more than a jointed skeleton, from which his hearers will turn with disgust. And if he preach them with bitterness and hate towards those who doubt them, he prepares the way for rationalism and indifference. On the other hand, life is not to be gained by rejecting doctrine, and railing at it, as some seem to think. This is only meeting one dogmatism with another—the positive with the negative. What is wanted is to present doctrine, *i.e.*, Gospel truth, with life, to speak the truth in love. Man must have doctrine for his head, and love for his heart. Christianity needs both a body and a soul. While the body cannot live without a soul, the soul cannot live in this world without a body.

Next, we may learn in regard to the form of preaching that, though the rules of homiletics are useful in their own way, especially in helping to correct errors, they are hurtful whenever they repress nature. Elaborate plans for introductions and divisions and perorations, which were once so much in fashion, have happily fallen into disrepute. Still some are apt to be led away by them. If you look into Claude's *Essay on a Sermon*, or into Simeon's writings, you will see how slavish the mind must become in trying to apply their confessedly elaborate schemes. Rules about making sermons are of use only so far as they help to cultivate nature, and teach us how to present truth clearly, connectedly, and impressively ; and to this there is no royal road in ready-made processes. The faculty must be gained by our own thought and practice, and by counsel as to how we can correct mistakes.

There are two advices which I must repeat, for they are all-important. Go to the Bible for yourself, and try to reach the meaning and touch the life of the special text with which you deal. Every text has a life; seek to seize it and draw it into the warmth of your own heart.

And then to your fellow-men in sympathy! Ask yourself what are their struggles and sorrows, and how this text of yours may help them ; and aim with all your might to bring these two together, the Bible and the heart of man. This will, with God's help, save you from the long error of the times we have been considering, and will give to your preaching spirit and life.

LECTURE XI.

IT has sometimes been said that Spener was the reformer of the life of the German church, as Luther was the reformer of its doctrine. This may place him too high, but it is certain that he was the most remarkable theological figure in Germany during the seventeenth century, and that he began a movement in the German church which long survived him, and which exercises an effect even on our country and our time. That we may understand his position, we must glance at the interval between Luther and him.

Luther was a preacher by his own natural gifts and by the grace of God, not by art and rule. Such a man gives a mighty impulse, but cannot himself train successors, and we noted, in last lecture, the comparative failure of those who sought to continue his preaching work by forming rules

The successors of Luther.

and writing books on homiletics. Indeed, from
the history of the Church, not excluding our own
country, it would seem as if after every great
upheaval, there must be a pause and re-action.
After the giants of the Reformation time, there
came a race of smaller men. They were distinguished scholars and hard students, but they
expected to bind the world by rules of grammar
and logic—all good in their place. They often
furnished fuel without fire, the fuel of the old
altar, but drenched with the water of cold secularism. There were dictionaries of arguments
and emblems and sermon-methods, to save the
preacher from thinking; there were books of
quotations from the Christian Fathers and the
Schoolmen, to save him from reading; everything
was provided for him, only the spirit and the life
were wanting. The Bible was still in his hands,
but instead of being studied as a living, gladsome
book, it was read through the spectacles of sketch
and skeleton makers. The doctrine of justification by faith was often in his mouth, but it had
become a dogma, a piece of hard surface orthodoxy, separated from heart and life, not connected
with the blessedness of forgiveness, nor leading
to a spiritual and active Christian course.

Then came the terrible Thirty Years' War, The Thirty
which barbarised the German people, provoked Years' War.
them by the despotism of the Pope and the
Emperor, and in many other ways left a legacy
of hatred and misery. Schools, colleges, churches,
were broken up ; and though the majority of the
nation clung more closely than ever to a nominal
Protestantism, they had lost in great measure
the knowledge and life of Christ. It was something like the twenty-eight years' persecution in
Scotland, which hunted out and killed the best of
the people, and, through the ignorance of the
curates and the profligacy of the rulers, introduced
an indifferentism and spiritual death, from which,
in many districts, we have not recovered to this
day.

Thus the place of Spener resembled that of our
Secession and Relief forefathers ; he was a repairer
of the breach, a restorer of paths to dwell in.
As we have already seen, there had been men of
light and power before him, but he was the man
appointed by God to make head against the evil
of the time, and to bring in a new movement.
We shall first sketch his life and then his work,
specially in regard to preaching.

Philipp Jakob Spener was born in 1635 in Alsace, Spener,
1635-1705.

which then belonged to Germany. He had truly
Christian parents, and from his youth up showed a
quiet, reflective nature, with a religious bent. A
strong impression was made upon him by the
Christian spirit in which a relative of·his own met
His training. her death. His first religious nourishment, apart
from the Bible, was drawn, as he himself says,
from Arndt's *True Christianity*, and from some
writings of Baxter, in all probability the earliest,
The Saint's Rest. His studies were pursued at the
university of Strassburg, under S. Schmidt and
Dannhauer, both thorough men; the latter of
whom wrote *The Milk of the Catechism* in ten
thick volumes, but was none the less a living
Christian. On leaving Strassburg, Spener, as was
then the custom, visited other universities, not only
in Germany but in Switzerland and France, where
Protestantism was comparatively free. He studied
Hebrew at Bâle under the younger Buxtorf, the
greatest orientalist of his time. At Geneva
he remained a whole˙ year, and was greatly
impressed by the piety and activity of the professors and ministers. He was himself a Lutheran,
but the constitution of the Genevan or Reformed
church commended itself to him in ˌnany respects;
especially did he admire the place which it gave

to the eldership and members. He was also moved by the fiery preaching of Labadie,* so different from the stiff and formal methods which then prevailed in Germany.

When he returned from his studies, his reputa- His career. tion had preceded him, and an attempt was made to secure him for a professorship in Würtemberg, but he accepted a place as preacher in Strassburg, where he also delivered lectures in connection with the university. Thence he was called after three years to an important post as Senior or chief minister at Frankfurt-on-the-Main, the scene of his first exertions for the reform of preaching and of religious life. In 1686 he was promoted to Dresden as Court-preacher to the Saxon Dukes, the descendants of the first friends of the Reforma-tion.† During his stay at Dresden, which lasted for five years, there were indications of jealousy among the clergy, and of dislike for his spiritual teaching at the Court ; and he was not reluctant to remove to Berlin, in 1691, where he was appointed

* A short notice of Labadie will be found in note D on page 199.

† The Dukes had degenerated sadly from the spirit of their ancestors. To secure the crown of Poland, one of them eventually became a Roman Catholic ; he lost the crown, but the royal family still remains of that religion.

to be Provost and Head of the Consistory under
the Elector of Brandenburg, the ancestor of the
kings of Prussia, who succeeded to the leadership
of German Protestantism when it was abandoned
by the Duke of Saxony.   In Berlin he spent the
rest of his days.

His activity.

His influence now extended over the whole of
Germany, and his life was one of great and incessant labour.   In addition to the duties of his office
as preacher and superintendent, he published 63
volumes in quarto, 7 in octavo, and 46 in
duodecimo, besides numberless pamphlets and
prefaces.   He had constant engagements from
8 A.M. till 7 P.M.   At the end of one year in which
he had replied to 622 letters, 300 remained
unanswered ; for wherever in Germany men were
stirred by the new Christian life they appealed to
him for guidance.   In order to overtake such work,
he withdrew entirely from company, and only
twice in nine years did he visit his garden.   He
took little share in polemics, and that only when
it was forced upon him, being a man of the most
charitable spirit, although he held fast by central
truths.   Towards the close of his life, the Germans
were divided in their attitude, some being strongly
opposed to him, others warmly devoted.   Yet

even his enemies admitted that his life was blame-
less, and that he was sincere in what he believed
to be the cause of God.   Having passed threescore
years and ten, he died as he had lived, testifying
that he was at peace with God through Jesus Christ.

Such was Spener's career ; perhaps the best
account of him, and of the movement which he initiated, is given by Freytag, the German novelist, in
his Sketches.   It is no wonder that even the secular
mind of Germany cherishes fond memories of him.
Had he been a Roman Catholic, he would be
represented as a saint, with an aureole of special
brightness round his head.

Of his general religious attitude, the most His religious
succinct explanation will be found in his *Pia De-* attitude.
sideria, or Pious Wishes, prefixed to an edition of
Arndt's sermons which he issued in the year 1676.
After describing the lamentable condition of the
German church, and bewailing it in the words of
Jeremiah, "Oh! that my head were waters," he
defines six desires which he cherishes for reform,
as follows :—

(1.) The larger circulation of the Word of God,
and private meetings of Christians for the study of
it.   (2.) The diligent exercise of the Christian
priesthood—*i.e.,* the co-operation of the members

with the minister for prayer and edification. (3.) The earnest conviction that knowledge is not enough in Christianity, and that we must also have life and action. (4.) A right bearing towards unbelievers, so as to carry on discussion with heart-felt love, and to seek not merely to answer them but to gain them and do them good. (5.) Such a course of theological training as will make students feel that they should seek progress in heart and life as much as in learning. (6.) A new way of preaching, in which the great aim will be to show that Christianity consists in the inner or new man, whose soul is found in faith, with the fruits of a good life as the results.

It will be seen that a number of those points anticipate the lessons of the revival in our own country at the end of last century, and that we

His view of preaching.

have much to learn from them still. At present we shall confine ourselves to his ideas about preaching.

The form of the sermon.

Of the form of the sermon and the rules of rhetoric, Spener makes little or nothing. He admits that they may be of some use in assisting the preacher to attain more clearness, and to divide his subject properly; but occasionally he decries them altogether as having done far more harm than good. He says that, though worldly causes may need the arts of oratory, in preaching the Gospel the truth itself and the conviction and earnestness of the speaker will, with God's blessing, gain the desired result. No doubt this view was a valuable protest against the formalism and pedantry of the time, but Spener pushed it too far; for logic and even rhetoric have their value for the preacher as well as for other speakers, and in this, as in all occupations, God blesses the use of means. Rules of logic and rhetoric do harm whenever they lead us to think more of the form than of the substance, and whenever they impair the individuality of the speaker; but they may guide us to present the substance in the best possible form, and may even help to develop and express our individuality. The injunction, "study to show thyself a workman that needeth not to be ashamed, rightly dividing the word of truth," implies that we are to do all in our power to make our discourse clear, impressive, and orderly. Yet the use of logic and rhetoric, especially with a weak mind, may pass into pedantry, and Spener's warning was needed for his time.*

* This may be seen by a reference to the French Roman Catholic preaching of that time, and to such English preachers as Tillotson.

The substance of the sermon. The two great essentials of preaching, then, according to Spener, are the substance of the sermon and the personality of the preacher. As to the substance of the sermon, he never wearies of insisting that it is to be found not in philosophy or science, but in the Scriptures, and that the man who knows the Scriptures best will, other things being equal, be the best preacher. The knowledge of philosophy is helpful, but a man who is mighty in the Scriptures will always be a better minister than one who is only or chiefly a philosopher. One must know them, however, not in a loose, disjointed way, but according to the "analogy of faith." Although given at different times and in divers manners, they form one book and have one plan. The two hinges on which all Scripture turns are Law and Gospel, to both of which the true preacher will have regard. He will preach the law not as the slave of Moses, but as the servant of Christ. He must so set forth its claims that men will feel that there is no hope for them in law, and that they are shut up to the Gospel. To Christians he will preach the law as a rule of life in its higher purity, which they are to follow as Christ's freemen out of love to Him. As to the Gospel Spener would have it preached always. Morality is nothing without it. The free justification of the sinner by faith in Christ is the necessary requisite for the keeping of the law in heart and life. Yet he insists very strongly upon the new life as a consequence of faith; indeed the emphasis which he lays on this distinguishes him from Luther. The great reformer dwelt upon justification because he was opposing the doctrine of salvation by works. Spener dwelt on the necessity for a new heart and life because he was opposing a dead, formal Protestantism. It was on this ground that some dogmatical theologians of his day charged him with denying the Lutheran doctrine of justification by faith; but the charge was utterly unjust. If anyone compares the first edition of Luther's *Commentary on the Galatians* with the second, he will see how the Antinomianism of the new sects that had arisen led him to insist more on the fruits of faith as necessary to Christianity, and it was this side of Luther's teaching that Spener developed. The new birth, the new life, heart-holiness as inseparably connected with faith—that is the key to the whole of his preaching and work.

As for the particular treatment of the sermon, His own method. though he disregarded form, he had his manner, and a rule of his own which he prescribes and fol-

O

lows. He calls it "the natural rule of the subject."
The first thing is to determine the meaning of the
text, and that by consulting the original, by exam-
ining the context, by comparing parallel parts of
Scripture, and by referring to commentaries ;
though these must always be sifted and judged by
the preacher with the help of God's Spirit sought
in prayer. After this comes the exposition of the
doctrine of the text, both in itself and in its relation
to other truths of the Bible ; and then its application
to different classes of hearers, which is made very
minutely and at great length, after the manner of
the Puritans. Spener has a long introduction to
each discourse, and sometimes two, a *general*, and
a *special*. Each one of these parts—the introduction, the exposition, and the application—is as
long as a good modern sermon. He is said to
have often preached for two hours. He com-
plained of himself that he could not be brief, and
that since he had not the gift of putting truth
into happy, memorable forms, he needed time for
impression. Yet his audiences gave him time,
though he was never brilliant, never used figures,
and was not impassioned. They were wearied of
the dull dogmatism of the previous school ; they
felt him to be a man of entire sincerity and

earnestness, bent on his sacred work; and his preaching had the variety that is gained from an independent study of the Bible, and independent views of human life. It was the heart that made him an acceptable preacher.*

Besides knowledge of the Scriptures, Spener required something in the personality of the preacher. He was anxious for a well-trained ministry, and two German universities, Tübingen in Würtemberg and Halle in Prussian Saxony, owe their origin to his exertions. But he always insisted that the preacher must himself be a Christian, and must speak from conviction. The truth he preaches must first be proved in his own heart, and then borne to his hearers by prayer. The most useful sermons, he said, are those in which there is least thought of self, and most thought of God and of the souls of men.

The personality of the preacher.

He had a strong aversion to polemical preaching; and his aversion was justified by the usage,

His aversion to polemics.

* Spener wrote out his sermons carefully and, after three
- readings, was able to preach them in their substance without the use of notes. He quotes, with approval, one of S. Schmidt's sayings, *Junge Blättler, alte Bettler*, which may be translated, "young extemporeness, old emptiness." Thoughts that occurred to him during delivery, he inserted afterwards into his manuscript.

then prevalent in Germany, of marching round the
walls of the Augsburg Confession, and doing battle
with the various enemies of the Lutheran doctrines.
He objected *in toto* to the introduction of polemics
into sermons, except when the text required it, or
when there was danger of the people being misled
by some doctrinal error ; and, even then, controversy should be left to those who were qualified to
handle the controverted point convincingly.   He
saw that the polemics of the incompetent were
more likely to awaken the doubts of believers
than to convince gainsayers, and he trusted to
the earnest declaration of the truth as the most
fitting method of preventing and removing error.
It was one of his maxims that sermons should
always be simple, since the common people form
the majority of almost every congregation. His ideal
preacher was a man eager to communicate to others
truths which he had tested in his own heart and life.

The success of   During Spener's life, his work produced remark-
·his work.   able results, and for some time after his death
its influence continued and even increased.   Some
of his opponents, such as J. B. Carpzov,* were

* Johann Benedict Carpzov, the opponent of Spener, is to
be distinguished from J. Gottlob Carpzov, the opponent of
R. Simon, Clericus, and Spinoza.

eminent men, but they were chiefly found among
the high and dry churchmen, whose motto was
quieta non movere, and who disliked the freedom
and life of his action. Throughout Germany there
was a marked reform in the style of preaching.
The new university of Halle, which became, under
his bosom friend Francke, of whom we shall
presently speak, the head-quarters of the movement, had soon more than a thousand students
fired with religious zeal ; and Halle became also
a great printing-house for Bibles, not only in
German but in the original languages.* The
religious education of the young was cared for as
it had never been before. Societies for reading
and studying the Scriptures were formed in many
parts of the country, and spread into Denmark
and Sweden and Norway ; into Holland, England,
Scotland, and America. Certainly we cannot
ascribe all this to Spener, for it was one of those
great religious movements, waves of the Spirit's
influence, which from time to time have visited
the world. But in Germany, and the neighbouring countries, he was the chief instrument in
God's hand for commencing and diffusing it.

* The valuable Hebrew Bible of J. D. Michaelis was issued
from the Halle press.

We must reserve for other lectures that more interesting period of the history of the German church which shows us how Spener's work developed in the Pietistic School, and led to a wide and deep reaction from which Germany is only now emerging.   We shall find it to be a period full of practical lessons as to what we should cultivate and what we should avoid.

NOTE D, see page 187.

JEAN DE LABADIE.

Jean de Labadie, not to be confounded with Abbadie, was born in 1610, in Guyenne, and died in 1674, at Altona. He was a singular man, of wonderful fire and energy, called the greatest and truest preacher of his time. Originally a Roman Catholic and a Jesuit, he became a Protestant through reading Calvin's *Institutes*, and had a strong desire to form a pure Christian community. He preached at Geneva with wonderful power and acceptance, and established Bible-meetings, house visitation, and strict discipline; passed to Holland where he formed a separate community; gathered devoted adherents, and exercised much influence especially on the upper classes; and moved finally into Germany where he died. His followers increased for a while, and spread to the West Indies and America, under the name of Labadists, but they are now absorbed in other churches. They may be compared with the early Quakers or the Irvingites, but they bore more resemblance to the Plymouth Brethren; and they had good and evil about them. The evil was an uncompromising and narrow temper, a desire to form a perfectly pure community for which they had peculiar marks, and so a leaning to spiritual pride and intolerance. Their good was great earnestness and self-sacrifice, and the value which they set upon the life of Christianity, as distinguished from form and doctrinal orthodoxy. They influenced Spener, Tersteegen the mystic, and ultimately Zinzendorf and the Moravian Brethren, though in their case in a charitable and Scriptural direction.

LECTURE XII.

PIETISM: ITS HISTORY AND LESSONS.

Importance of
Pietism.

IN speaking of Spener and his work, we have indicated his relation to that religious movement of his time which is commonly called Pietism. But Pietism is so important in itself, and in its effect upon many parts of Europe, that it deserves separate consideration. We shall, therefore, deal to-day with its growth, its decline, and some of its lessons.

Part of a
general
movement.

Germany was evidently prepared for such a movement, and not Germany only but other countries. We find similar manifestations in Holland and Denmark, and in England and Scotland in various forms of Puritanism, followed by Methodism. We can trace the movement even among Roman Catholics, in Jansenism and Fénélon, and in abnormal shapes in Madame de Guyon and Madame Bourignon. Indeed, throughout Christian

200

Europe there were traces of weariness of dry dogmatic teaching and incessant polemics, and of a
wish to find relief in a religion of feeling. Whilst
Spener, more than any other in Germany, gave
voice to this movement, he was the child as much
as the father of it, and it cannot be understood
without reference to another German who, after
Spener, held the chief place in promoting it, and in
giving it shape.

August Hermann Francke* was born at Lübeck Francke,
in 1663, and died at Halle in 1727. He conse- 1663-1727.
crated himself early to the ministry, and, being told
that Hebrew and Greek were "the two eyes of
Bible knowledge," entered with the greatest ardour
into the study of these languages. In one year,
under the care of a learned Rabbi, he read the Old
Testament in Hebrew seven times. He acknowledges, however, that his aim was to become a
learned man, not to know the will of God. One His conver-
day, in preparing a sermon upon the words, " Peace sion.
be unto you, as My Father hath sent Me, even so
send I you," he suddenly felt that he had not heard
these words, nor received any such commission.
A terrible darkness came over him, and in the
inward struggle which followed, the whole of his

* He was a contemporary and correspondent of Boston.

life rose before him "as if he were standing on
the high tower of Lüneburg and looking down on
its houses." He fell down and prayed that, if
there were a God and a Saviour, he might know
them in forgiveness and love. His prayer was
answered, and he looked back to this season as
the birth-time of his soul. " Thenceforward," he
says, "I was in earnest for God and willing to
suffer all for His sake, and from that time also I
had more to suffer."

We cannot here give even a sketch of the
varied events of his life. Amidst continuous work
and severe struggles, he was sustained by a naturally cheerful heart and by reliance on God, and
was crowned at last by eminent success. He was
opposed, like Spener, by the hard and dry party,
calumniated and driven from his post, but re-
instated to labour with increased activity.* While
Spener's sphere was Frankfurt and Berlin, that of
Francke was the newly-formed university of Halle,
which became the head-quarters of the Pietists, a
name at first given derisively by the enemies of the

His pastoral work. movement. He was not only a professor in the
university, but minister of one of the town churches.

* An epitome of the controversy between the Pietists and
the Orthodox will be found in note E, on page 218.

The congregation was in a broken and desolate
state. The previous minister had been deposed
for gross immorality, and his example had told on
the people. There was sensuality among the rich,
misery and discontent among the poor ; while the
other ministers of the town drew their stipends
without caring for their flocks, and preached the
dry, thrashed straw of formal phrases. Francke's
church was at once crowded through the attractive
power of his preaching. It was not sensational,
nor filled with figures and stories, but drawn from
the Bible through his own heart. It was full of
faith and warmth, simple and direct, referring constantly to Christ, and to life through Him. All
the doctrines were in his sermons, but they were
more than doctrines, they were filled with spirit
and life ; and the presence of these makes the
difference between orthodox and evangelical.[*]
Presently he opened his morning family worship
to his neighbours, and gave a short exposition
of the Bible. The room was crowded ; he had to
move to the church ; and this informal meeting
became a regular morning service. He began to
seek out the young who were growing up in
ignorance, and held catechetical classes which

* A sketch of one of his sermons will be found on page 219.

were frequented by the old. He circulated little
tractates on Christian knowledge, on the Bible, on
prayer, on family religion, and against prevailing
His orphan-   vices. He took special pity upon the children who
age.   had been made orphans by the German wars, and
provided food for the most destitute of them in his
own house, placing a box at the door for contri-
butions—the first instance, perhaps, of a ragged
school. The largest room in his house was filled,
and he put it under the care of some of his senior
students.   Finding that constant personal influence was required to do the children any real
good, he arranged for lodging them in Christian
families.   Encouraged by a few large donations, he
resolved to found a home for them ; and at length
he raised an immense building, or rather pile of
buildings, in which, at his death, one hundred and
thirty-four infants were lodged and trained. With
this were joined schools for teaching the children
of poor parents, and others for giving a higher
style of instruction to those who could pay for it.
In these there were about two thousand children
when he died. He also set up a great Apothecary
Institute for supplying medicine and medical
advice, and an establishment for printing the Bible
in different languages, and other books for the

people. Those buildings still excite the wonder of every one who visits Halle, and the remarkable little book in which he tells how they were reared, *The Footsteps of God in the Building of the Orphan House at Halle*, may well be reckoned among the classics of Christian faith.

At the same time he was carrying on his work His university in connection with the university. He delivered work. lectures in successive years on the various branches of theology — on Dogmatics, on Homiletics, on Casuistics or questions of conscience, and on the Bible. His motto was, *theologus nascitur in Scripturis*, and he gave himself systematically to the special study of the books of the Old and New Testaments. He founded the Collegium Ministeriale for the exercise of preaching and catechising, and the Collegium Orientale for the study of the Old Testament, in which it was the rule that all the discourses should be in Latin, and that the Old Testament should be read in Hebrew once a year. At the same time, it was his desire that the studies should be carried on, not so much in the method of a science, as with a view to personal edification. He had a saying that theology is *Christianismi cultura uberior*, " the richer culture of Christianity ;" and in everything he made

Christ the beginning and the end of his work.
He taught that the motive of all study is the
glory of God ; that the means is the knowledge
of His truth in the Bible ; that the object is the
conversion of man by word and example. In this
he was supported by his colleagues, and the effect
was great. While Wittenberg, the university of
Luther and Melancthon, had become the habita-
tion of a dead and formal orthodoxy, Halle was
the home of living faith. As yet rationalism was
unknown in any prominent part of the Church, but
outside of the Church there was much infidelity.
Halle had soon eight hundred theological students,
and before many years twelve hundred, a greater
number by far than attended any other of the
German universities ; and the students spread the
The spread of movement throughout Germany. Before the death
the movement. of Francke it was felt everywhere, and extended
into the neighbouring lands. One cannot but
admire the lofty faith, the untiring energy, the
administrative power and tact of this good man.
Although he was assisted by others into whom he
had breathed his spirit, his health repeatedly broke
down under the burden of toil and care ; and he
had to seek for recovery in journeys to different
parts of Germany and to Holland. These journeys

became serviceable to the Christian cause, for wherever he went he removed prejudices, changed enemies into friends, and planted the principles of a living religion. At length he became conscious of the final failure of his strength, and in his last lecture he gave a farewell blessing to his hearers. Lingering afterwards with some friends in the garden of the Orphan House, he traced his life experience, and poured out his heart in a fervent prayer of thanksgiving for the gracious leadings of God. Not long afterwards he fell asleep.

One would have thought that German Christianity was now entering upon a long cloudless day. And, indeed, for a season those influences were productive of great good. We may say of the generation of ministers reared under Francke, as of Israel in the days of Joshua, that they "served the Lord all the days of the elders that outlived him, who had seen all the great works of the Lord that He did for Israel." But there were other forces already at work. The infidelity which became so prominent in the middle and at the end of last century had its seeds in the ground and was shooting up. It has been said by enemies that the seed was sown by

The rise of counter influences.

Pietism, but it may rather be said that Pietism
delayed the growth. For the infidelity of the next
age appeared in England before it came into
Germany, and it was strongest in France, where
the only Pietism was the short-lived and limited
school of Jansenism. Yet it is true that Pietism
failed to deliver Germany from unbelief. In the
time of Frederick, named the Great, and his friend
Voltaire, it invaded all ranks. Under Semler, the
father of modern rationalism, it proceeded to sap
the Bible, book after book, and to carefully remove
every trace of the supernatural by glosses and
fanciful explanations. It assailed the Canon under
Reimarus. Then at last under Strauss, taking
Hegelianism into its service, it sought to resolve
the gospels into myth and legend, left Christ a
shadow, and denied the personality of God and of
the soul. This spirit pervaded Germany until it
turned the ministers into teachers of little moralities, emptied the churches, and formed a mass of
indifferentism, which the believing men of the
present day are slowly endeavouring to leaven.

Failure of
Pietism.

Although German Pietism did not cause this
infidelity, we may naturally ask how it is that it did
not prevent it. This is a very important question,
bearing as it does on our teaching, our preaching,

and our Christian life, and we shall try to give
some thoughts by way of answer.

There is an easy way of answering which some
take. They say: "Things never abide in one
stay; men will have change, and they are right to
seek for change, since, as the poet says, 'one good
custom would corrupt the world.' When they
weary of dogmatism they take to pietism, when
they weary of pietism they take to rationalism."
There is enough of truth in this to make it plaus-
ible. A great mass of men—we may say the great
mass of men—are fickle, and like the old Athenians
are bent on hearing "some new thing." But we
who believe in a Bible, in a Christ, and in a Church
of the living God, believe also that there is something fixed, that the ground we stand upon is not
shifting sand, and that if there be change, not in
forms merely but in essential truths, there is a real
reason for the change. Further, since we hold
that religion is primarily of the heart, with conversion and regeneration as its central elements, we
may be sure that if these truths failed to secure
permanence when they were so earnestly impressed
by men like Spener and Francke, there must have Its defects
been defects in the method of their work, real with regard
to :—
defects, although perhaps not apparent at the first.

P

In seeking to indicate its defects, we may classify
them as they concerned the mind, the heart, and
the active life.

(1.) The mind.   1. As to the mind, it cannot be said that the first
leaders of Pietism neglected it, for they sought to
give the rising ministry a thorough knowledge of
the Bible, and also of Bible doctrine. Yet one
can see that they made this training bear very
largely, if not almost exclusively, on the question
of conversion and the state of the heart. Now,
these are not the only aspects of Christianity.
There is what the apostle calls "the building up in
our most holy faith," when we "leave the principles
of the doctrine of Christ, and go on unto perfection." There is the light which the Gospel casts on
the works and ways of God in the world, on the
plan of the universe, and on the varied forms of
human life and action. Among the leaders of the
Pietistic movement there was an avoidance of such
themes, and this grew into a prohibition of them
on the part of many of their followers. They
distrusted science and literature and those healthy
modes of thought and feeling which are also part
of God's truth and God's world. ˙ Thus the preaching of the later Pietists became dull, tame, and
monotonous, not merely unattractive to men of

the world, but deadening to Christians, because
it did not furnish food for thought and for spiritual
growth. While it is right that we should aim at
conversion in our preaching, and also that we
should seek for revivals, we shall lose all the blessing
which these may bring into the Church, unless we
cultivate growth, and lead Christian men into the
treasures of knowledge and understanding. The
want of breadth and variety and freshness in their
supply of mental nourishment had much to do
with the failure of the Pietists.

In connection with this we cannot overlook their
notable neglect of the arts of oratory, which was
aggravated by the undue attention they gave to
speaking and writing in Latin. They gained no
proficiency either in clear or in coloured language,
and indeed were gradually unfitted to make any
powerful use of their native tongue. If we are to
maintain popular interest in religious truth, we
must bend all our strength towards making our
speech telling and pointed ; we must not think
that even Bible truth, if it is served out in dull,
heavy fashion, with length as a substitute for
strength, will produce its proper result.

2. A second reason for the decline of Pietism (2.) The heart.
lay in its relation to the heart. It is true that the

very strength of the early Pietists lay in their appeal from the dead dogmatism of the understanding to the living experience of the heart. Yet the heart cannot continue to live on its first experiences. These must indeed remain, but in new forms; like the life in a tree, which grows naturally into leaf and flower and fruit, but dwindles and decays when crushed back on its root. If the Christian heart constantly reverts to the fact of its conversion and examines its own moods and motives, it becomes morbid from its self-inspection, conceives doubts and phantoms, and pines away into an unhealthy subjectivity. Those who are acquainted with James' *Anxious Enquirer*, Edwards' *On the Religious Affections*, and other such books in our own language, know that with all their excellence this is their danger. While there are frivolous, superficial people who need to be told to go into themselves, there are Christians who need to be told to go out of themselves, to be less concerned for the state of their hearts, and to pay more attention to Christian truth and Christian work. Sometimes it needs courage to say this plainly to those who think that they show their Christianity by discussing and exhibiting their feelings and their motives, but no honest Christian minister will shrink from telling them the truth. The prevalence of this introspective habit in the days of German Pietism produced many excesses and eccentricities in religious life; it assumed heights of asceticism that were inconsistent with a real belief in God's guidance of the world, and with the fulfilment of the duties of the Christian Church. This led Spener himself to say that "he had more to fear from the follies of his friends than from the attacks of his enemies."

There came to be associated with this an affected language about spiritual experiences, real in the first gush of emotion, but sought out and mechanised when it was no longer fully real. Not only was this injurious to the individual, it sounded hollow to the hearers. While speech should be "with grace," it should be seasoned with salt, with enough of salt to keep it fresh. Christian ministers lose their influence if they rigidly avoid the ordinary methods of conversation, and abstain from discussing serious topics in a free and open way.

This, then, was the second error of the Pietists; they tried to detain the heart in a state of self-inspection, and they cultivated language about it that became unreal.

(3.) The active life.

3. This leads us to the third of their faults, which concerned the active life. In the beginning of the movement there was, indeed, a considerable amount of Christian effort, especially at Halle. One might find there the germs of most of our modern religious movements — of Home Missions, Ragged Schools, Bible-circulation, Tract Societies, and Foreign Missions. Francke, more than any man of his time, anticipated that practical aspect of Christianity which has marked the present century. But elsewhere it was different. The societies that arose throughout Germany aimed chiefly at edification, and confined their attention to their own members, as "brethren" and "sisters" who possessed a higher amount of religious life than other Christians. Spener hoped at one time that the whole Lutheran church would be pervaded by a personal awakening; but the opposition he met with disappointed him, and led him to foster these select companies, *ecclesiolæ in ecclesia*, little churches within the church, as they were called. They lacked the power of united government, discipline, and action, and they tended to keep their members aloof in a self-satisfied isolation, not only from the ungodly world but from the formalism which prevailed in the church around them.

This isolation, and the sense of superiority which it nourished, led to a species of religious pride, and their very pity for others was ready to pass into uncharitableness and contempt. Had they been able to form separate and independent churches, as the Methodists did in England, and our own fore-fathers in Scotland, those consequences might have been largely prevented ; the religious history of Germany would, it is true, have seen more denomi-nations, but also more Christian activity, with a healthier development in the train of its great spiritual impulse. But the Lutheran church at that time had a very strong feeling against any-thing like Separatism or free self-government of churches, and it is a question whether the civil authorities of the time would have permitted separation. So it happened that the Pietists, cut off from healthy independent action, became gradu-ally isolated companies or coteries, with a large amount of spiritual pride, and a growing narrow-ness which kept the name Pietism from rising to the honourable significance of Methodism and Nonconformity in England. It passed through stages of decay, and sank at last into a party, like that well-known section of the church of England which, though once represented by large-minded men, ultimately became a narrow *ecclesiola in ecclesia*, and drove such men as Frederick Robertson and Charles Kingsley into prejudices against evangelical doctrine.

Yet this was not the whole outcome of Pietism. God can make His truth outlive and triumph over human error, and in another lecture we shall try to show how men like Spener and Francke were, in their noble earnestness and self-denial, doing lasting work.

Lessons.   Meanwhile, we may learn this, that in our preaching we must aim at dealing with all the breadth of man's nature. If we address the mind alone, we shall make hard, cold dogmatists; but if we address the heart alone, we shall produce weak and narrow sentimentalists. Our aim should be both light and life. Again, when God sends times of quickening, through conversion and revivals, we should be specially careful to lead men out from dwelling on moods and frames, into the more bracing elements of Christian edification and Christian service, into the breadth of God's Word and the activities of God's world. Lastly, we should be thankful that the history of Christianity in our country has saved us from being an *ecclesiola in ecclesia*, living in morbid and

inactive self-congratulations. That is the heresy
of " schism in the body," of which Scripture speaks.
Our fathers formed a Christian church which has
power of free independent action, and which finds
in that action life and health and strength. For
what the individual needs, the Church needs—
action to help her to recognise and to preserve the
truth, and to bring her at the same time into
sympathy with all who are seeking to do good to
men in Christ's name and for His sake.*

* See Note G, on page 221.

Note E, see page 202.

The Controversy between the Pietists and the Orthodox.

On the Orthodox side, with bad temper, were Mayer of Hamburg, Schelwig of Dantzic, J. B. Carpzov, and Deutschmann; and in a good spirit, Ernst Löscher of Dresden, a pious and learned man. The watchword of the Orthodox was, "The Church and the doctrines;" of the Pietists, "The Individual and Life." The Orthodox held by the Confession; the Pietists by the Bible. The Orthodox looked to ordinances as means of quickening; the Pietists, to the Holy Spirit. Their special differences gathered round the following questions :—

(1.) Is knowledge or life (will) first in conversion? The Orthodox said "knowledge;" the Pietists ultimately admitted that knowledge is first logically, but they held that really they are simultaneous.

(2.) Can an unconverted man have a saving knowledge of the Gospel? In answering this in the negative, the Pietists were led into confusion; and they eventually said that an unconverted man may gain much knowledge that appertains to salvation, it being felt that otherwise there could be no response, and conversion would be mechanical.

(3.) In what sense does faith justify? The Pietists answered, "in virtue of the germ of life which God discerns in it." The Orthodox charged them with confounding Justification and Sanctification. Löscher says : *Fidem justificare non quatenus agit vel suam activitatem exerit, sed quatenus recipit et habet.*

(4.) Can an unregenerate minister be a means of conversion? The Orthodox answered: "Yes; the Church acts through him ; " the Pietists said : " Nothing good can come through him ; but good may be done by the Word of God in his mouth."

(5.) Can Christian men reach perfection in this life ? The Orthodox said " No ; " while the Pietists spoke of a modified perfection, which, though not sinless, may be full and rounded.

(6.) In what relation does the Confession stand to the Bible ? The Orthodox insisted on adhering to the former, *quia* not *quatenus*, ascribing to it a kind of inspiration ; the Pietists inclined to accept the Confession *quia*, so far as its chief points are concerned, but to leave room for a *quatenus* in secondary matters.

In addition to the above, which may be compared with the summary given by Kurtz (Vol. II., sec. 46), there were differences with regard to Eschatology, the Pietists looking for a literal Millennium, the Orthodox for a time of general improvement. As to secular amusements, the Pietists forbade many which the Orthodox permitted as ἀδιάφορα.

NOTE F, see page 203.

SKETCH OF SERMON BY A. H. FRANCKE.

LUKE viii. 4-16—The Parable of the Sower.

Introduction : Not enough to hear the Word of God, we must take heed what and how we hear, and ask if we are bearing fruit from it.

Theme stated : How we are to act so that the Word of God may come to a true, ripe, and rich fruit.

Short prayer bearing on the subject.

I. A man must learn to know the right seed, and that by looking to the Good Sower, Jesus Christ. It is in His

Word, the Word of God, specially the Gospel Word—"Thy sins are forgiven thee." This is the beautiful and precious little seed which, when falling into the sinner's heart, brings the sweet and joyful message of grace, and springs up in the soul as righteousness and peace and joy in the Holy Ghost. We also know the right seed by its power. Man's seed cannot overcome sin or fill the heart ; power comes only from Christ's hand.

II. A man must see that the field is prepared. Here the husbandman may be taken for a copy, and the parable followed. (1.) The heart must be freed from the hard wayside surface ; the thinking, speaking, or doing of evil makes the ground so hard that the seed cannot enter ; there must come the plough of the law, the stern plough of Sinai. (2.) The heart must be freed from the rock below the surface. The understanding often takes the seed and talks ot it ; the fancy takes it and is pleased with it ; while the heart beneath is rocky and callous. The heart must be broken—a contrite heart. The rock must be pierced. We need repentance to open it for the seed, and for this we must plead with God who alone can take away the hard and stony heart. (3.) The heart must be free from thorns and thistles—*i.e.*, the worldly mind, the love of worldly pleasures, the anxiety of worldly cares, which deprive the seed of room for growth. Therefore, pray the Lord that He may tear out such thorns and thistles, clearing the field for the precious seed.

III. A man must work and wait for the seed to grow. Here, again, the husbandman is our example with his harrows and his roller waiting through weeks and months in sunshine and rain, in drought and frost, in weariness and fainting of heart, till the grain is ripe. Therefore (1.) the Word must be kept in the heart, not in the memory only, hidden there and pondered. Parents, hide the Word in your children's hearts. (2.) It must be commended in faith and prayer to God, who is the God of the harvest, of the early and latter rain. (3.) It must be waited for. It does not grow in a day, at least in its fulness. It needs the cross, and often many crosses to drive it in and cover it up. (Then follow words of sorrow for the small spiritual harvest in Germany after so many years of waiting, and the sermon closes with a suitable prayer.)

It will be seen that the substance of the sermon is Scriptural and evangelical. The form is easy and natural, following the passage; the illustrations are homely; and there is a constant endeavour to come into contact with the hearers. There is a tendency to diffuseness and repetition in the language of the sermon, which was one of the faults of the Pietists.

Note G, see page 217.

The Bible, the Church, and the Individual.

The growth and decline of Pietism show us that while there are three great factors in Christianity—the Bible, the Church, and the Individual—healthy Christian life is maintained by giving each of these its proper place.

If the Church be exalted to the repression or depression of the Bible, we have Romanism or High Churchism. The individual life withers from want of contact with the quickening power of God's Word, while the activity that remains tends to externality both in motives and in manifestations, or retreats into Asceticism.

If the Church be exalted to the repression of the Individual, we have formal Orthodoxy and rigid Confessionalism; the tendency then is to narrowness and intolerance of spirit, and to mechanism and partisanship in work.

If the Individual be put above the Bible, we have either

Rationalism or Mysticism. The Individual selects for himself according to his inner light, whether that be the light of
the bare understanding or of unregulated feeling; he thus
becomes his own Bible.

If the Individual be placed above the Church to its
depreciation, and as a critic, we have Brethrenism and
Atomism. This promotes a spirit as intolerant as that of
hard Orthodoxy.

It is also possible to set the Bible unduly above the
Church and the Individual by a rigid literalism, which
regards it as a book of legal precepts and restrictions,
instead of as a history of revelation supplying us with facts
and principles. This attitude also leads to hardness, and
produces fanaticism. Many points of Church government
and individual duty must be determined by principles, which
can be reached only by a liberal and intelligent method of
interpretation.

Interpret the Bible in its breadth; stir the depths of individual life; employ the Church for both of those purposes;
so Romanism, Brethrenism, and Rationalism will be best
encountered.

LECTURE XIII.

THE OFFSHOOTS OF PIETISM: BENGEL AND ZINZENDORF.

THE later history of Pietism is very sad and yet very instructive. It reached its strongest period about the time of Francke's death, and then it entered upon a course of decline which continued to the middle of last century, when it almost disappeared. Those who followed its great leaders—viz., Francke the younger, Joachim Lange, and others, had neither their mental power nor their spirit. They became narrow and ascetic, dark and bigoted, and for the freshness and strength of feeling of the earlier men, they substituted an affected talk and a withdrawal from the ordinary employments and enjoyments of human life. They divorced Christianity from humanity, and there came a recoil, a revolt against their aberrations in behalf of the bare, cold understanding which assumed the name of reason. This is

Recoil from Pietism.

223

one of the most usual movements in Church
History. One-sided, over-strained mysticism leads
to its opposite in a one-sided rationalism which
leaves no room for feeling and rejects everything
it cannot understand. This spirit found its expression in Semler, the father of modern destructive

Semler,
1725-1791. criticism. Curiously enough, Semler made his
appearance in Halle, where he was appointed a
professor in 1751. His chief attention was directed
to the Canon of Scripture. He was a man of great
acuteness and unwearied industry, and of wide but
unregulated learning, strangely deficient in guiding
principle and unable to see whither his conclusions
were carrying him. In the latter period of his life
he shrank from some of the conclusions which
others drew from his views, but in the beginning
his bold utterances knew no bounds. They gained
a new importance from their appearance in so
orthodox and pious a university as Halle, though
they were to be found half a century before in the
writings of Richard Simon, Leclerc, and Astruc.
We have not time now to trace the development of
these views. It must suffice to say that at the end
of the century no trace of Pietism or orthodoxy
survived in Halle except in the person of the
venerable Georg Knapp, who remained faithful

among the faithless, and whose lectures on theology * will well repay a perusal.

Is this, then, the end of the Pietism of Spener Survivals of
and Francke, and of the life which it poured into Pietism.
the Lutheran and Reformed churches of Germany?
Does that fresh, noble river that promised such
fertility end in a waste of sand? There are two
rivulets from it, which were small at first but
became rivers that afterwards approached each
other ; and it is to these that I turn your attention
to-day.

Johann Albrecht Bengel, who was born near J. A. Bengel,
Stuttgart in 1687 and died in 1752, is a name of 1687-1752.
the very first importance in the religious history
of Germany, and especially of Würtemberg. His
great work is his *Gnomon* or Index to the New His Gnomon.
Testament, which should be in the hands of
every student, and which has done more for the
study of the Bible than any book since the *Commentaries* of John Calvin. It contains, as the title
implies, finger-points towards interpretation, full
of pregnant meaning and of that insight which
amounts to genius, and which comes from the
enlightening of natural gifts by God's spirit. In

* Translated and annotated by Dr. Leonard Woods, of
Andover.

its original shape the *Gnomon* formed two moderate-sized octavo volumes, which were edited in Latin by Bengel's son, with a short life prefixed. It has given tone to the best German commentaries of modern times, those that unite thought and learning with reverence and piety; and it was of God's providence that such a book was being prepared just before Semler began his cold-blooded and destructive criticism at Halle. Semler dealt with details without regard to spirit or unity; Bengel dealt with details but with a regard for unity. We may give a brief resumé of his principles, which are important to all students of the Bible.

His principles. Holy Scripture shews a connected divine economy. The same God who in the Old Testament calls Himself the God of Abraham, Isaac, and Jacob, is in the highest sense the Father of our Lord Jesus Christ. He has revealed in the Bible His one clear and perfect word, and has fulfilled in the New Testament what He promised in the Old. The Holy Scripture is itself the best vindication of the truth of its contents. Its effect on man is of a kind that can be ascribed only to God. For this effect, however, it is necessary that we should not pick out separate parts, but appropriate and imbibe the whole.

While the thoughts of the different writers must be understood in their grammatical and historical sense, each part must also be referred to the complete revelation taken as an intelligible unity. Further, as interpreters, we must carry nothing of our own into the Scripture ; we must take out of it only what is there, nor dare we disregard anything that it contains:

Besides writing the *Gnomon* and other books on His attitude. the interpretation of Scripture, Bengel was occupied during his long and active life in teaching, in preaching, and in superintendence. He was a man in whom piety, learning, and sagacity or balance of mind, were finely blended. His piety had grown from early training in a religious home, but it was quickened and moulded, as he tells us, by the writings of the Pietists and afterwards by intercourse with them. He did not, however, connect himself with the Bible unions which Spener and Francke formed in the course of their visits to Würtemberg, and when the later Pietists showed a separatist spirit he held aloof and pursued his work steadily and in all charity. His judgment preserved him from extremes both of hard dogmatism and of heated fancy, while l e was far removed from the rationalistic tendencies

which were fast rising. His preaching was
thoroughly evangelical, though he did not dwell
upon conversion as constantly as did the Pietists.
"That doctrine," he said, "is very important; it
is the finger-hand of the clock, but we must
remember also the round dial-plate—all duties in
their turn." His preaching was also more exposi-
tory than that of the body of the Pietists, and had
therefore more of the breadth and variety of
Scripture. His weakness, if we can call it so,
was that he dealt rather frequently with prophetical chronology. He fixed, *e.g.*, upon 1836
as the year when a great catastrophe would befall
the kingdom of evil—a catastrophe still delayed.
Some of his general conjectures, however, have
been remarkably verified, and are quoted by the
Christians of Würtemberg, as Fleming's *Fulfilling
of the Scriptures* used to be quoted among us.*

His charac-
ter.

The character of Bengel shows a rare combination of moderation with depth. It may be illustrated by one of the extracts from his journal
quoted by his son :—" My greatest burden is not
my weak physical frame, or my relative afflic-

* Bengel was led towards this line of study by reading
Vitringa on the *Apocalypse.* Examples of his conjectures
will be found in Note H on page 239.

tions, or the attacks made on me, though from all these I have suffered. It has been hidden in the heart, the burden of eternity. Eternity itself in its infinite moment has pressed upon me, and sometimes entered my soul like a sword." This, he said, caused him to be taken for sad among the joyful, and for joyful among the sad. He died with great calmness, pointing to his breast when the words were quoted, "Living or dying, I am the Lord's." His celebrated scholar Oetinger, the Christian philosopher, says of him, "He died according to his desire; for his wish was not to leave the world with spiritual pomp and triumph, but in a common way, as when one is called to the door from the business of the house."

It was through Bengel, on the side of thought and Bible study, that the Pietism of Spencer and Francke revived in Germany after the reign of rationalism.*

The other channel through which Pietism reached later times was Zinzendorf and the Moravian Brethren.

* In Würtemberg the influence of the old Pietism is still felt. Those who adhere to it in fellowship meetings, while they also attend the ordinary church services, are reckoned at about 30,000. Some of them are very practical, and supply labourers for the mission field. Their standard books are those of Arndt and Bengel. Another section of a more

Brethren. We put these together, because they are both included in the history of a movement which is full of romantic interest, and which can be verified at each step. The Moravian or Bohemian

Their origin. Brethren are said to have had their rise among scattered Waldensians who fled from persecution. They were in their turn subjected to bitter harassment, and were compelled to conceal their views except in their homes and at private meetings.

Their revival In the eighteenth century, when a breath of revival was passing over all the Protestant churches, it visited them in their loneliness. There was a powerful longing for renewal and unity which was met in an unlooked-for way. One, Christian David, a carpenter in a Moravian village, was impressed by a sense of sin, and driven to seek for rest. Born and brought up a Roman Catholic, he knew nothing beyond his own church. A Bible which fell into his hands brought him to a degree of knowledge, and he had to leave his native land. He went to Berlin and joined the

speculative temper, whose meetings I have attended at Wildbad, in the Schwartzwald, read Oetinger and Fricker; while a third is notably given to singing hymns with lively popular melodies. The most noted preacher of the Bengel school was Georg Conrad Rieger, one of the most gifted men of his time.

Lutheran church, but he found it at the time cold
and dead. Thence he passed to Görlitz, in Silesia,
where he met with believing, warm-hearted Christians, who instructed and encouraged him. He
conceived a great desire to do something for his
own countrymen, and revisited Moravia several
times. He came at last in contact with the hidden
" Bible Christians," and gave them news of the
Christian world outside. They also were seized
with a desire to find some place where they would
be free to read the Bible and to profess their
faith. David left them, bent on securing the
fulfilment of their wish, and in the course of his
search he was introduced by the friends at Görlitz
to young Count Zinzendorf. This was in May,
1722.

A place of refuge was provided by Zinzendorf, Their settle-
on the northern slopes of the Giant Mountains, ment at
Herrnhut.
whither many Moravian families fled, leaving
house and lands for the Gospel's sake. Here they
raised a village, which became the mother of all
their communities, and which they named Herrnhut, " the Lord's watch." From this name they
are called in Germany Herrnhüter, " the Lord's
watchmen." Although Moravian in origin, and
connected with the ancient church of the *Unitas*

Fratrum, they became ere long more German than Moravian, and spread through the rest of Germany in communities that took Herrnhut for their parent and model.

Zinzendorf.   That we may see their connection with Pietism, we must turn to Count Zinzendorf, the adoptive father of the community. He was descended from an old and noble Austrian family, who had been forced to emigrate into Germany from having embraced Protestantism. Born in 1700, he was reared in a religious home, and when ten years old, was sent to Halle, where for six years he was under the influence of Francke. At an early age he became decided in his religious life, and he His character. never swerved till he died. He was a man of lively fancy and poetic temperament, with considerable power of judgment, which, however, was ready to be carried away by his ardour and restless activity. His devotion to the Gospel took the form of an intense personal love to the Saviour, sometimes marked by an over-sweetness and familiarity which made his hymns distasteful to Bengel, whose depth disliked great demonstrativeness. Bengel and Zinzendorf were men who show in what different moulds Christianity may be cast; the one full of thought and regulated feeling, the

other full of impulse, demonstrative expression,
and action.

Zinzendorf devoted his whole life to the com- His devoted-
munity which he had been led by Christian ness.
David to found. All his means, all his powers of
body and soul, were expended upon it. He wrote
its hymns, he drew up its regulations, he attended
universities that he might reduce its theology to a
system, and he received license as a regular
preacher that he might set an example to its
ministers. He took on him the care of all the
churches, and attended to the minutest concerns
and to the humblest members. He travelled
through Germany, into Austria, Russia, England,
the West Indies, and America, to found communities and establish missions, and everywhere he
was fervid and unwearied in work. There were
present in him qualities that are seldom united—
a simple, child-like faith, great elasticity and
geniality, the power of organising and administer-
ing, and an indefatigable activity.

As a preacher, he attracted thronging multitudes. His preaching.
In Berlin, the highest State officials, artisans and
servant girls, officers and common soldiers, stood
side by side in his crowded audiences. His
sermons, or at least sketches of them, have been

printed from the notes of one of his scholars.
They are founded on the doctrine of justification
by faith, but they have poured into them the spirit
of John, caught from the school of Francke. The
ransom paid by Christ, does not, to his mind,
bring merely an outward pardon but an inward
redemption from the power of sin; the fervour
with which this truth is pressed home, and the
knowledge of the human heart which he possessed,
constitute the power of his preaching.

The United
Brethren.

Without entering into the history of the church
which he founded or renewed, the church of the
United Brethren, we may mention some of its
leading features.   It held in the main by the
doctrine of the Augsburg Confession, placing
emphasis upon the necessity of spiritual life.   Its
views as to the authority of Scripture were at first
somewhat vague.   Like many mystics, the Moravians tended to put the inner light over the Word
of God, and to select those parts of the Bible
which edified them, disregarding the rest as
unimportant or uninspired.   Their historian, Plitt,
acknowledges that this method, which left them
without a fixed objective guide, was apt to land
them in rationalism; but in the end they worked
themselves clear of this danger.   They made a dis-

tinguishing feature of the oneness of the Christian Church (*unitas fratrum*); and, while they formed themselves into a separate organism, they acknowledged the true Christianity of all who have the spirit of Christ, without which acknowledgment, indeed, the largest church reduces itself to a mere sect. In its action, accordingly, their church set itself to quicken what it called the διασπορά, the Church scattered throughout the world, and spoke of itself as merely the πρόσωπον, or face, which represented the unity of Christendom. It was especially active in mission work. There had been individual missionary efforts before this, but the Brethren were among the first Protestants to send out missionaries as a church, or rather the first to view the Church itself as a mission both at home and abroad. Their work in Greenland, in the West Indies, and in North America is celebrated.

Their missions.

> "See Germany send forth
> Her sons, to pour them on the farthest north;
> Fired with a zeal peculiar, they defy
> The rage and rigour of the Polar sky,
> And plant successfully sweet Sharon's rose
> In icy wastes, and 'mid eternal snows."

Their simple faith was unconquerable. Everyone has heard of the two Moravians who offered

themselves as slaves that they might gain access
to the negroes, and of those who entered the leper
enclosure with the prospect of remaining in it for
life. When Zinzendorf himself was approaching
the Island of St. Thomas, where their missionaries had been persecuted and imprisoned, he
said to his companion, a humble Moravian from
Herrnhut, " What if we find no one?" He calmly
replied, "Well, *we* are there;" whereon Zinzendorf
exclaimed, " *Æterna gens Moraviorum!*"

To the Moravians, then, we owe a stronger
conviction of the unity of the Church of Christ,
as well as a powerful stimulus to missionary
enterprise. On these questions they have led the
van.*

The later
influence of
those schools.
These are the two offshoots from the Pietism
of Spener and Francke which gave it a permanent
interest and influence—the school of Bengel
led to a deeper and more comprehensive study
of the Bible; and the school of Zinzendorf and
the Moravian Brethren transformed the *ecclesiolæ*
of Spener into an *ecclesia* that exercised an

---

* Plitt is the great historian of the United Brethren, but
his work is in MS. It has been condensed by Burkhardt
in his full article on *Zinzendorf* in Herzog, in which he
corrects mistakes in Kurtz.

important influence on the Church and the
world. Bengel said of himself, " I shall be forgotten at first, but I shall be remembered again,"
and the influence of his *Gnomon* reappeared
when the reign of the Illuminism of Semler was
over. It is seen in the best modern commentaries—those which are marked by the interpretation of spiritual insight and of the analogy of
faith as distinguished from that of mere grammar
and detail. In a similar way the Moravian church
may be said to lie at the root of the great
Methodist movement, which has done so much for
all English-speaking communities. When John
Wesley, in his first religious fervour, was ready to
be carried away by the mysticism of William
Law, he met with Peter Böhler, a Moravian, who
revealed to him the way of God more perfectly,
and showed him the great doctrine of justification which set him at liberty in keeping God's
commandments. The Wesleyans took from the
Brethren many points in their system—the watch-
night, the love feasts, the idea that the whole
Church is a missionary society, and the spirit of
Christian song, so marked in Methodist communities. Both John and Charles Wesley were led by
the Moravians to explore the treasures of the

German hymns, some of which they have translated, besides transfusing their general spirit into
their own compositions.

In later times another link was formed.
Schleiermacher, the founder of the new school of
German theology, which rose to protest against
the superficialism of the school of Semler, was
educated in a Moravian community, and owed to
its influence the principle with which he started
—the religion of feeling. This connection is well
traced in the finest of Tholuck's smaller works,
Guido and Julius.   .

So true it is that no work of faith or labour of
love is ever wasted. Though, like the old fountain
of the Greeks, it sink below the sea and seem lost
in sand and bitter waters, it rises in another land,
and, as a streamlet of the river of life, makes glad
in after years the City of our God.

NOTE H, see page 228.

EXAMPLES OF BENGEL'S CONJECTURES ON
RELIGIOUS LIFE.

The spirit of the time, he says, will become increasingly
one of scepticism and naturalism. The powers of nature
and reason will be so extolled that men will lose sight of the
supernatural; people will be paid for attacking with their
pens the bases of Christianity. Everywhere men will
declare for the sufficiency of bare morality; and not only
with the higher but with the lower classes free-thinking and
mockery of faith will take the upper hand. The Western
Empire will last for sixty years after 1740 A.D. (it really
ceased in 1804), the face of the world will be changed, and
the old maps be useless. The Latin tongue will not be
current. Marvellous tales and romances, be they true or
feigned, will be prevalent, and amusement the chief thing
sought in reading. If anything spiritual is introduced, it will
be in attractive tales, and the form of the representation,
not the improvement of the mind and heart, will be the
chief thing sought for. The doctrine of the internal word
will work immense mischief when it is carried out to its
consequences. Those who use it will say that they wish for
"the kernel without the husk"—*i.e.*, Christianity without the
Bible, and, from subtle beginnings, they will advance to
destructive consequences. Scepticism and superstition will
prevail together. People who have not an inner taste of
truth will thus fall into the hands of Rome. Socinianism
and Romanism seem far enough asunder now, but they will
then work together, and that will knock the bottom out of
the vessel. It is a great mistake that in Protestant churches
we have not begun sooner with foreign missions. I..

beginnings are made in the East and West Indies, which give a hope that other lands will receive what we refuse ; soon greater and brighter things will follow.

In the end, he proceeds, there will be a time of victory, when the Kingdom of God will bring in an overflowing fulness of the Spirit, and a deliverance from the wrong and suffering which men have inflicted on one another through their wickedness. Christians will still walk by faith and not by sight, and they will have to contend with sin and meet death. The law will remain, the Gospel will be preached, the commemoration of the death of Christ will continue till He comes ; but these will have a higher power. Kings and magistrates will exist, but they will go about among men as their brethren. Family and social life and husbandry and handiwork will continue, but extravagance and luxury will be unknown, and men will live in charity and mutual benevolence.

Many of the evils which Bengel foretold have come and still remain ; surely we also see the beginnings of the fulfil·ment of his hopes ?

LECTURE XIV.

THE Illuminism or Aufklärung, as the Germans name the next stage of their religious history, has its roots in the early part of the eighteenth century, but it does not appear in full force till 1760, and it lasts till the beginning of the present century, when it took new shapes and found new opponents. It thus coincides in the main with that period of our own Church history which we call the reign of Moderatism.

Before entering on it, however, we may speak briefly of a preacher who stands half-way between Pietism and Illuminism, the well-known Church historian, Johann Lorenz Mosheim. He died in 1755, and must have been over sixty years of age at the time, but the year of his birth is not certainly known. His birthplace was Lübeck, and

J. L. Mosheim 1693-1755.

241   R

the chief spheres of his activity were Kiel, Helmstädt in Brunswick, and Göttingen, where he was
both a professor and Chancellor of the university.
He was a man of universal learning, at home alike
in history, in ancient and modern philosophy, in
every branch of theology, and in the modern literature not only of his own country but of England,
France, and Italy. He gave lectures and wrote
on almost every subject except science. As a
theologian, he does not belong to the school of
the Pietists, but seeks to hold the balance between
reason and feeling. While he generally maintains
the orthodox faith, he tones down its strong
features, and presents it in such a way that it
awakens a sense of chill. His history of the
Church is a history of the circumference rather
than the centre, of the community rather than the
religion. It shows Christianity in a state of
perpetual war with heretics and heresies. Yet
his narrative, so far as it goes, is clear and free
from bias, and has still its value for the student.

His theory of   Besides being the most learned man, Mosheim
preaching.   was the most popular preacher of his time. His
lectures on Homiletics, which were published after
his death, explain his distinctive theory of preaching. "A sermon," he says, " is a discourse in which,

following the guidance of a portion of Scripture, an assembly of Christians, already instructed in the elements of religion, is confirmed in knowledge or roused to zeal in godliness." This, which he terms "edification," addresses both the intellect and the will, and is the sole aim of preaching. It follows that whatever is not for edification should be left out, and that whatever is serviceable for edification should be carefully adapted to the hearers. This leads to the question of form, and Mosheim lays down these rules:—that it should be in keeping with the dignity and importance of the subject; that it should be lively and have as much ornament as does not interfere with clearness; and that the language should, as far as possible, be that which is used in ordinary life among cultivated people.

Mosheim acted on these rules, and his popularity was of a corresponding character. His audiences, which were often so large that soldiers were required to keep order, were composed not so much of the masses as of the middle and upper ranks. He was the preacher of the educated and the enlightened; his style and manner were novel in the German pulpit, and awakened the greatest admiration. *His own preaching.*

It will be seen that this is widely different from the preaching of the Pietists. The special points *Different from the Pietists'*

of difference are these :—(1) His object is edification, not conversion.   (2) He takes a portion of
Scripture for guidance (Anleitung), not for the
purpose of ascertaining its meaning and enforcing
it.   (3) Further, he deliberately leaves out what is
not for edification—a method which often comes
to mean that preachers omit doctrines which they
dislike.   (4) There is also a difference in the
importance which he attaches to culture, form, and
language.

We may remark here that, while special attention to form is frequently a sign of a preacher's
conscious divergence from the opinions or senti-
ments of his audience, preachers who are in full
sympathy with the popular doctrine of their time
generally pay less attention to form.   This should
not be so.   We should be as careful of the form of
our discourses when we agree with our hearers as
when we differ from them.

On the whole, however, the preaching of Mosheim
was orthodox, although showing a measured moderation of feeling and a tendency to tone down or
avoid some Bible doctrines.

Rise of
Illuminism.
This brings us to the commencement of the age
of Illuminism, which came in like a flood.   There
were influences now at work unknown in the

previous century.* In Scotland, Hume was
writing his *Essay* against miracles, and Blair was
the great preacher. In England, it was the age of
the deists who followed Tillotson, the English
Mosheim ; and the old Presbyterian church of
Howe, Baxter, and Henry was passing along the
road of culture and progress, to drop one after
another of the Christian doctrines, till it became
the church of Taylor of Norwich, Price, and
Priestley, and the sparse Unitarianism of our day.
In France, Voltaire had taken the place of Pascal
and Bossuet, and, worse than Voltaire, the materialism of the Encyclopædists was sowing the seeds
of the Revolution.

The deism of England and the materialism of Its theology.
France invaded Germany, and found the soil more
than half prepared. Wolf, the successor of
Leibnitz in philosophy, but much his inferior every
way, had set up his system, which was, that whatever could not be demonstrated could not be
believed, being at best only a probability or a
possibility. Everything in heaven and on earth and
in the water under the earth was bound to stand
and explain itself to the enlightenment of the age.
The theology of the Illuminism was in harmony

* See Rothe's *Geschichte*, section 105.

with Wolf's philosophy.   It would have neither
the doctrine of the dogmatists nor the feeling of
the Pietists, but a "religion of common-sense."
At first the Illuminists did not attack the authority
of the Bible, but presented a number of ingenious
explanations of its statements.   The burning bush
of Moses was the sun shining on a desert shrub
covered with drops of dew.   The angels at
Bethlehem were the aurora borealis, the fancy of
the shepherds having supplied the rest of the
narrative.   The cures of the sick by Christ were
effected by animal magnetism.   When He walked
on the sea, He was only on the shore, but seen
through the morning mist.   His teaching about
Satan and about the Old Testament prophecies was
an accommodation to the prejudices of the Jews.
His recorded resurrection is to be accounted for
by the supposition either that He was not dead or
that His disciples were under a hallucination.
So they plodded through the Bible, laboriously
ejecting everything that did not agree with
their "common-sense," till a more advanced class
arose who said that it required more faith to
believe their explanations than to believe the Bible
as it stands.   But this belongs to a subsequent
period.

The preaching of this period was different in different parts of Germany.* In some places, as in Würtemberg, the country of Bengel, and also around Elberfeld and Bremen, the old Pietism held its ground, sharing only in the improvement of form to which Mosheim had given an impulse. But in places where Illuminism prevailed the matter of the sermons was entirely changed. Some preachers, unable to find in the Bible, as they read it, topics of sufficient interest, gave lectures upon economical or social subjects, such as agriculture, vaccination, and the making of wills,—or upon subjects taken from the natural sciences, such as the structure of fishes and birds. Most of this school, however, a very numerous one, took to "moral preaching." Sometimes they changed the language of the Bible, in order to make it, as they -said, more rational. For conversion or regeneration, they spoke of amendment of life ; for justification, of forgiveness on condition of repentance ; for the Holy Spirit, of the exercise of the higher reason ; for the atonement of Christ, of the spirit of sacrifice which He has taught us by His example, and so on. Sermons in our day

---

* See Schuler's *Geschichte der Veränderungen des Geschmacks im Predigen.*

preached and published with blast of trumpet as being new and up to the coming time, may find their parallel in volumes on which the dust of a hundred years has gathered. I have waded through three thick octavo volumes of sermons by the most noted preachers of the period, and other three volumes containing a history of the change in German preaching by a man who hailed the advent of rationalism as the dawn of a new day, and I had to cut the pages of the books from the first to the last. Yet some few men—the best of the school—may be briefly mentioned.

J. J. Spalding, 1714-1804.

Johann Joachim Spalding was born in Pomerania in 1714, and died in 1804. He was a very diligent student and minister, and wrote some books that attained great popularity. His first, *The Destiny of Man*, went through many editions, and was translated into French. He says of it very modestly that it made an impression merely because he had written it in a simple, straightforward style, and that there were many who could do far better if they would give up the attempt to be fine and clever. In another work, on *The Utility of the Office of the Preacher*, he seeks to present his subject in such a light as to save the ministry from the attacks made on it by the infidelity of the day. He is evidently very sincere and earnest, but the ground he takes shows the character of the time. After a strong appeal to preachers to consider their obligation to instruct and improve those who are entrusted to them, he discusses how this may be done. Resting upon the distinction, of which we hear a great deal at present, between religion and theology, he insists that a preacher is to teach not theology but religion. He is to leave out metaphysical doctrines, as unintelligible to common people, and indeed useless in any case ; among these he reckons the doctrine of the Trinity, the two natures in Christ, the atonement, the depravity of man by nature, and the power of faith without works. He advises the preacher to confine himself to the teaching and example of Christ, and to be most earnest and minute in impressing on men all their relative and social duties.

Spalding's books excited considerable controversy. The celebrated scholar, Ernesti, who took part in it, declared that no ordinary man with Spalding's views could honestly baptise children in the name of Father, Son, and Holy Ghost, or could read much of the New Testament with any intelligence. Spalding's first sphere of labour was in the country, where he was a most diligent pastor, but could not gain the sympathy of his hearers, who still clung to the old Bible doctrines. He was removed to Berlin in 1764, where his simple natural style, and his amiable, upright character made him a great favourite. He was certainly one of the best rationalists of that generation, though the atmosphere which he breathed, and his easy accommodating nature, kept him from those deeper views of Christian truth which since then have penetrated Germany.*

Zollikofer, 1730-1788. Georg Joachim Zollikofer was born at St. Gall in Switzerland in 1730, and died at Leipzig in 1788, having been minister there for thirty years. He was considered the most eloquent German preacher of his day, and was called "the Cicero of the pulpit." On his monument at Leipzig one reads: "He lives on here by his teaching, and he lives on there in the sphere of souls, where Socrates and Jesus live." It may be inferred from this that he did not belong to the stock of Luther or Spener, of Bengel or Zinzendorf. He was the

---

* Spalding's position is illustrated by the fact that besides translating Butler's *Analogy* into German, he translated several professedly deistical books both from French and from English, such as *The Principles of Deism fairly stated.* A sketch of one of his sermons will be found on page 260.

child of his time, and his preaching was of forti-
tude and tolerance and charity, as the way to God
which Jesus has opened up by His teaching and
example. His subjects are such as these—dili-
gence, patriotism, national faults, and moderation ;
and his method is entirely topical. The general
fault of Zollikofer, and indeed of most of the
preachers of the time, is that the subject is turned
away from its context and connection, and the text
becomes little more than a motto. The sermon on
moderation, *e.g.*, is based upon 1 Peter iv. 7,
" But the end of all things is at hand ; be ye therefore sober, and watch unto prayer." Nothing is
said in the sermon of the reason for moderation—
"the end of all things is at hand ;" nor of the
means—"watch unto prayer." The deepest currents and springs of Christian life had escaped his
view. With those serious deductions, it may be
said that his sermons, which have been printed in
fifteen volumes, are remarkable for their knowledge
of human nature, for the skill displayed in what
the French call "invention," or the raising of
topics, and for the exactness and force of their
expression. When one reads that the delivery of
them corresponded with their form, and was indeed
faultless, it is easy to understand his great popu-

larity.   The language of James was commonly
applied to him—the perfect man who never
offended in a word.*

Reinhard,
1753-1812.

The last of whom we shall speak in connection
with the period of Illuminism is Franz Volkmar
Reinhard.   It is perhaps scarcely fair to class him
with the Illuminists, for he strove very hard to
resist their influence, and had a longing after
better times than those in which he lived ; but he
had not the strength of deep conviction that makes
a Luther and a Spener, and so he failed to rise to
the first rank.   Nevertheless, such a high estimate
was set on his sermons that thirty-nine volumes of
them have been printed, and if you were to
ask any ordinary German to name the greatest
preacher since the time of Luther, in nine cases
out of ten the answer would be Reinhard.   Not
that his sermons are now read, but such is his
fame.

Reinhard was born in the Ober-Pfalz in 1753,
and died in 1812.   The great scene of his activity
was Dresden, where he was Chief-preacher, though
he filled Germany with his renown, and also with
his labours.   Instead of following his career, which
from the very beginning of his studies excited

* A sketch of one of his sermons will be found on page 260.

attention, and raised the highest hopes of him, it may be more useful to show the character of his preaching, and to give some of his own thoughts about sermons.

There can be no doubt that he yielded, so far, His position. to the influence of his age, and that his views of Gospel truth want the thoroughness of statement and the clear ring which distinguished the preachers of the Reformation, and which we shall also find in later German preachers. His treatment of duty, the favourite theme of his time, is not baptised as it should be in the doctrine of the Cross of Christ. There is a tendency to furl the banner, and he sometimes half draws the sword from the scabbard ; none the less he is a decided supernaturalist, has a portion of the warmth of the old Pietism, and laments and struggles against the coldness and the secular spirit of the time. He preaches the doctrine of the free grace of God in Christ. One extract will show this, and will be at the same time an example of his manner :—

"It is not to be denied, my brethren, that there Illustrated. are moments when the awakened conscience speaks with a remorseless claim ; when it shows us our sins in all their magnitude ; when it makes us feel with deep conviction and with humbling power the want of any good in us ; when our guilt before God, and the punishment we deserve, are set before us in a light that strikes us to the ground and leaves us in a condition the most helpless. Woe, then, to the sinner who feels himself so convicted, so condemned, so agonised, if he does not know the hope of the Gospel, if it has not been proclaimed to him that we are justified freely by His grace through the redemption that is in Christ Jesus! Happy then all who know this Gospel and hope in it! They will grieve for their sins, but not despair; they will humble themselves before God, but look up to Him with trust; they will seek to be holy as He is holy, and yet have no confidence in their attainments. Their desire will be to be accepted in the beloved, and to fall asleep at last, calm and comforted, on the bosom of a mercy that gives us everything with Christ. And so grace, mercy, and peace be with all who love our Lord Jesus Christ. Amen."

In a sermon to those who are wounded in conscience, he says :—

"You are miserable; miserable indeed, who feel the stings of a wounded conscience; nothing on earth can ease your pain ; no abundance of worldly wealth, no brightness of power and honour, no

intoxication of pleasure will help you. What the
world offers becomes ever more distasteful, and
fills you at last with loathing ; but I rejoice the
more to lead you to the fountain of healing which
is opened in the grace of God through Christ,
since for you, specially for you, this fountain
stands open. For you the comfort of the Gospel
is pre-eminently ordained. Well for you that you
feel your guilt, that your conscience is awakened
and shows you your need, that with a recoil of
terror you perceive how great is your danger and
how little you can do in self-help. The pain you
feel is salutary. You are troubled, as the apostle
says, 'after a godly sort,' and this godly sorrow
works repentance which needs not to be repented
of. Only remain by this repentance. You must
feel that in God's sight no flesh can be justified,
and that it is impossible for you to pay the debt
you have incurred. Be willing to be justified without merit by His grace. Grasp and take home
the assurance of this word, 'He that spared not
His own Son ;' for so it is, my brethren, God himself must declare whether after so many sins He
will be gracious, and He alone has the right to
settle the conditions under which He will forgive.
He himself has declared and made known

the order to which every sinner must submit.
Therefore praise God for His love, that Christ
died for us when we were sinners, and we shall
be saved from wrath when we are justified through
His blood. Look on the death of Jesus as an
atonement for sin. Lay hold by faith of God's
pardon through Him, and live no more to sin, but
to Him who died for you and rose again."

Nothing seems to be wanting here as a statement of the way of pardon, and yet one feels that
it is not the tone of Luther and Spener. It is not
merely that it is less direct, more rhetorical, and
redundant, but that he presents the Gospel as
working more in the way of doctrine, and less in
the way of life. There is an erroneous method of
preaching Christ in us and not for us; but there
is also an erroneous method of preaching Christ
for us and not in us, converting and quickening us
by His Holy Spirit. Strange, also, as it may seem
after the passage we have read, Reinhard does not
appear to have held the true and proper divinity
of the Saviour. Jesus was, he said, in the most
intimate union with God, but not himself very God.
This creates a weakness in the centre of his preaching, which kept him from bringing the deliverance
which his time needed. He seems at seasons to

have felt what was wanting, but the chill and the mist by which he was surrounded benumbed and dimmed his vision. His sermons, too, have in their form a kind of mannerism and monotony that would make the reading of many of them a great burden. They aim at a logical precision in the divisions, which gives them a stiff and scholastic air, and which was relieved only by the free and graceful delivery to which he attained.

He has left us a very interesting paper explaining his ideas of preaching, and his own mode of preparation for the pulpit. He worked out each sermon with the greatest care. First he sketched a scheme in which the chief thoughts were outlined in logical order, and on this he set great value, both for its own sake and as an aid to his memory. His memory for words was very weak, and, despite all the exercise he gave it, did not improve. But he had a memory for the logical outline, and he constructed his discourse accordingly, filling up the parts of the plan as a painter might do with a sketch. The committing of the sermon was to him the most disagreeable part of his work. But he did not shirk it. Beginning on Monday, he committed a section every morning, so that on the Saturday the whole sermon was

His idea of preaching.

S

fast and firm. While he was committing one thus
piecemeal, he was working out another, and by
the time he had the first committed, the second
was ready in his desk. The sermon, in his view, is
a piece of art, to which, as to its outer form, both
logic and rhetoric must contribute, but logic is the
more important. Its thoughts must come up in
regular order, group themselves in proportion, and
lead to proper conclusions. The language should
be suited to this, simple, clear, pointed. The
preacher must never forget that he is above all
a teacher; he who makes it his chief aim to
awaken and move robs his office of much of its
value, for if we are to reach the heart it must be
through the understanding.*

Reinhard and
Spener con-
trasted.

Reinhard was an able, conscientious, and in
many respects a useful man, but he stood as far
distant from the school of Spener as it was
possible for one to stand who was not a rationalist. Spener's element was feeling; Reinhard's,
the understanding. With Spener, form was disregarded; with Reinhard, all must be according
to the logic of the schools. With Spener, the

* A sketch of one of his sermons will be found on page
262; an extract from his *Geständnisse* is given in Note L on
page 286.

great aim was to comfort and move; with Reinhard, it was to fill and convince the reason. We
may surely hold that there is a method by which
these may be united; but Spener's idea must in
any case form our basis. Men must live before
they learn. The order is—first conversion, then
edification. In Him is life, and the life is the
light of men; only if we have life, do we, through
the truth spoken in love, grow up unto Him in all
things which is the head, even Christ.

NOTE I, see page 250.

SKETCH OF A SERMON BY SPALDING.

Luke ii. 33-40—Simeon and Anna in the Temple.

The whole life of a Christian can, and should be, the service of God.

I. The whole life can be divine service, for—
1. Every benevolent deed in God's name is service.
2. The common work of life, with the feeling of religion, is service.
3. The pleasures of life, when innocent and God-grateful, are service.

II. Our whole life should be divine service, for—
1. All our life belongs to God, as its Author and Owner.
2. All our life may thus be made true happiness.

The division of this sermon is natural: the defect, as concerns substance, is want of depth and grasp. The choice of subject illustrates the pericopic system, for the portion came round in regular course and only a part is selected, that there may be variety another year.

NOTE J, see page 252.

SKETCH OF A SERMON BY ZOLLIKOFER.

Proverbs iii. 21, 22—" Keep sound wisdom and discretion ; so shall they be life unto thy soul."

The difference between what happens (Glück) and what makes happy (Glückseligkeit).

Definition : "What happens " is all the circumstances and changes that affect our position in the world ; what makes happy is what gives satisfaction and peace.

I. Show the difference between what happens and what makes happy.

    1. What happens is without, what makes happy is within.

    2. What happens is not in our control, what makes happy is.

    3. What happens is passing, what makes happy is abiding.

    4. What happens has a limit, what makes happy is boundless.

    5. What happens can be only a means, what makes happy is an end.

II. Show the importance of attending to this distinction.

    1. Every one cannot have good *hap*, every one can have true *happiness*.

    2. A man is not happy through what happens to him, and he is not unhappy through what does not happen.

    3. To think, not of what may happen, but of what makes happy is the way to all true wisdom, genius, virtue, and lasting power.

This plan is very ingenious and clever, but the second head is a repetition of the first, and would have been better as a brief application. In regard to the substance, what makes truly happy is never stated. We are told things about it, not what it is. The sermon is introduced by a prayer which begins, " God, &c.," and which might be taken for a thesis, were it not in the second person singular.

NOTE K, see page 258.

SKETCH OF A SERMON BY REINHARD.

Phil. iii. 8—"Yea doubtless, and I count all things
but loss," &c.

Theme : The feeling that to be a Christian is to have a
higher happiness.
  I. Description of the feeling.
    1. It does not renounce all other kinds of happiness.
    2. It is superior to them all.
    3. It controls the whole character.
  II. Justify this feeling.
    1. It is acceptable to God.
    2. It is useful to the world.
    3. It is advantageous for time and eternity.
  III. Apply this so as to—
    1. Judge the state of our hearts (unsers sittlichen
        Zustandes).
    2. Regulate our conduct.
    3. Seek the welfare of our fatherland.

He rose to a higher style than this in later life, as we have
shown.   This is a specimen of his moderate tone.   The
marrow of the text is not reached—the excellency of the
knowledge that I may win Christ and be found in Him.   He
is guided by the usefulness (Nutzbarkeit) of religion.

Professor Palmer, in his article in Herzog, gives instances
of the way in which Illuminism weakened his language.   He
covers plain Bible language with words about conditions,
and circumstances, and relations, and hypotheses, and terms
drawn from the Wolfian school, that look as if, to use
Milton's words, " he thought our religion had been guilty
of the first trespass, and needed fine rounded phrases to

cover its nakedness ; " *e.g.*, he defines saving faith to be reliance on the death of Jesus and acquiescence in this arrangement on the part of God.   Instead of saying that there is no
condemnation to those that are in Christ Jesus, he says that
" God remits to them the unpleasant conditions that are
suspended over them in a future life."   There are certain
words that act as non-conductors, and these are examples
of them.

LECTURE XV.

HIDDEN LIFE IN THE ILLUMINISM.

Extent and influence of Illuminism.

THE Illuminism, which was the first period of decline in evangelical faith, lasted from about 1750 to the early part of the present century, extending steadily till it had taken possession of the greater number of the pulpits and professors' chairs.* There were degrees in its influence. In a few places evangelical warmth remained, in others there was orthodoxy without life—a form of sound words. But as a rule it transformed Christianity into a system of morality mixed often with the secular topics of the day. The result was not such as to encourage those who think that in our day preaching of a similar kind will gain the ear of the masses. No doubt some men of rhetorical power drew crowds to listen to them, as crowds

* This is well illustrated in Reinhard's *Geständnisse*. An extract will be found in Note L on page 286.

264

will gather to any intellectual display ; but in no generation are the majority of preachers great orators, and when the people found the pulpit occupied with bare moralities and cold secularism, they gradually fell away from church attendance, discovering that there was more to interest them elsewhere—in the fields, in art galleries, and even in beer-gardens. The change was, as we have said, gradual, for men were held for a while by old habits, and the Illuminist preaching had a kind of novelty at first, so that the rationalists deceived themselves, and boasted in some places of the large congregations which listened with curiosity to their reckless speculations or their profane sensationalism. But when the heart was not met nor the spirit stirred, a great weariness began to grow, and the churches became more and more empty, till only some women and a few old people were to be seen in them. And so it remains in many parts of Germany to this day ; for, though the professors' chairs and the pulpits have now more faith in them, it takes a long time and much hard and earnest work to reclaim the masses from indifference. It is easy to slip down—

> Sed revocare gradum superasque evadere ad auras,
> Hoc opus, hic labor est.

Unchecked by denominations.

Had it been in our country, denominations would have been formed outside the national church, and these would have kept up life and ultimately quickened the older church by their example and their influence. But this way was not open to the Germans. As I indicated in a recent lecture, they had a great fear of what they called Separatism, and the Government would not at that time have permitted it.

Hidden life.

What remained, then, was for life to draw together where it was possible within the national church, and I shall turn attention in this lecture to some cases where this occurred—to some watch-men of the night, or waiters for the morning, as we may call them ; wells of water they were to those around them in this march of the German church through the dry wilderness.

Oetinger and Wizenmann.

They were, as we have said, of different kinds. In Würtemberg there was a scholar of Bengel, Oetinger, who died in 1782 at the age of eighty, and one of his scholars, Wizenmann, who had a brief career. Both of these had and still have influence with a certain class of minds in Germany. Oetinger belonged to the theosophist school, and was in his deepest nature opposed to the rational-ism of the time.

There was Jung-Stilling, who was a professor, Stilling, first at Heidelberg and afterwards at Marburg. 1740-1817. In his later years he lived in the palace of the Elector Palatine, at Carlsruhe, as Court-counsellor or spiritual adviser. He was a man of remarkable but eccentric genius, with a gift of insight that gave him the reputation of a seer, and carried him at times into extravagances. He had correspondence all over Germany with those who were called "the quiet in the land," the evangelical believers in that time of noisy unbelief; and he died, worn out with labour, with the words, "Lord, cut the thread and give me rest."

There was Lavater of Zurich, a Swiss pastor. Lavater, He is known to many only by his theories and 1741-1801. researches in physiognomy; but apart from, or rather notwithstanding these, he was one of the most remarkable men of his time. He was an intimate friend of Goethe, Herder, and other notables; beloved and revered by them for the simplicity and loftiness of his nature, and for the charity and boldness with which he confessed the Lord Jesus Christ, whom most of them would not receive. His nature had such a thirst for the divine that Goethe compared him to "a dry plant to which the least drop of the feeling of God's

own presence brought more joy than other men
have in the possession of all the good things
God can give with His hand." His most characteristic book is *Pontius Pilate,* written on the
question : What is truth? He has poured all
his heart into it; indeed he said of it, "that
book is myself; he that hates it hates me, he
that loves it loves me;" and it was in fact
received with scorn on the one side, and with deep
affection on the other. He died from a treacherous
blow dealt by a French soldier at the taking of
Zurich. When the assassin was brought before
him, he refused to identify him, and exclaimed as
he departed, " Pray, pray !" The longing of his
nature is expressed in his beatitude, " Blessed are
the home-sick, for they shall reach home." Yet
in that age there was no more uncompromising
and heroic confessor of Christ.

There were several others of the same school,
chiefly in South Germany, all marked by a spirit of
warm mysticism, with that tone of love to Christ as
a personal friend which we find in the letters of
Samuel Rutherford and in Halyburton. This spirit
seems to belong not merely to particular temperaments, but to special times, when the very influences which chill some natures call out in others

the resisting warmth of love unto death. While
we have a Judas and a Peter at the cross, we have
also a John. There are, however, two circles of Two circles—
which we may speak specially, since with each of
them a remarkable man is connected.

The first was at Münster in Westphalia. In the (a) At
neighbourhood of that town the Princess Galitzin Münster,
represented
had her seat, and it became the resort of Germans by—
who were interested in general literature, but
specially of those who still were concerned for
religion. Most of them were Protestants, although
the Princess was a Roman Catholic. At that particular time Romanism was not ultramontane, the
Jesuits were in discredit, and the tone of Roman
Catholic devotion was that of Fénélon or Pascal.
The Princess was a woman of genius and of high
accomplishments. She had been one of the gayest
of a gay circle, when the hollowness of the prevailing life impressed her, and she turned another
way. While attracted by all questions that touch
the mind and soul, by literature, art, philosophy,
she was most frequently engrossed with religious
topics, which were to her of the deepest personal
moment.

In her doubts she found special aid from Hamann,
Johann Georg Hamann, whose name constantly 1730-1788.

recurs in the history of the thought of that day. He was not a minister nor a priest, nor did he make any marked profession of belief, but he had a powerful religious influence over all who came into contact with him.   Similarly, although he neither founded a system of philosophy, nor wrote any epoch-making book, his conversation and his occasional writings filled men like Jacobi and Goethe with the highest admiration of his acuteness and depth and force of intellect.   The name by which he was known among them, was *Der Magus aus dem Norden*, the Wise Man of the North.*

His career.   There was something of romance in the changes and struggles of his life.   He was born in 1730 at Königsberg, in East Prussia, the country of Copernicus and Kant and Herder.   The son of religious parents in humble life, he was driven from place to place till he reached London.   There he fell into sin and dissipation, had to seek support by playing on the lute, and was at last struck down by disease. His distress led him to study the Bible as he had never done before, and he persevered in reading it till he became a new man.   Having found in it a cure for his own sin, he learned that it supplied a test of all human knowledge and philosophy.

* Oetinger was known as the Wise Man of the South.

Returning to Germany, he set himself with wonderful energy to complete and extend the education he had begun in youth, and erelong he proved himself equal to the first thinkers of his time, and superior in depth to its greatest theologians. He could not rest in the cold deism of Mendelssohn ; he needed a stronger positive basis than the subjective faith of Jacobi ; the Stoicism of Kant had in it neither enough of humanity nor enough of divinity for him ; and he regarded the pretentious and shallow Illuminism of the day with a dislike that bordered on hatred and contempt. He had a strong originality that made room for him wherever he went, and when he appeared in the circle of the Princess Galitzin he was its presiding power. He died suddenly, when on a visit there, at the age of fifty-eight, and was buried in her garden with the inscription on his tomb: "We preach Christ crucified, to the Jews a stumbling-block, and to the Greeks foolishness." He was perhaps the first to strike an effectual blow at that form of the Illuminism which is known generally as "the flat rationalism of Germany."

A few extracts from his writings will show his attitude and style :— *His attitude and style.*

"Our bodies could more easily live without

heart and head than can our souls without Christ. He is the head of our nature and all our powers, and He is the spring of a movement which can no more stand still in a Christian than the pulse can stop in a living body. The Christian alone is spiritually living, because he lives with God and in God, and this implies that he lives also for God."

"Of all the religious parties which profess to show the way to heaven, and to communion with the Being of beings, we Christians should be the most miserable if the foundations of our faith stood on the shifting sand of the fashionable critical learning. No ; the theory of the true religion is so fitted to every child of man, so capable of being woven into the essence of his soul's life, that it is too high for the most daring heaven-storming giant to reach it, and too deep for the most subtle word-critic to undermine it."

"All the miracles of Holy Scripture take place again in our souls. The Holy Scripture should be our grammar, our dictionary, out of which all the modes of Christian speech should grow. Every mode of thinking that visits the world of fashion, every slight change of feeling, colours ordinary language. Surely the way of Christians (call them a sect if you will) must give them a new tongue

and speech. The language used in the holy city
should betray the genealogy and fatherland of its
citizens, and show that they, παρὰ φύσιν, contrary
to nature, have been grafted on the heavenly olive
tree. If a preacher would be edifying, his Galilean
dialect must strike the ear. Though the Ishmael-
ites of our times make sport of it, our discourse
should sparkle with that dew of the morning in
which the Sun of Righteousness was first reflected.
The speech as well as the doctrine of the pulpit
should furnish the treasures of the East, where lies
the cradle of our race and our religion."

"Bengel has a happy expression, *Te totum
applica ad textum: rem totam applica ad te*, apply
thyself wholly to the text: apply the matter of it
wholly to thyself. But this is *hysteron proteron*,
the first should be the last. The more the
Christian realises that, in this book, the matter
concerns himself, the more will his care be bestowed on the letter of it. The criticism of the
letter may be the pedagogue to Christ, but Christ
takes the place of the pedagogue. The spiritual
man receives a power of judgment which is surer
than all the introductory rules of grammar or logic."

"The testimony of Jesus is the spirit of prophecy; and the first miracle in which the majesty

.T

of His incarnation shows itself is that in which He
changes the books of the first covenant into good
old wine, a miracle which passes the skill of the
critical master of the feast, but is known to lesser
men who draw the wine. Read, says the African
Father, the prophetical books without Christ, what
wilt thou find more insipid and empty? Put Him
into them, not only will they be pleasant to the
taste, they will fill thee to the full."

"The history of the Jewish people has always
been for me the only universal history, and that
nation the image, not only of Christendom but of
the whole human race. Every Jew I look on is to
me the greatest of all the wonders of God's providence, greater than Noah's ark or Lot's wife or
Moses' burning bush."

"Nature is a book, an epistle, a parable, that
tells its meaning by signs. Granted we know all
the letters and can put them into syllables and
words, we must know the language; physical
science gives only the A B C. I trust the visible,
the material, in nature, as I trust the dial-plate
and hands of a watch; but the secret wisdom lies
behind the dial-plate, in springs and wheels and
artist's skill."

"Do you know, dear friend, why Job received

sheep and camels, oxen and asses, in double
number, but not his children? This I have read
in an old book is a proof that his lost children
were alive, and that the dead are still counted
before God; and this before it occurred to the
Phædos to give us metaphysical proof for what
is embedded in the majestic promises of the
Scripture."*

"I love strong thinking, gentle dealing." "The
door to the highest university is death." "Sorrow
in the world is the one proof that we are not at
home in it. If we wanted nothing, we should be
no better than the heathen, or than the philosophers
who have fallen in love with dead matter. This
holy home-sickness is the salt with which the
sacrifice is kept from the corruption of the present
time. Thus the prince of this world, dark as he
looks, is the *diaconus*, the servant of the blessed
God; over the church-yards, as over the flood, there
hovers the raven, but after it the dove." "True
knowledge and love of one's self is the measure of
one's knowledge and love of neighbours." "So
long as we believe on Him who thus loves men,
we shall be in no danger of hating them."

---

* This is also found in Matthew Henry *in loco;* whether
he borrowed it or not, it is hard to say.

(b) At
Hamburg,
represented by
M. Claudius,
1740-1815.

We pass now to another school of believing men, which had its centre at Hamburg. The chief figure in it was Matthias Claudius, a man whose attitude in some respects resembled that of Jacobi. They differed, however, in this, that while Jacobi found the voice of God in the receptive feeling of the soul which drew material from outer knowledge and assimilated it, making every man his own Bible, Claudius rested on God's revealed Word, which verifies itself to the soul as a divine revelation, and proves its own truth, both as a whole and in its parts, the more it is studied. He differed from Stilling and Lavater in that he had less of the mystic, and from Hamann in that he did not approach Christian truth so much on the philosophical side as on that of the old Pietist and Puritan, while he possessed modern culture. He had a curious mixture of clear common-sense and deep pathetic feeling, of true humour edged at times with sarcasm, and of a strong faith that infused itself with genial warmth into his life, and carried him safe and unhurt through the cold scorn of rationalism.

His life.

He was born in Holstein in 1740, and studied at Jena. He was afterwards engaged in business at Hamburg, but he kept up acquaintance with art,

with literature, and, above all, with religious questions throughout his long life. He died in cheerful
acquiescence with the will of God, in the house of
Perthes, the famous bookseller, who was his son-in-
law. In the *Life of Perthes*, which gives a most
interesting picture of the state of Germany during
that half century, there are many references to
Claudius, including a beautiful description of his
quiet home, where, with his family, he read classical and English literature, cultivated music and
poetry, being himself a poet, and blended the
earthly with the heavenly, without an effort and in
perfect harmony. Perthes says : " I found him full
of happy humour, as did Ewald, the zealous
adherent of the Illuminism, who expected to find
him a dark and bitter fanatic. But his faith of
reconciliation with God was not a mere doctrine,
but a condition of the soul that filled his inner
nature and shone through his life and his home.
He could laugh at many troubles and attacks
which would have half vexed to death the humanity
and toleration of the preachers of our day." At
that time, and in that district of Germany, there
were a number of like-minded men — Count
Reventlow, the Counts Stolberg, the elder Cramer,
the Niebuhr family, from which came the famous

historian, and Perthes himself, who was at first an
Illuminist, but advanced to full sympathy with
evangelical truth. The home of Claudius was at
Wandsbeck, two miles from Hamburg, a pretty
little village—one broad street of quaint houses
with little gardens in front and behind, a pleasant
"beck" or brook, and a remnant of the original
oak-forest that once covered all North Germany.
The favourite seat of Claudius in his meditative
moods is still pointed out beneath one of the
gigantic oaks, and on his monument, hard by, is
his name, "Matthias Claudius, 1815," carved deep
on a great boulder that must have been brought in
ages long past from the Norwegian hills, a twin
brother to that which bears the name of Gustavus
Adolphus on the field of his death at Lützen.

His writings. His works consist of fugitive papers on various
subjects, chiefly religious, in the form of short
treatises, letters, dialogues, and poems. They
appeared in a journal called the *Wandsbeck
Messenger*, corresponding somewhat to Addison's
Spectator, and have been collected into four small
volumes. They form a book well worth reading
for those who can feel an interest in strong faith
held fearlessly in the face of unbelief, supported by
a shrewd and powerful intellect of the philosophic

type, and suffused by a mixture of imagination
and feeling that turns from humour to pathos, from
pathos to bold but never bitter irony—a peculiar
book in which the Christian and the human, the
glad and the sad, are never far from each other.

This is the way in which he criticises the
Paraphrasis Evangelii Johannis, a pretentious
commentary made up in the style of the day—all
surface, no depth; all words, no insight.

" I have, from my youth up, read the Bible with
delight. There are such beautiful things in it,
dark and deep though they be, which make one's
heart fresh and gladsome ; but most of all I like
to read in John, there is something so wonderful
in him, the dusk and night, and through it the
quick darting lightning—a soft evening cloud, and
behind the cloud the great full-bodied moon.
There is something so full of pathos and loftiness
and foreboding of far-off things, that one is never
weary of it. Always, when I read, I seem to see
him at the Last Supper lying on his Master's
breast, and his angel holds the light to me, and,
at some passages, falls on my neck and whispers
his sayings in my ear. I am far from understanding all he says, but frequently it seems as if what
he meant were floating before me, and even when

His spirit.

I look into a passage that is quite obscure, I have
the presentiment of a great and glorious meaning
which I shall one day understand.   Therefore it
is that I grasp so eagerly at every new interpretation of John, but most of these only curl the edges
of the evening cloud, and the full moon behind
enjoys undisturbed repose.   I think this reverend
author's commentary must be very learned, and
it would take him studying words twenty years
before he could write it."

His treatment   We may give an instance of the way in which he
of philosophy
and the Bible. deals with philosophy and the Bible in questions
of faith.   His cousin writes him a letter, saying
that his head is turning round with the disputes
about the relations of the orthodox to the philosophical theologians.   It seemed to him that to
set religion right by philosophy was like setting
the sun right by his own wooden clock.   Yet he
had been told that philosophy was the broom to
sweep all the rubbish out of the temple, and that
he ought to take his hat off much further to a new
philosophical teacher than to an old orthodox one.
Here is part of Claudius' answer :—

"Philosophy is good, and people are wrong who
try to laugh at it, but in matters of faith philosophy
stands to revelation, not as little to much but as

earth to heaven. I cannot explain it better than
by the chart which we made, when boys, of the
pond behind the garden. We used to sail on the
pond, and had made a chart of all the deeps and
shallows, and thereby we got round it safe and
sure ; but if a whirlwind, or the queen of Otaheite,
or some great power or potentate were to take thee
up with thy canoe and thy chart and set thee
down on the ocean, cousin, and thou wert to try
sailing there by thy chart, that would not do. The
fault is not in the chart ; for the pond it was good,
but the pond, seest thou, is not the ocean. Here
thou must have another chart. From this thou
mayest so far judge whether philosophy be a
broom to sweep the rubbish out of the temple. It
may in a certain sense be such a broom; thou
mayest call it a hare's-foot brush to touch the dust
of the holy statues, but he who should set there-
with to cut and hew at the statues would do a very
foolish thing. Paul, who had tried all ways of it,
and knew the Sadducees or philosophers of his day
very well, and could reason with the best of them,
tells us that the peace of God passes all understanding.

"Since, then, the holy statues of the temple are
above men's understanding, it is rational in the

true sense of the word to let the old shapes remain ;
if he be an orthodox pastor who says that, you
cannot take off your hat to him too far, yet you
must ask what kind of orthodoxy."

Here is another letter, the first of a series to
Andres:—

"Thou mightest gladly hear of our Lord Jesus
Christ, Andres; who would not?   But perhaps
thou comest to the wrong quarter, for I am no
friend of the new views, but hold fast to the Word
I hate to break my head clearing up all religious
mysteries, for I think they are mysteries, and were
meant to be so till the time comes.

"If we cannot see Him, Andres, we must believe
those who have seen Him ; for me there is no other
way.   The facts recorded in the Bible, all His
glorious sayings and doings, are indeed not Himself, but only witnesses of Him, the little bells
of His vesture.   Yet they are the best thing we
have on earth, and they are such that it makes one
comforted and joyful when one hears and sees that
man can become something else and something
better than we now see him to be. . . . I know of
nothing dearer and more delightful than to speak
of help and deliverance, and he who does not feel
this has never himself been in need, nor seen others

in need. Does not the woman who has found her lost penny call her friends and neighbours, and say, 'Rejoice with me?' But what a loss was that from which gold and silver could not have saved us!

"Dost thou remember our first voyage, when we tried the new canoe, and I fell into the deep water? I had given up all for lost, and was thinking how death would taste, and what my poor mother would say, and then I saw thine outstretched arm and held on. And I see it still, Andres, if I only stumble on thy name, or even light on a capital A.

"But here a Deliverer from all loss, from every evil, a Redeemer from sin, a Saviour who went about doing good, and had not where to lay His head! Through Him the lame walked, the lepers were cleansed, the deaf heard, the dead arose, and to the poor the Gospel was preached ; whom winds and waves obeyed, and who took little children to Him and embraced and blessed them. He was with God, and was God, and might have kept His divine blessedness, but He thought of the wretched in the prison-house, and came to them concealed in the uniform of misery, that he might make them free with His blood. He thought not of toil nor of shame, and was steadfast till death that He might finish His work. He came into the world to save the world, and left it with a crown of thorns.

"Hast thou ever heard the like? Do not thine hands fall down in helpless wonder? It is indeed a mystery, and we cannot comprehend it, but it comes from God and out of heaven, bearing heaven's seal, and dropping with God's tender mercy. One might well be tortured and crucified for the conception of it, and he who can bring himself to laugh and mock must needs be mad. But the man who has his heart in its place will lie in the dust, and pray and give praise."

Power of the Hidden Life. There can be no doubt that the utterances that came from men like Lavater and Hamann and Claudius kept alive the faith of many who were trembling for the ark of God. They were as watchmen answering the call, "Bless ye the Lord, all ye servants of the Lord, which by night stand in the house of the Lord;" they help us to believe in the perpetuity of God's truth, and remind us of the words of Luther: "I have seen two wonders. The first was that I looked out of the window and saw the stars of heaven and the whole beautiful firmament of God before me, and yet, though there was nowhere any pillar on which the Maker had fixed the arch, the heaven did not fall in, but stood on that arch quite strong. And then I wondered that though the stars are quite safe, they seemed to tingle and tremble as if the heaven certainly would fall in, for they cannot grasp the pillars nor see them ; if they could do this they would not tremble."

NOTE L, see page 264.

THE PREVALENCE OF THE ILLUMINISM.

The following extract, which is somewhat abbreviated, from Reinhard's *Geständnisse*, illustrates the attitude of the Illuminists—

"I became a preacher at the time when our Illuminist theologians had succeeded in making the Christian doctrine so clear and intelligible that nothing remained but pure rationalism. Any man who wished to get a name for learning or praise from the journals must declare some book of the Bible not genuine, or call some doctrine traditional, and therefore false. He who ventured before the public without paying homage to the spirit of the time, might reckon on being met with contempt as behind the age. How little I have escaped this fate, how sarcastically and bitterly the editors have dealt with me, you well know.

"Let me tell you, then, how I have never been able to reconcile myself to this new rational theology. I came to the conviction that one can be truly consistent by following either reason alone, or Scripture alone. The one constitutes a naturalist, the other a supernaturalist. The rationalist holds the Bible to be no more than any human book. He agrees with it where it ʿagrees with him, but no further. With the supernaturalist, the Bible is the rule by which reason judges and rectifies itself. Reason examines its claims, interprets its meaning, and then it listens with reverence.

"If a man tries a middle road between these, he can never be consistent. It is mere caprice if he takes a little from reason and a little from the Bible, and those who try this plan can never agree with one another, for one will give reason more, another less. Most of the theologians I have

met, of the rationalistic kind, have tried this wavering, cap-
ricious, half-way plan. I say *most*, for there were some who
knew quite well where they were going, who were out-and-
out rationalists, believing nothing positive in religion, yet not
caring to say this, and keeping quiet. Most of the Illuminist
theologians, however, did not know what they wanted, nor
whither their road was leading. They thought only that they
were much above the common crowd in rejecting first one
and then another part of the old system, but they did not see
that to be consistent they would have to reject much more,
and perhaps all. So everything was at sea. Very few
knew where they were. Sometimes reason, sometimes the
Bible prevailed, and every truth was ready for surrender.
They were very angry with Lessing when he laughed at this
wretched patchwork of the rationalist theology, and said
that it disgusted him, and that he preferred the old consistent orthodoxy with all its rigidity. For myself, I felt I must
be either an out-and-out rationalist or a supernaturalist.
Now, I could not be a rationalist. It seemed to me that
Revelation had too much to say for itself to be set down as
a fancy or deception. The more I considered the discords
and errors of mere reason in religious things, the more
I felt that Revelation was not only a desirable benefit,
but an indispensable need. The Gospel, moreover, had
been so helpful to my own nature from my earliest youth,
I had so many experiences of its power, that I would have
gone against conscience and all sense of duty if I had
renounced it. And so I had no further choice. If there
was no consistent middle path, and if I had to choose
between rationalism and supernaturalism, I was obliged to
hold by the Bible, and to accept what could be proved from
it. I honour all conscientious inquiry, I am open to all
light, but my rule of judgment, my guide in perplexity, is the
Gospel of Christ."

LECTURE XVI.

TRANSITION PERIOD: SCHLEIERMACHER.

Schleier-
macher,
1768-1834.

His general
position.

THE life of Schleiermacher forms an epoch in the religion of Germany; it stands between the period of rationalism in its superficial form, and the period of a higher faith. Schleiermacher himself is the bridge between these. He has the elements of two different men in him, the man of doubt, and the man of faith. It is not at all uncommon to find these two in the same person, but the peculiarity of Schleiermacher is that in him the elements co-existed till the end of his life, and were even blended in a system. Pascal had doubt as well as faith; probably his doubts at one period of his life went deeper than Schleiermacher's, but he ended by overcoming them, and his *Thoughts* form a clear consistent book which another thinker can make his own throughout. But there is probably no man who has made the

288

system of Schleiermacher his own so as to be able to rest in it. This may serve to illustrate the distinction of the German mind from the French, and we may also say from the Scottish, for in this the Scottish has more sympathy with the French than with the German.

Personally, Schleiermacher was a very remarkable man. He was so distinguished in different departments of knowledge, that he made them for the time his own, and he has left his mark deep on most of them. He was a philosopher, and his commentary on Plato would itself have made him celebrated. He was a philologist of the first rank. He was at home in every branch of theology —in the criticism of the Canon, in exegesis, in church history, in apologetics and dogmatics, in ethics and practical theology. On all these his writings created movement by the freshness, if not always by the soundness of his thinking ; and he has gained for himself one of the first places in the roll of German preachers. It is in this last character that we shall chiefly consider him. He began with preaching, and he continued to preach to the last. It was his favourite task, even when he had work of all kinds in hand. Our estimate of the importance of preaching in modern times will

U

surely rise when we think that a man of such gifts found in it the most fitting field for the exercise of his great qualities of mind and heart. To-day we shall first give a brief sketch of his life then a short view of his peculiar theological position, and finally we shall look at his relation to preaching.

His training. He was born in Breslau in 1768, and died in Berlin in 1834. His father was a military chaplain in the Reformed church, of the old faith and manners. He sent his son for education to a Moravian school, where he was for several years under the training of the good simple-hearted Brethren. This period of his life formed the link between him and Spener to which we have referred, for though in many things he afterwards left the faith of the Brethren, he never lost the early religious feeling that was then unfolded, and in his later life he seemed to return to sympathy with them. From the Moravian school he went to Halle, in opposition to his father's wish, and there studied under Semler and other teachers of the school of the Illuminism, of which Halle was then the centre. Their influence was ingrafted on his early Pietism, and his future partook of these two—his heart was with Pietism, his mind with the Illuminism, although ever fighting with it and rising above its shallow forms.

He was ordained in 1794 to a country charge at His career. Landsberg, but removed in two years to the chaplaincy of the Charité at Berlin, where he attained great celebrity both in the pulpit and in literary intercourse. He was appointed Court-preacher in 1803, and became a professor and University-preacher at Halle in 1804. But when, after the unfortunate battle of Jena, Halle was torn from Prussia, he removed to Berlin and resumed his work there. He was an ardent patriot, and while, during the French dominion, Goethe occupied himself in studying Chinese, Schleiermacher and the philosopher Fichte entered the ranks of the volunteers in the War of Liberation. He continued in Berlin till the close of his life, revered and beloved. He had a weakly constitution, but, by careful attention to regimen and to hours of work, he went through Herculean labours, and his biographer says that while he was subject to moods of deep depression he did not trouble others with them. His death was one of simple faith. In the midst of bodily weakness, he preserved his clear intellect and sustained himself by profound speculative thoughts, which, he said, were to him identical with the deepest religious feelings. On the last morning he observed the Communion with some Christian friends, breaking the bread with his own hand, as is the custom in the Reformed, as distinct from the Lutheran church. In partaking of the cup, he said with regard to the words of dedication: "On these words of the Scripture I rely; they are the foundation of my faith; in this love and communion we are and ever will remain united." He then sank back on his pillow, and passed away after a few minutes of troubled breathing.*

His theology. Schleiermacher's theological system, if we may use a term which he himself might have rejected, is of a peculiar and mixed character. It is indeed rather what the Germans call a stand-point than a system—a central position from which a great many things shade away into dimness and uncertainty in the distance; and the central position itself seems at times to shift. The whole of it belongs to a period of transition. The religious authority is not placed in Scripture, as by orthodox theologians; nor is it placed in the bare reason, as by the rationalists, but in the religious feeling, which

* Steffens' description of Schleiermacher will be found in Note M, on page 304.

Schleiermacher holds to be inherent in man, and to have been especially quickened and unfolded in Christianity. This idea is the centre of all his thinking. Proceeding from this along the line of secular and church history, he reaches the origin of Christianity. He holds that its main features cannot fairly be doubted, and that the beginning of its development is manifestly due to certain documents termed by us the New Testament—documents which are still the source of quickening in the individual soul. He handles the New Testament very freely, after the manner of Semler and the other critics; although the authority of parts of it is shaken, he is not distressed, finding that enough is left to support his spiritual life. To the Old Testament he gives a secondary place, and of it he makes very little use either for proof or for illustration.

Now observe what he discovers from the New Testament, or rather from the religious feeling when brought into contact with the New Testament. He does not appeal to proof-texts or express statements, but to the general spiritual bearing of its teaching, and the way in which that is verified by our own spiritual life.

Man is a sinful being—every individual sharing

in the sinfulness of the race; no one is able to
deliver himself from sin; the deliverance comes
from God, and from God in Christ. Who Christ is,
Schleiermacher never clearly says. He will not
call Him the true God; He is the first-born Son,
the type and original of humanity, the only sinless
Being that has ever appeared in our world, not
merely the blossom but the root of the race, from
whose perfect nature Adam fell away. We are
redeemed through Him, not by an atonement and
justification as the beginning of a new life, nor
merely by His doctrine and example, as the
rationalists say, but by His life and power entering into us and renewing us, so that holiness is the
beginning of forgiveness. As to the supernatural
elements in Christ's life on earth—His miracles,
His resurrection, His ascension—Schleiermacher
seems to admit them, but he rarely gives them
prominence, for the religious feeling does not
attest them as it does His saving power. He
believes in immortality, in a final judgment, in
eternal blessedness, and even in the doctrine of
election, connecting it, however, with the hope of
the subjugation of evil in some form in the future
life.

Its tendency.   This is, in brief, Schleiermacher's theology,

suggesting at some points that of *Ecce Homo.*
Some of his positions are the same as those of
F. D. Maurice, though Maurice differed from him
in holding distinctly the divinity of Christ, and
also in giving higher authority to the Bible, including the Old Testament. There can be no question as to the deep sincerity, earnestness, and lofty
character of Schleiermacher, nor as to the fact that
he struck a deadly blow at the old rationalism by
his deeper views of sin and redemption, and his
more exalted conception of the work of Christ;
but his was a position that could not be maintained. He himself was wounded in the heel by
the arrow of doubt. The shifting sands of restless
criticism that were blowing about him prevented
him from seeing clearly the real and the positive.
Yet, after all, his face was not towards rationalism, but away from it. It is this that marks the
difference between men, not so much where they
stand as whither they are looking and going, and
teaching others to go; and Schleiermacher was
the man who bade the Church turn from the
theology of the surface understanding to the
deeper theology of religious feeling and faith. His
followers, Ullmann, Nitzsch, Tholuck, and Müller
moved forwards.

Views on preaching. We come now to what Schleiermacher has to say about preaching. His views must be chiefly ascertained from his practical theology, but we may take these in connection with his own example, although we shall afterwards have to say a few Its basis. words specially about the latter. As to the basis of preaching, he appeals not so much to the Word of God in the Bible as to the religious feeling of the preacher. This is quickened and unfolded by the Bible as by no other book, but the inward experience of each preacher can alone verify the teaching of the Bible and give it power. The Its subject. subject of preaching must always be distinctly Christian. Upon this point Schleiermacher is very decided and explicit, and in his own sermons he adheres to the principle most thoroughly. One cannot but admire the way in which he brings the person and influence of Christ to bear on all things in human life—the heart, the personal conduct, the family, the nation, the Church. Yet there is a vagueness about the presentation of Christ. He does not answer the question, Who is He, that I may believe on Him? We have the fragrance of Christ but no clear view of Him—Christ exciting religiosity, not Christ the object of intelligent religion. Even when the historical Jesus is presented, He is seen through a haze, and we cannot tell distinctly who He is, or what He has done. This defect arises naturally from the subjectivity of Schleiermacher's conception.

He holds that the primary object of preaching is Its object neither to instruct nor to incite to action, but to awaken feeling—religious, Christian feeling. The hearers are to be considered as already Christians, not in the Sacramentarian sense (for in this he does not believe), but in virtue of the religious feeling which is latent in all men, and of living in a Christian country where they cannot but have come under Christian influence. With this idea, he addresses all his hearers as "Christians," and dissuades preachers from using any other manner of address. It will thus be seen that his conception of the object of preaching is tinged with the same subjectivity as marks his idea of the basis and the subject, showing the same want of outline and point and distinct aim. There is an elevation, a beauty, a fulness, but it is like the evening cloud that melts away and leaves a sense of pleasure, not a tree with firm trunk and branches rooted in the solid ground, covered with fruits that can be plucked and carried home. I do not mean that his sermons fail to serve a purpose; but, as he himself says, the purpose is not instruction nor action, but influence.

The structure of the sermon. With this general idea of preaching his special views about the structure of a sermon coincide. He holds that each sermon should have a text, and that the text should not be used as a motto. In order to have unity, the sermon should deal with something contained in the text, but not necessarily with the whole of it nor even with the chief thought in it; it may be but a fragment of it, or a secondary thought. His own preaching is topical, not textual, and so distinctly topical that all his sermons which I have seen have titles prefixed. The introduction is generally the disengagement of the topic from the text — breaking the shell as it were, and taking out the kernel, or so much of it as is needed. When the kernel is extracted, the shell is thrown aside. As for the plan or arrangement of the sermon, he does not attach much importance to logical proportion. The end should be kept in view and the road to it, while way-marks should be set up and announced; but what is wanted is such unity of feeling or free flow of feeling as will produce an impression on the hearers, and the subordinate topics should be arranged with a view to this, rather than to logic.

The great thing in a sermon is the right tone, and
this is to be gained in two ways : first, by drawing
the feeling proper to the subject from the Word
of God, or rather from Christ in the Word ; and
secondly, by coming into sympathy with the
hearers so as to penetrate them with the tone. In
keeping with this, the close of the sermon should
gather what has been said into a unity, so that the
discourse may terminate, not with its last thought
alone, but with the weight of the whole, bearing
upon the heart and life. For the manner of the
sermon, he would have it to be of the nature of a
two-fold dialogue—a questioning of the Scriptures
as to what they teach about the topic, and a
questioning of the hearers as to how it is to profit
them. Not that questions are to be put in so many
words, but this is to be the mental attitude of the
preacher, in order that he may learn the truth and
apply it ; and he may sometimes put his points in
the form of literal questions.

With regard to style, we should remember that
the sermon is not poetry but prose. It should
be prose, with life and colour, yet not too highly
idealistic. If the poetic enter, or if poetry be
quoted, it should be at the close of some period
which is shaped as a climax. The choice of words

The style of
the sermon.

should be chastened and modest, not sensuous, not heaping up epithets or making appeals to angels and spirits and the powers of nature, but simple and natural. The gesture of the preacher should correspond to the matter. There are two extremes to be avoided—indifference, and affected force ; and this will be secured by unconscious sympathy of look and action. If there is a study of manner, it should be that general study which is not perceptible in any particular case.

His own preaching. In the main, Schleiermacher himself conformed to these rules ; indeed, they were given from his own experience ; but we may add some few facts about his preaching. His sermons were not in general written before they were delivered—*i.e.*, he neither read them nor delivered them *memoriter*, but gave them after very full and careful meditation.* The unbroken flow and the correctness which he attained by this method are remarkable, and were the result of long practice and of close concentration on his subject. The sermon grew in his mind

---

* Of the ten volumes which remain to us, some were reproduced without alteration from the shorthand notes of his friends and admirers; but those which he himself revised were changed considerably, for he held that a spoken and a printed sermon must differ, in order to produce the same effect. A sketch of one sermon is given on pages 305-7.

throughout the week, until it gradually took shape; then, having marked down the course of each part and the transitions on a piece of paper, which he called his " bill-of-fare," he was ready.   It is certain that this method would suit very few preachers, and even these few would have to pursue it with great care and thought.   For ordinary men it would be ruin, yet ordinary men might cultivate it at shorter services and devotional meetings with good results.   The way to do so is to fill yourself with the subject, and to begin by leaving short parts here and there open for expression at the time, gradually extending these till they form the greater part of the address.

There are defects both in the substance and the style of Schleiermacher's preaching.   In the substance, his defect, as we have seen, lies in the want of objectivity, especially in regard to the person and work of Christ.   There is a dimness in the view which he presents of the Lord Jesus, warmly and sincerely as he loved Him, and the dimness is caused by his undervaluing teaching, and by his looking within to his òwn feeling more than without to the Word of God.   His style, too, has its defects.   There is an absence of Bible language, and one cannot but see how his style has suffered

The defects of his preaching.

from his neglect of the Old Testament. He would have gained in picturesqueness and force, besides presenting another side of truth, had he dealt more with the history and the prophets of the Old Covenant — had he followed the example of Bossuet and the advice of Hamann.* His style shows also a want of concreteness. He seldom introduces figures from nature or touches from the beautiful hymns of Germany, though he was a lover of both. The structure of his sentences, too, tends to monotony. The periods are so long, involved, smooth, and harmonious, that short sentences, even if abrupt, would give relief; they are like the large rolling waves of mid-ocean that fold out but do not break with shocks of thunder and spray. But with all this, his style has great beauty and soothing power—of a Ciceronian not of a Demosthenic kind; and while his teaching may not always be Biblical, there is the felt presence of the Spirit of the Bible visiting a wide and varied extent of human experience.

His preaching differed from all that went before it. It wanted the passion and direct purpose of Luther, and, as we have seen, it wanted the central truth in which lay so much of Luther's power. It

* See above, pages 272-3.

wanted also the fervour of the Pietists, and their searching discrimination of the spiritual life. It had not even the clear, logical outlines of Reinhard. Yet it had qualities of its own which went deep down through the dry, barren surface of rationalism like an Artesian well, and touched the great springs of feeling, and taught men that there is something more in religion and the Bible and Christ than the easily understood commonplaces which Illuminism declared to be the whole. So Schleiermacher led the way to a new and better time.

NOTE M, see page 292.

HEINRICH STEFFENS ON SCHLÉIERMACHER'S APPEARANCE.

" I must here introduce a man who made a new epoch in my life. It was Schleiermacher, who at the same time with myself was called to be 'professor extraordinarius' at Halle. He was small of stature, full of life in all his movements, with expressive features. There was a kind of sharpness in his glance which repelled some men. In fact, he seemed to look through people. His face was rather long and finely cut, the lips firmly closed, the chin projecting, the eye lively and fiery, with an earnest, concentrated, and steady gaze. I have seen him in all the changing relationships of life—deeply thoughtful and sportive, mild and indignant, moved by joy and sorrow. But the prevailing expression was a deep calm that pervaded and governed his disposition. Yet there was nothing monotonous in the calm, for an inner sympathy broke out through it with a sort of childlike kindliness. He was so quick that while he was engaged in the closest conversation nothing escaped him. He saw all, heard all that was passing around him, even to a whisper. Art has made his features immortal. The bust of him by the sculptor Rauch is a master-piece ; and one who has known him so intimately as I have is almost frightened to look at it. It seems to me at this very moment as if he were before me, and as if he were about to open the firm, closed lips for some telling word."—(*Was ich erlebte*, V. 141.)

Note N, see page 300.

A Sketch of one of Schleiermacher's Sermons.

Romans vi. 4-8.

Christ's resurrection, the image of our new life.

The sermon begins: "Glory and honour be to God, and peace be with all those who with joyful heart call to each other, 'The Lord is risen indeed.' Amen."

The introduction, which is brief, gathers together the sense of the paragraph, so as to justify the theme announced.

I. Our new life is like Christ's resurrection when we consider the manner of its rise.

His resurrection was from death and through it, not an easy death, but sore and with struggle. (This is described.) So in us the former life must die, and die by a crucifixion. Our sins, our evil desires must be nailed to a cross and buried in the grave. But then comes life, and it comes from God, from heaven. (Here is a favourable specimen of his style.) "When the hour comes which the Father has kept for His own power, then to such a soul under some form appears His life-giving angel. Yet how little do we know of the work of the angel at the resurrection of Christ! We do not know whether he appeared to the Redeemer or not; we cannot fix the moment when he rolled the stone away from the grave and the Redeemer stepped forth in new life; no one was there as witness, and those who might have seen it with their human eyes were dark with blindness. So we do not know how or in what form the angel of the Lord touches the soul that sinks into the grave of self-annihilation, to call forth in it the divine life. It rises concealed in this deep grave-like stillness, and not till it is in life can it be perceived. Its proper beginning

X

hides itself, as every beginning does, even from him on whom
it is bestowed. But this is certain, as the apostle says, that
the Lord was raised through the glory of the Father (and
so, in the words of the Redeemer, no one cometh unto the
Son except the Father draw him), *that* glory of the Father
which called forth the Redeemer from the grave, and which
always awakens in the soul that has died to sin the new life
which is like the resurrection of the Lord. Yes, amidst all
that heaven and earth show us, there is no greater glory of
the Father than that He has no pleasure in the death-like
state of the sinner, but that in some way the almighty
mysterious quickening call sounds forth to him, Arise, and
live."

II. Our new life is like the resurrection of our Lord in its
constitution and manner of acting.

It is the life of the same person and it is in close connection with the previous life. As Christ's resurrection was
the opening of a powerful and energetic life, so is ours.
His journey to Emmaus, His conversation with the disciples
about the Kingdom, are illustrations of this. Such should
be our new life. But, with all this power and action, the
life of the risen Redeemer in another sense is retired and
hidden. It is not before the world. The eyes of men were
holden, and He appeared only to those who belonged to
Him in love. So Christians have a peculiar life which they
do not obtrude on the world, an experience known and com-
municated among themselves. (Here he draws some fine
distinctions as to how Christians should be seen by the
world and should act on it, while they yet have their own
Christian fellowship).

III. Our new life is like the resurrection of our Lord,
because we cannot combine it meanwhile into one connected
whole.

Christ's resurrection was realised in some moments and
hours, conversations and acts; then He disappears from

sight and we have to wait for Him again. So with our new life ; not that it is confined to times of fellowship with others, or to special moments of higher vision, else we may fear that it is visionary ; but we lose sight of it often in trial and in the busy acts of life. Yet when we lose it in ourselves we may find it always in Him. The sermon concludes with a prayer addressed to the Redeemer.

This is a very favourable specimen of Schleiermacher's style, ingenious and yet just in the conception and carried out with much delicate thinking, while the language folds round the thought closely and gracefully. What one desiderates is to learn how the life of the Christian has its origin in connection with Christ. We are, as the apostle says, baptised into His death. How comes His death to be a seed of life, so that our union to Him in His death makes His life also ours?

LECTURE XVII.

MEDIATING SCHOOL: NITZSCH AND THOLUCK.

THE "flat rationalism" of Germany, which rested on the common understanding, and denied what it could not explain, died away in the first quarter of this century. As it decayed, two other tendencies arose. The one originated with Schleiermacher, to whom we have already referred, the other with Hegel, who was a contemporary of Schleiermacher. Hegel's sphere was philosophy, but he included religion in his system, and sought to reconcile Christianity with his philosophy. Different schools of religious thought arose upon the Hegelian basis, some positive and some negative; but, as the tendency of Hegelianism was pantheistic, the negative school prevailed, and ended in the absolute rejection not only of Christianity but of religion by such men as D. F. Strauss. Hegelianism as a philosophy is extinct in Germany, and survives only in various forms of communism and naturalism. As its theological side produced no remarkable preacher, we leave it for the present, and turn to the other movement which sprang from Schleiermacher.

The general name given to this movement is the Mediating School, because its object has been to reconcile religion and science, faith and reason. It corresponds to the movement of Lamennais and Montalembert in France, which was defeated by the power of Ultramontanism or Jesuitism, and finally crushed by the Vatican Council of 1870, and the Decree of Papal Infallibility. We may hope better things for the Mediating School in Germany. Its principle is to find so deep a root for religion in man's nature, and such a correspondence to this in the Bible and in Christianity, that it can look upon the inquiries of science in every form without any fear. The most noted German theologians of recent times belong to this school— men like Neander and Julius Müller, Ullmann and Olshausen, Sack and Dorner, and also Nitzsch and Tholuck. We shall select Nitzsch and Tholuck, as each of them has his own distinctive character.

Karl Immanuel Nitzsch was born in North Ger-

The Mediating School.

Nitzsch, 1787-1868.

many in 1787, and died in Berlin in 1868. He
was descended from a family of eminent theologians, and his father, who was superintendent of
the Church and Preachers' Seminary at Witten-
His life. berg, gave him the name Immanuel from his
admiration of Kant. Young Nitzsch received his
first education at Wittenberg, before that university
was united to Halle. He became preacher there,
and continued at his work through the siege of
the town when it was held by the French against
the Germans. During every sermon there was a
French officer stationed behind the pulpit, pencil in
hand, to note down any suspicious word. When
in 1815 the university was united with Halle, he
remained at Wittenberg in charge of the Seminary
and of his other duties, till his health broke down
under manifold labour. Then he retired to a
quiet country charge, and when he recovered, he
was appointed in 1822 professor of Dogmatic and
Practical Theology at Bonn. Here his chief work
was done. His success as a professor soon placed
him at the head of German doctrinal theology.
He continued to preach regularly, first in the
university and then in the town church. He also
took the guiding part in church affairs, especially
in seeking to consolidate the United church

(Lutheran and Reformed), to which his heart was devoted. He was called to Berlin in 1847, and lived there till his death.

Two events troubled his public life; the first was the outbreak of 1848, which let loose a flood of atheistic communism in Berlin and other parts of Germany; the second was the conservative reaction against this, which, in the form of rigid Old-Lutheranism, attacked his beloved Union, and sought to break it up. Still he held on bravely, with faith in God and devotion to the principles of Christian truth and Christian charity. When he had passed his eightieth year, he had repeated paralytic shocks, which all but separated him from the outer world, without, however, injuring the intellect that had been one of the strongest of his day. Among his last words to his old friend, Twesten, were these, "I can no longer hear or see or work; I can only love."

To understand what Nitzsch was as a preacher, we must know what he was as a theologian. On the objective side he was in advance of Schleiermacher—*i.e.*, while he held by feeling as the centre of religion in the soul, he advanced to more positive views of the Bible, of the person and work of Christ, and of doctrine and duty as connected with

Nitzsch as a theologian.

Him. It was as when a soft hazy mist, through which objects are dimly discerned, gives way to clear outlines of landscape under a fresh breeze of air. We refer here to the matter of his teaching, for the manner of it is unfortunate. He has his peculiar phraseology and structure of sentences— cumbrous and involved, thought within thought, but strong, deep, and solid. His theology is like that of Vinet, a fine balance of the objective and subjective, of the Bible and the heart; but while in Vinet it is in clear-shaped forms like vases of precious ore, in Nitzsch you find it in the nugget, and can even trace the laborious smelting of it from the granite into the ore. But those who use patience find that Nitzsch always has gold.

His views of preaching. He has given his views of preaching in his *Practical Theology.* According to him, preaching is the exposition of the divine Word, specially the word about Christ in its bearing on man's nature and the changing occasions of his life. It aims at the enlightenment of his mind and the change of his will, laying hold of that sense of need which is at the root of faith ; the beginning of this is renewal or conversion, and the continuance of it is edification. While he thus adopts Schleiermacher's conception of feeling, he lays more stress upon the need both of doctrine and of action.

In every sermon, he says, the preacher should consider: (1) The aim; an aim which can be briefly stated, and which must be kept in view throughout ; (2) the collection of material bearing on this, which is to be found principally in the Bible and in the heart; (3) the arrangement or division of the material, which should be simple and yet comprehensive ; (4) the carrying out of the plan under each division, and in this the main aim should always be kept in view; (5) the language ; and (6) the action. Instead of going over these in detail, we shall specify some of the most important of his views, and some of his own characteristics.

With Luther, he is of opinion that every preacher Two-fold aim should be both a reasoner and a rhetorician, *i.e.,* of preaching. should deal both with instruction and with exhortation. Instruction without exhortation becomes dry and pointless ; exhortation without instruction loses itself in empty harangue. Another consideration by which he seeks to check mere speculation or emptiness is that the preacher should keep before him some moral or spiritual aim, and ask himself: " Am I seeking in this for the edification

of the hearers?" The moral purpose, in his view,
should always predominate; by which he does not
mean to favour "moral preaching," but rather to
indicate that all the parts of the sermon should seek
a definite end in man's moral nature, that truth
should lead to righteousness and grace to love.

Language. As to the language of preaching, he commends,
above all, that of the Bible. Faith he says, is our
wisdom, and the Bible speech is its classical
tongue. He cannot bear the words deity, virtue,
obligation, &c.; they are not only unscriptural, but
cold and powerless; and he has equal objections to
the talk of the modern school "categorical," "tran-
scendental," &c., which may befit the Chair, but is
out of place in the pulpit.

Delivery. The delivery of the sermon should be free—*i.e.*,
without use of manuscript, as is almost universally
demanded in Germany and on the rest of the
Continent; and while there should be thorough
preparation, there should also be an endeavour to
gradually escape from the use of verbal memory
to the giving of the thoughts from a resting upon
the thoughts themselves. The advantage of this
acquirement is so great that no one should be satis-
fied till he has made a strenuous effort to reach it
and in most cases it can be gained.

When we consider Nitzsch himself as a preacher, His own preaching. we must confess that he has not reached his own standard. His style wants clearness and simplicity. He has not the skill to construct balanced and proportioned sentences, or to carry the intelligence of the hearers readily along the line of his thought. Thoughts come in the midst of thoughts as parentheses and qualifications, till the attention flags, and men must have listened to him more for profit than for pleasure. He was conscious of this defect, and laments it. He attributes it to his having read more of philosophy than of history in his early life, and to a tendency to follow thoughts down to their tangled roots rather than up into the clear open daylight. It is instructive to compare his style with that of men who, holding the same religious views, are pre-eminently clear—with that of Vinet, whose clearness comes from the admirable arrangement of his periods, which fall into their proper places like soldiers on drill; or of Andrew Fuller, where it comes from the perfect naturalness of saying much but only one thing at a time; or of Dr. Chalmers, whose sentences are built up paragraph after paragraph, while the attention is yet kept awake, and the understanding vivified through the fire which pervades every part of the discourse.

Its merits.   Still Nitzsch aroused the increasing interest of those who continued to hear him. He had two striking qualities; he penetrated into the deep things of the Bible, and into the deep things of the human soul. He was not an exegete, but, approaching the Bible with his own heart, psychologically rather than philologically, and thus carrying with him the hearts of men, he brought forth out of his treasure things new and old. All the grammars and lexicons' a man can use will do nothing without this. He believed, as an old writer has said, that " the heart and the Bible were made for one another." If there are unknown places in our hearts, it is because we do not know the Bible, and if there are unknown places in the Bible, it is because we do not know our hearts. The preaching of Nitzsch had neither beauty nor elegance nor fire, but his sermons were a mine for thoughtful hearers and are still of high value for students and ministers.

Tholuck,   Friedrich August Tholuck belonged to the same
1799-1877. school of belief as Nitzsch, but he was very different in many ways. His strength did not lie in doctrinal theology nor in penetrating argument, but he was an exegete and critic furnished with all the materials of learning. He was an apologist

with deep power of feeling and a vision of the ideal ;
he was a church historian ; he had an interest in
all branches of human knowledge, and an acquaintance with them that was encyclopædic. He had a
memory of prodigious power, and his knowledge of
the languages of the dead and the living made him
at home in the original literature of every important tongue of the East and of the West. With all
this he was one of the humblest, simplest, and most
lovable of men. We have to speak of him specially
as a preacher, but first a few things about his life.

He was born at Breslau in Silesia in 1799, and His life.
died at Halle in 1877. His father, who was a
goldsmith and jeweller, intended him for his own
business, but he showed so little aptitude for it, and
so much taste and ability for learning, that his
course was determined for study. He turned
specially to the languages of the East, and became
familiar not only with the Semitic, but with the
early Aryan—the old Persian and Sanskrit. So
intent was he on study that he sat up whole nights,
dipping his feet in cold water and drinking tea to
keep himself awake. He thus laid the foundation
of a weakness of sight and constitution that
attended him through life, though it did not
diminish his energy. During all this period, how-

ever, he was not merely indifferent to Christianity, but viewed it with prejudice and dislike.

When he had exhausted Breslau, he went to Berlin, and came in contact with some of its most noted professors, Diez, Hegel, and others, who were struck by his eagerness for knowledge. Attraction to Neander first turned his thoughts to religion, but intercourse with a Christian man, Baron von Kottwitz * of Silesia, determined him. He was led through him to study the epistles of Paul, which he had not previously read, and he says himself that, through the great mercy of God, he thus found wisdom and life in Christ crucified. He now devoted himself with the greatest zeal to the study of theology with a view to the Christian ministry. Such was his reputation that he was called to Halle in 1826 as a regular professor of theology in room of Knapp, the surviving representative of the old Halle Pietism. His commentary on the Romans, his works on Eastern Mysticism, and above all his little book on Sin and the Redeemer, *Guido and Julius*, had made his position known.† The whole Faculty of Halle

---

* Kottwitz is the " Patriarch " in *Guido and Julius*.

† Extracts from *Guido and Julius* will be found on page 326.

rose like one man against him, and urged the Government to rescind the appointment. The Government stood firm, and the Faculty were reconciled only through the broken health of Tholuck, which seemed to indicate that he would not trouble them long. But his case was like Calvin's and Baxter's, who did their work along the brink of the valley of death. For fifty years he was professor and preacher, and he went through his labours not only resolutely but joyfully, like Mercury, the celestial messenger, who has wings to his feet. At first he had scarcely a friend in Halle, but he soon began to strike his roots. Session after session the number of his students grew, till he became the light of the university; his class-room was crowded, and the largest town church was filled to overflowing when he preached. The old reign of rationalism passed away with its last chief, Gesenius; and Tholuck, with Julius Müller and Guericke and Ulrici, restored something like the feeling that prevailed one hundred years before in the days of Herrmann Francke. While he lived he was probably the best preacher in Germany, and when he died it was felt that one of the finest-moulded Christian natures had left the world

Contrast between Nitzsch and Tholuck.

We have said that he differed from Nitzsch, and we may express the difference by saying that Nitzsch instructs, Tholuck stirs. Nitzsch pursues the truth into details and applications, and works it curiously in the lower parts of the earth, whereas Tholuck presents it in masses of ideas and visions like broad landscapes or sunlit clouds. Nitzsch labours with his subject as a strong man with a load, Tholuck pours it forth like a full clear river reflecting all things in earth and sky. The preaching of Nitzsch is composed of the solid material of Christian doctrine and duty ; Tholuck's sermons, while filled through and through with Christian truth, teem with illustrations from all the stores of his learning — literature, poetry, art, treasures of the East, " barbaric pearls and gold." In a word, while Nitzsch's preaching is to the Christian understanding, Tholuck's is to the Christian heart and imagination. In this respect it resembles the preaching of Vinet and of Adolph Monod.

Tholuck's writings.

His *Sermon on the Mount* shows him at his best as a commentator ; his simple style may be learned from his popular *Commentary on the Psalms* and his *Hours of Devotion*, both of which have been translated into English ; and his change of heart is seen in that beautiful little book, *Guido and*

Julius, to which I have already referred. He has not written any special work on homiletics, but his views can be gathered from his sermons, and from his prefaces to them.

He has three discourses on the second chapter of 1st Corinthians. The first deals with the contents and tone of the sermon: the contents are found in Scripture with the centre in Jesus Christ, the alpha and omega; the tone is distrust of self and confidence in God. The second discourse deals with the origin and aim of the sermon: its origin is the teaching of God's Spirit in the preacher's own heart, for he must speak as a living witness; and its aim is not intellectual demonstration, but a manifestation of the truth to the heart and conscience. The third discourse is on the efficacy of the sermon: it is from faith to faith, the Holy Spirit working in the heart of the hearers.

His views about preaching.

It will be seen that he views the preacher as a witness-bearer, who should seek to stand as a conducting rod between the Holy Spirit in the Word and the Holy Spirit in the hearts of the listeners. His own sermons all move in this atmosphere — " I believed, therefore I spake " — and it was doubtless this which made him the

Y

instrument of such extensive spiritual quickening to his generation.

Dislike of conventionalism. He has a strong dislike of conventional rules for preaching, and wishes that the sermon could be brought back to the old homily of Chrysostom's time, leaving the preacher free to open his heart in a gush on any subject, though but indirectly connected with his text. He is probably right in objecting to such complicated rules as were laid down by Claude and the German schematists of the seventeenth century. They prescribed so much scaffolding that there was no room for the builder —no fresh individuality. On the other hand, if preachers were left to their own will without being bound particularly to their text, it would lead in many cases to intolerable diffuseness, and the disjointed nature of the discourse would put it out of the power of the people to follow and recollect

His own method. it. Tholuck himself has always a plan, and sometimes a very striking one. He does not despise the use of alliteration, and even of rhyme, to fix the thoughts in the memory.* He is specially rich in illustration, almost too rich, glancing from heaven to earth, from earth to heaven, in figures both of the fancy and imagination.

* Plans of two of his sermons are given on page 326.

But that which always gives interest to his Secret of his power.
sermons is the heart that is in them. He is never
dry, never cold, being always in contact with
his audience, hearing them, as it were, and asking
them questions. He is an admirer of Luther and
Hamann and Matthias Claudius and Bunyan, and
is one of those who mingle the divine with the
human, and the ideal with the real, who make
the Word flesh that men may see it to be full of
grace and truth. "A true sermon," he says, "has
the heaven for its father and the earth for its
mother. Why is it that so much of our preaching
goes coldly over the head and heart? Because
earthly affairs are treated only in the light of
this world. They have the earth for their mother,
but not the heaven for their father. And why
do other sermons go over the head and heart
altogether? Because, though heavenly things are
dealt with, they are not carried into the streets,
the homes, the workshops of the earth. They
have the heaven for their father, but not the earth
for their mother."

Tholuck's feeling and earnestness pervade the
whole of his sermons, but he reserves them specially
for the close. Here is an example from a sermon
on the dying thief :—

An example.   "Sinner, while thou standest on this side of the grave, it is never too late for thy repentance. But beware of presuming on this. There is a 'too late.' Oh, word of terror, how hast thou fallen like God's thunderbolt on many a human heart! See the father who hastens from the burning house and thinks the lives of all his dear ones are safe beside him. He counts; there is one wanting; he hastens back. Amid the rushing streams of fire the roof crashes in, and he sinks helpless to the ground. He is TOO LATE! Who hastens through the darkness of the night on his flying horse? It is the son who has wandered in the path of sin, and who would hear from the lips of his dying father the words, 'I forgive thee.' He is on the spot—at the very door. It is TOO LATE! The voice of his mother says, 'Thy father's spirit is gone,' and he falls into her arms and breaks into a bitter cry. See the criminal on the scaffold, and the executioner with uplifted sword. The crowd stands awed and shuddering. Who is visible on the distant height with eager gestures? It is the King's messenger. He brings pardon. 'Pardon' is first whispered softly on the verge of the throng, and then gathers into a cry. But the blow has fallen, it is TOO LATE! Yes, frightful is that word, rung in many a human ear since the earth began. But who shall describe the anguish when, on the boundary where eternity meets time, the voice of the righteous Judge shall declare that it is TOO LATE? Long has the door stood open, the wide door of heaven, and His messengers have called, 'To-day, to-day, if ye will hear His voice.' Man, man, what wilt thou do when the door shall be shut and the word heard from within, 'It is TOO LATE?' Strive, strive now to enter in at the gate! As frightful as is the truth that eternity speaks that word, so joyful is the voice from the Cross of Christ—while thou art on this side of the grave, IT IS NEVER TOO LATE. · Therefore, to-day, if ye will hear His voice, harden not your hearts."

NOTE O, see page 322.

PLANS OF TWO OF THOLUCK'S SERMONS.

Gal. iii. 19—"Wherefore, then, is the use of the law?"

  1. It is a standard to measure our defects.
  2. It is a sword to pierce our conscience.
  3. It is a seal to certify that we are in the way of grace.

Rom. viii. 18—"If children, then heirs."

  1. Wherein the witness of sonship is seen.
  2. How it is a pledge of eternal life.

A strict criticism would reject the first head as not properly in the text, but it is really needful for the exposition of the second.

EXTRACTS FROM *Guido and Julius.*

In the circuit of their Seminary there was no Emmaus; no spring flowers flourished there, nor groves of Academus. The new temple of reason was built on the mouldering ruins of the old porch of the Stoics and the deserted walks of the gardens of Epicurus. The Director of the Gymnasium, an aged man, revered the pineal gland as the seat of the spirit, and had often indulged the speculation, whether the Creator might not have furnished man at creation with a third hand or a third foot, instead of a heart. It was his office to teach religion. Most assiduously he dragged a skeleton, his own workmanship, day after day into his lecture-room, and shook the thing of bones till a shudder ran through the school. Nor were the other masters of a better kind—philologers, who in all their vocabularies had not one word of life-giving power. The preachers of the town were part orthodox, part neological, but all lukewarm and devoid of energy. What they had of religion was picked up at foreign volcanoes. No wonder that the flame in the souls of these youths shone more faintly, as it vainly turned to the right and left, eager for fuel, but finding none. . . .

With secret tremor the young men looked in on the floods of boiling passion, on the cataracts of unbridled desires in their souls, and they heard no voice that could control them. Their principles were stationary clouds, their resolutions mists flying across them. . . .

There is a bold, mocking spirit in man, to which nothing is holy, not even his virtue when it is merely his own creation.

LECTURE XVIII.

THE UNBROKEN TESTIMONY: HOFACKER
AND HARMS.

W E have been looking at the changes in German
theology and preaching in the decline of
Pietism, in the rise of "the flat rationalism," and
in its decline before the Mediating school of
Schleiermacher, Nitzsch, and Tholuck. What
has been said applies to a great part of Protestant
Germany, but not to the whole of it.

Variety of religious life in Germany.
Germany is a country with forty-five millions of
inhabitants, not including the Austrian dominion;
and of these fully two-thirds are Protestants. If
we were to hear one speaking of the history and
characteristics of "British preaching," we should
naturally ask if his remarks applied to England,
and if so, to what part of England, if they applied
to Scotland, to Ireland, and to Wales, and further
if they applied to all religious denominations. We
should probably find that no general remark was

328

equally true of all the districts and of all the churches of Great Britain. So it is in regard to Germany. The state of religion is different in different parts of it; and though there are not so many denominations as with us, there are as many, if not more, shades of religious life. Some provinces and districts have been comparatively free from rationalism, and have carried down the doctrine of Luther and Spener to our time. We wish to speak to-day of this " unbroken testimony;" and we shall select two instances, one from the south and one from the north—Ludwig Hofacker and Claus Harms.

The ancient Swabia, now the kingdom of Würtemberg, has always been noted for its depth of feeling. Richter and Uhland, who belonged to this region, show its characteristics ; it was the country of Bengel and Oetinger and many of the early Pietists.

Ludwig Hofacker was born in Würtemberg in 1798, and died in 1828. His father was a minister of the old orthodox school, but earnest and full of life ; his mother was quiet and deep and spiritual. Besides Ludwig, there was another son, Wilhelm, five years younger, who also became a minister, and when he died, in 1848, left a name scarcely

(margin note:) Hofacker, 1798-1828.

inferior to that of his elder brother. Their biographer, Albrecht Knapp, says: "How well would it be for Germany if more mothers were to give their native land such heralds of eternal life!" Some of Ludwig's sermons were printed while he lived, but most of them after his death. Above 100,000 copies were sold in Germany. My own copy is from the ninth stereotype issue, so soon did the plates wear out. His books have been translated into French, Dutch, Danish, Russian, and English; and in old German families in America the books you find most frequently are Arndt's and Hofacker's sermons. There must have been something remarkable about a man who left such an impression after a life of only thirty years. Short notes of his life, taken from his journal, are prefixed to most editions of his sermons, with a portrait of him—a fine Roman face, youthful almost to boyishness, a broad brow surmounted by the little clerical cap worn in those country districts, and great full eyes that seem to be looking out into eternity.

His life.   He was intended at first for business, but his heart did not lie to it. He would be a minister, and yet it could scarcely be so, for he had no particular seriousness or love of study. After preparatory education at the Pädagogium or chief school of the little town of Esslingen, and the Cloister-school of Schönthal, he proceeded in 1816 to the university of Tübingen, which afterwards acquired an evil reputation through Strauss and Baur. Here he showed a jovial, restless temperament, being more frequently in the beer-house than among his books, with a strange power of influence over those with whom he came into contact. But he was free from vice, and he had a conscience, for he resolved that before he became a minister he would seek for a change of heart.

The change came before the time he fixed. A His conver-restlessness took hold of him. He felt that he had sion. no footing for mind or heart. Putting to himself Pilate's question, What is truth? he could not find an answer. He resolved to write down what he was sure of, but each thought vanished as he tried to find expression for it. He happened to read at this time an account of the death of Jung Stilling, and he saw that Stilling had something which he firmly believed, and on which he could base his happiness. Jakob Böhme fell into his hands, but confused him with the mystic idea of a holiness that was to become his justification. At last, from the Bible itself, he obtained a view of reconciliation without the works of the law, which he never lost. This was just as he was finishing his student course, and before he left Tübingen he received a blow which left a mark upon the rest of his short life. Crossing the street on an intensely warm day, in August 1820, he had a sunstroke, fell unconscious, and was seized by a nervous fever which returned again and again, and made his work but a series of intermittent efforts. Like the touch of Jacob at Peniel, it weakened him physically but made him a spiritual hero.

His work.   He began his work by preaching for three months at a small country village called Pleiningen, and the people so felt the power and earnestness that were in him, that they came from all the neighbouring villages and crowded the church. Then he broke down, and for two years he was laid aside. He grew spiritually during those years, and rose with a more simple and penetrating faith, that made him speak as if he saw the invisible. He preached in Stuttgart, the chief town of Würtemberg, every Sabbath for two years. The effect was wonderful. People flocked from distances of twelve and sixteen miles eager to listen; some even making journeys of two days. To find room it was necessary to be in church an hour beforehand. An eye-witness

describes the immense area—seats, passages, every
space crowded with a mass so dense that an apple
could not have fallen to the ground, silent and
waiting. And when Hofacker spoke of the love
of the crucified Saviour, and seemed to draw them
to His feet, the heads of the listeners bent invol-
untarily under his spiritual power. " I remember," he says, " comparing them unconsciously to
a cornfield with the heads of grain bowing under
the sweep of the wind. Though he disliked
appeals to mere feeling, sometimes a universal
weeping was perceived as the words of the Cross
came home to the hearts of the hearers. In those
days I could see crowds of travellers, staff in hand,
hastening to the town to find some spot where they
could hear a few words of the sermon. There was
a rare outpouring of the Spirit of God, and the
name of Christ was praised by thousands who
before had little concern for their souls' salvation."*

Hofacker's health broke down again and forced
him to leave Stuttgart, but he returned, only half
recovered, to his work of preaching. The flame

* This reminds us of the account given of the effect of a
sermon in which Richard Cameron appealed to the hills
around him : " Look to these hill-tops there, over the Shaw-
head. Take them in your view ; they are all witnesses.
Look to them ; they shall all be witnesses when you are

had gone with his bodily vigour, but there was a
white heat, a deep concentrated fire, that was as
powerful and, if possible, increased his popularity
throughout the whole of Würtemberg.   But it was
not for long.   In the spring of 1828 he preached
his last sermon on " Jesus, the conqueror of death;"
and, after much suffering, he fell asleep.   The last
whispered words heard by his friends were "Saviour,
Saviour!"

Character-
istics of his
preaching.

When we read Hofacker's life and look into his
sermons, we see that the marvellous effect of his
preaching was not produced by what is commonly
called eloquence.   There is no appearance of the
arts of oratory, about which indeed he seems never
to have thought.   There is no depth of thinking
or loftiness of imagination.   There is little beauty
or freshness of illustration, little even of appeal to
the emotions.   Still less is there any novelty of
doctrine or strangeness of speculation.   If we read
his sermons merely for what they bring to the
intellect, we should say "we have heard all this
again and again, with far more of art and orna-

dying that you were invited and obtested to take Christ ; "
"and thereupon," says the narrator, " he fell in such a rapture
of calm weeping, and the greater part of the multitude, that
there was scarce a dry cheek to be seen among them, which
obliged him to halt and pray."

ment and scientific treatment." I do not mean
that his sermons are marked by any degree of
ignorance or carelessness. Far from it. He had
studied the Christian system, and he had studied
the Bible. His sermons were evidently thought
over and planned. They are not rhapsodies nor
disjointed remarks. They have all an aim, and
the divisions and treatment are often happy and
striking. But it is not in these that their power lies.

Apart from the power of the Holy Ghost, of Source of its
which we do not here speak, it had three sources: power.
—(1) the strong impassioned conviction with
which he pressed home the great central truth of
the love of God in Christ, with its two poles, sin
and righteousness; (2) the deep earnestness and
sympathy with which he spoke—a solemn insist-
ance on the danger, a kindly yearning love for the
souls of men ; (3) the directness and intense force
with which he went to his aim. His object was to
come to close quarters ; or, as one of his hearers
said, he "shot with rifle balls." So he used the
simplest, clearest, most telling language, and put
his sentences in the directest forms. His brief
ministry was one strong, piercing cry, "We
beseech you, in Christ's stead, be ye reconciled
to God."

Its limited scope.   Yet his sermons were not repetitions. In the
beginning he was afraid they would be so.   After
his first sermon he thought he had said all he
could say—-that he had shot his one arrow and had
no more.   But in his distress he seemed to hear a
voice saying, "Poor man, that does not lie on thy
head.   Look to Me; if I do not help thee, thou
art soon done."   And, though his sermons have
always the one aim, they are very varied, and reach
it by different roads.   Thus he says, "I have but
one sermon: come, sinners, and look on Christ.
I preach the Lamb that was slain; that draws
hearts—oh, brothers, that draws hearts.   It is a
pity that we have so many words in the pulpit that
do not go to Him.   But I have found that he who
preaches Christ never runs done.   We get done
with our wisdom, for it is a vessel, and a vessel
has a bottom; but the love of Christ is an abyss,
and out of his fulness we receive grace for grace."
"We should preach," he says again, "more like
missionaries, as if we were going to the people for
the first time; we make too many words and
forms of speech, far too many; and they miss the
message.   We should speak more simply and tell
them they have a Saviour, and who the Saviour is,
and what He has done, and what love He has to

men, and what blessings He has in store. We cannot be plain enough, I might say common enough."
He gives his reason for preaching in one strain:
"The trumpet that wakens men is more powerful
and piercing when it does not follow the range of
the scale, but keeps at one penetrating note."

With all this, he is aware that there are different kinds of preaching. He says: "I do not know
that mine would tell for more than two years in
one place. People become accustomed to the
sharp searching tone, and it ceases to affect them."
He compares himself to a driver who presses the
sheep to enter the fold, while others must look
after their nurture there.

This is true; and it suggests to us that Christian Lessons.
ministers whose gift is rather for edification, should
have no jealousy of evangelists, but rather welcome
them; and also that the Christian Church, when
it finds a man with the evangelistic gift, should
appoint him to a special office. Still, we may all
learn from men like Hofacker to be evangelists as
well as pastors, and to seek often to present the
first truths of the Gospel in the simplest and
directest way. It is only at revivals that men are
raised up who have this power in the highest
degree—men who stand like Stephen in the very

presence of God, and declare what they see. They are placed along the Church's line of march, to be witnesses to an invisible world and to rouse both people and ministers. If we cannot reach their power, we may learn from them that men are most moved when we bring them to three places—Sinai, Calvary, and the Great White Throne; sin, righteousness, and judgment—these are the powers of the world to come, and we must learn to use them with God's help in some way, if we are to speak in demonstration of the Spirit and with power.[*]

C. Harms, 1778-1855.

Claus Harms was born in 1778, and died in 1855. His life, which thus began earlier and ended later than that of Hofacker, was different in many ways, more coloured and combative, and more connected with ordinary secular interests. Yet he was the instrument of a revival of faith in the north, as Hofacker was in the south of Germany.

His youth.

His father was a miller, a well-to-do man as we should say, of good character, who lived at Dithmarsch, in the province of Holstein, which was then connected politically with Denmark. The way in which young Harms repeated hymns and

[*] For a sketch of one of Hofacker's sermons, see page 346.

went through his school work, made the parents think of making him a minister. But the father changed his mind, partly from fear of the stirring, restless character of the boy, and partly from having lost the means of educating him. Claus, however, was resolute, and with great difficulty made his way to the university of Kiel.

The faith of his youth had by this time been shaken, and he was at sea on almost every religious question. A friend lent him Schleiermacher's *Reden.* He sat down to read them on a Saturday afternoon, read and re-read them through the night and the next day, with scarcely any sleep; and when he finished, he was done with rationalism. It took him, however, a good while to find his way to a new life; he needed, as he said, to "bury dead rationalism in its grave." Ever afterwards he looked on Schleiermacher as his spiritual father, though he went on to more positive standing-ground, or rather he went back from all the schools that sprang from Schleiermacher, to the position of Luther and the Augsburg Confession pure and simple. *Influence of Schleiermacher.*

When near the end of his student course, he began to preach for his minister at Kiel, and the people liked him so much that they repeatedly *His preaching.*

asked when they would hear him again.   He
preached in the country for a while with the same
result, and then returned to Kiel.   He spoke from
deep conviction, and had a fresh, striking way of
putting things; and men flocked from all sides to
His struggles   hear him.   He had his difficulties.   The university
at Kiel.   at Kiel was against him; he was "an obscurantist,
a darkener of the light of reason, a retailer of old
worn-out ideas; he and his Bible and Luther!"
The middle-classes of Kiel were given to money-
making, and had grown vulgar; they thought to
show that they were men of culture and progress
by chiming in with the university.   Besides, they
liked to dine well, and it had been arranged that
Harms should preach in the afternoon just in the
middle of the dining-hour.   Yet he held on without complaining.   People who dined sparingly
came to hear him; the students, who found that
rationalism was getting old and that Harms was
new, also came.   Then followed the professors;
old Eckermann, the father of Kiel rationalism,
never missed an afternoon; and the hotels and
restaurants had to arrange their hour for dinner so
His victory.   that the guests might hear Harms.   The victory
was now complete, as when Shimei, who had
thrown stones at David, came back to welcome

him in his triumph. But it took a number of years.

Meanwhile Harms' name and views had been Growth of his influence. taking possession of Holstein and Schleswig, and were known far beyond. He republished the *Theses* of Luther, with others of his own bearing on rationalism, and a fierce contest ensued. About two hundred pamphlets were written by the angry rationalists, but Harms had the best of it. His style was so clear, so bold, so full of trenchant wit and humour, that everybody read what he said, and the current flowed strong on his side. People were weary of the dry moral harangues of the friends of reason, and wanted something for their heart and spirit. He was now the hero of the time. The university that had laughed at him made him a Doctor of Divinity. The King of Denmark invited him to the Lutheran church in Copenhagen ; the Emperor of Russia asked him to settle in St. Petersburg ; and the King of Prussia offered him the place of Court-preacher in Berlin, vacant by the death of Schleiermacher. But Harms declined these offers and remained at Kiel, busy as ever.

Besides preaching, he occupied himself with the His varied activity. ordering of church affairs ; with the school-system,

seeking to make it Christian; with the hymn-
book, restoring it to evangelical strength—it had
been watered down by the rationalists; with
popular literature, trying to purify it; till his
sight gradually failed, first one eye then the other,
leaving him at last in total blindness. But he
visited families, he dictated books, he preached
occasionally, and at length died quietly, after a life
of long and varied labour, at the age of seventy-
seven.

His strength.   It will be seen from this brief sketch that
Harms was a remarkable man and preacher, and
it may also be seen in part wherein his power lay.
First of all, he planted himself on the central truths
of the Bible—sin, salvation, justification, and faith,
as these had been set forth by Luther, whom he
recognised as his master in theology. Next, he
had a deep conviction of their truth, and spoke
with all his heart. Lastly, he spoke simply and
directly according to his own nature, as Hofacker
did, though his nature was different from Hofacker's.
He was not so searching, arresting, subduing in
spiritual power, but more broadly human and fresh,
having a quaint fancy and a love for old confes-
sional forms—an eloquent Matthew Henry.*

* For a sketch of one of his sermons, see page 346.

Among many volumes which he gave to the His views of press, there is one in three parts on *The Preacher*, preaching. *The Pastor*, and *The Priest*, and a tractate *Mit Zungen*, With Tongues, from which we may gather his views of preaching. The first thing he requires of the preacher is a right spirit—that a The spirit of deep holy earnestness should fill him; and he refers the preacher. to the tongues that descended at Pentecost, as emblems of a permanent qualification for which preachers should always seek. This may be strengthened by occasional retirement for hours, and even days, of meditation and prayer. He holds the necessity for spiritual "retreats," quoting Moses, Elijah, John the Baptist, and Paul; and he thinks that a man will always come forth from such privacy with increased power.

Next, he says that the Bible is to furnish the Material for material for preaching. Without this, the spirit preaching. would want guidance. But he does not approve of the "homily," nor of adherence to the exposition of parts of the Bible, nor of the textual method. Indeed, he makes light of instruction, and would have appeal made, not to the understanding but to the heart and conscience. In this we think Harms to have been decidedly wrong; for the awakened heart cannot grow without teaching, and the field of teaching must be the truths of the Bible. His objection to textual preaching, with his exclusive use of the synthetic or topical method, is also, we think, a mistake. Indeed, Harms did not, and could not, adhere strictly to his own rule.

Language. As to the language of the sermon, he would have it usually Biblical, and, when not so, then of the simplest and most natural kind. He denounces the use of book-language as suited only for reading. Conversational language, the language of the people, is the proper dialect of the preacher—short, strong, kernel-like expressions, without circumlocution or phrase-making. But Bible language is always the best. We get our religion from the Bible, and it should be our mother tongue. "The nearer the Scripture," he says, using a phrase of Hamann's, "the nearer the skies."

Delivery. With regard to delivery, the idea that the sermon may be read does not even enter his conception of the work of preaching. The question with him is whether it should be pondered thoroughly and spoken from the thought, in Schleiermacher's later manner, or written and committed to memory. He thinks that for most preachers the latter is the better plan, and that, with some labour at first, almost every one will in this way reach a natural and easy delivery.

As to speaking, he enjoins three *L*'s. The three *L*'s are—loud, longsome, loving ; to which I would add—loud without bawling, longsome without drawling, loving without whining. For tone and emphasis and gesture, he would leave the preacher chiefly to nature, though care should be taken to correct defects and awkwardness. The three *L*'s.

From this it will be seen that, while Hofacker and Harms were different, they had the essentials in common. They held the same Gospel and maintained it in a time of coldness and defection. They brought to it the same deep conviction, drawn from personal experience. They had a true love for their work and for men's souls, and they addressed themselves to their task in the most direct way, using all plainness of speech. There were diversities of operations, but the same Spirit. Without that which was common to both of these men, our preaching will be to some extent marred ; with even a portion of it, we shall, with God's help, have abundant success. Hofacker and Harms.

NOTE P, see page 338.

SKELETON OF ONE OF HOFACKER'S SERMONS.

Matt. xv. 21-28—The Faith of the Woman of Canaan.

I. The nature and the form of her faith. It was great—
1. Because she followed its impulse without regard to the judgment of men.
2. Because it broke through all obstacles.
3. Because a deep, unconquerable trust in Christ lay at the bottom of it.
4. Because it was accompanied with deep humility.

II. How this faith was born in her.
1. She heard of Jesus and took the word to heart.
2. A terrible affliction was pressing on her.
3. She saw and knew of no other helper.

This division is a fair specimen of Hofacker's method. It is quite simple and artless, while a rigid logic might pick faults in it; *e.g.*, the first and second sub-divisions of the first part do not exclude one another. The power of his sermons, however, does not lie in their arrangement, but in their spirit and their fragrance. It is not from his head but from his heart that we may learn.

NOTE Q, see page 342.

SKELETON OF ONE OF HARMS' SERMONS.

John xvi. 16-23—He selects from the verses the idea "a little while," and speaks of its value to the Christian.

1. It chastises the sorrowful.
2. It checks the joyful.
3. It spurs the loiterer.
4. It pierces the careless and self-confident.
5. It strengthens the struggling.
6. It upholds the dying.

His divisions are clearly cut, briefly expressed, and memorable, and much may be learned from them. Sometimes they are too numerous, there being in some cases as many as twelve. But the illustrations are never long, and the style is terse and picturesque. *E.g.,* in enforcing the fourth head of the above sermon, he says : "Who are the careless? We cannot seek them out or count them ; but let each man step forward to this word with his heart. Who is the careless? The man who has behind him a youth full of sins, his riper years guilty without repentance, and who, because in old age he has been forced to give up some sins, is confident that all is right. Man! thou hast built thine house upon a fire-vomiting hill, and thou dost not know it. Before thou art aware, in 'a little while,' it will burst out and hurl thee into an abyss where thou shalt no longer stand erect. Thou dost not fear this? Even that is thy carelessness— thy sinful carelessness."

LECTURE XIX.

BIBLICAL PREACHERS—STIER AND KRUMMACHER.

BY this title we do not mean that those of whom we have been speaking are not in accord with the Bible, but that the two men whom we here name made use of the Bible in a way that brought them closer to it, not only in its reality but in its shape and formation.

R. Stier, 1800-1862. Rudolf Stier is well-known in this country by his commentaries, especially *The Words of the Lord Jesus.* It is a question whether they have not sometimes been used to the weakening of self-reliance and self-development; there is always this danger, when a commentary passes beyond exposition into exhortation or into minute indication of lines of treatment. Yet there is perhaps · no one of the German writers, with the exception of Lange, who has been of so much direct use to ministers in the preparation of their sermons.

348

Though born in the Duchy of Posen, which His education.
is mostly Polish, he was of German parent-
age. His father, who was in the Government
service, intended his son for the law. The education of young Stier was not carried forward very
systematically, owing to the want of "higher"
schools in the neighbourhood ; but he made great
efforts in after life to compensate for this. At
the university of Berlin he entered the law classes ;
but he found the study uncongenial and dry ; and
after some trouble with his father, he gained
permission to change to theology and to enrol himself under Neander, who was then enthusiastically
followed in the Berlin university. It was not
decided religious conviction that led him to this
decision. He was of a poetic and idealistic nature ;
and the poetry of the Bible, with its dreams of a
nobler humanity, had great charms for him. He
lived in a constant ferment of excitement about
some great poet or some new movement. In 1818,
he removed to the university of Halle, and became
a leader there in the Burschenschafts or debating
and patriotic clubs.

Presently a great bereavement—the loss of His conver-
his betrothed—shook his whole nature and turned sion.
the stream of his enthusiasm into the channel

of religion.   It was a period in Germany when many heard the words of Christ as if for the first time, and when sudden conversions were more frequent than in calmer seasons.   He speaks thus of the change in a letter to Tholuck, who was one of his friends.   " As truly as I live, and live now truly for the first time, I know that One lives outside us, who can enter our hearts in a way above reason ; and I now know that the natural man, with all his poetry and fashions, is like a blind man without light.   He, He alone, is the light of the world." He now threw himself with immense energy into the study of the Bible as the source of all true knowledge, and published in 1824 his first book, *Hints on the believing Interpretation of the Scriptures.*   It is brief but very suggestive, and contains the principles of the numerous works that followed.*

His career.   In the same year he was offered the office of Lecturer and Teacher in the Mission-Institute of Basel, a great school of evangelical missionaries, and he gladly accepted it.   There he remained for four years, laying the foundation of his works,

---

* He himself drew the spirit of it from a remarkable man, J. F. Meyer (not the commentator), who is little known in this country ; a sketch of Meyer will be found in Note R, on page 366.

and drawing out a plan for life, which he nearly accomplished. His health, however, broke down under his great labours, and, in 1829, he undertook a pastoral charge near Merseburg. He afterwards laboured in Barmen, a stronghold of the evangelicals ; at Schkeuditz, near Magdeburg ; and at Eisleben. In some of those places he was not very successful, owing to his retired student habits, and to the want in his preaching of that concreteness which he recommends in his homiletical writings. For ordinary hearers he was too minute, analytical, subtle ; indeed he exemplifies the truth that it is easier to tell what right preaching should be than to practise it. Yet in other places, where Bible instruction was valued, he was followed by crowds. Tholuck gives this anecdote of him. In Magdeburg, where he was very popular, one of the country people was asked what kind of man he was, and answered, " He is a religious mystic." " But what do you mean by a mystic ? " " I mean a man who does what he preaches." His last charge was at Eisleben where Luther was born and died, and there, after a life of constant study, he was cut off by a stroke of apoplexy at the age of sixty-two.

He was a man of strong faith, of piercing, power- His character.

ful intellect, and of decided originality, who left
his mark on everything he handled. Withal, he
had a certain rockiness of nature that brought him
into collision with those about him—a flintiness
that gave out sparks when he was struck or when
those truths were struck that were dear to him.

His distinctive
attitude.
His views of preaching were different from most
of those which we have considered. Schleiermacher spoke from the deep religious feelings of
one who was in Tertullian's phrase *naturaliter
Christianus;* and, while he found the reflex and
completion of his feelings in the Bible, he took
from it only what melted into them. Nitzsch
went to the Bible with his heart, but not less with
a clear deep understanding, and thus became a
preacher of doctrine. Tholuck went with his heart
and with a rich imagination, and became a Christian
orator. Hofacker went with intense spiritual conviction, and became an apostle of repentance and
reconciliation. Harms went with the Confession
of his church, and preached, as an evangelical or
orthodox churchman, the circle of things to be
believed and to be done. But Stier went to the
Bible alone, and to all the Bible, and in approaching it he sought to strip himself of everything
that would prevent him from receiving its full

impression and from reflecting it in its rounded completeness on his fellow-men. This is why we have called him a Biblical preacher ; and to understand his position we must define his views of the Bible, which are themselves very important and instructive.

He approaches the Bible with the persuasion His view of the that, beyond and above the particular writer, Bible. *auctor primarius est Spiritus Sanctus.* He does not overlook the fact that the human medium gives its own shade and colour, but he is chiefly concerned with the divine light that shines through. There is always a deeper sense and a wider reference than the outside critic finds in the immediate occasion. The Bible is one book, with a pervading plan—the history of salvation—and with the living breath of the Holy Ghost through it all. No part, therefore, can be interpreted by itself ; each part must be taken in the light of the whole, and has always some reference to the whole. He thus comes upon the doctrine of inspiration from what we may call the "inside." He finds the Bible to be a living word wherever he goes, a word that as far as he studies it has life in every part, and witnesses in a thousand ways, to his mind and heart and will, that it is not only above himself

2 A

but above all the natural powers of man. He thus supplies a wholesome counteractive to those numerous critiques which regard only the human side and mince the Bible into little dead fragments. His commentaries are peculiarly stimulating from their lively style of argument, and their edifying character makes them very suggestive to the preacher.

His ideas on preaching.

In a tractate entitled the *Keryktik,* which is addressed specially to preachers, Stier declares that the Bible is the living fountain of all Christian teaching, and that wide, deep acquaintance with it is the first qualification for preaching. The preacher's work is to make the Scriptures living and efficacious; so he becomes a follower of the apostles and prophets, and speaks with their authority—*i.e.,* with the authority of God. "If," he·says, "the cultivated pagans of the day wish to hear something else, it is because they wish to hear, not God's Word that they may learn and obey, but the preacher's oratory that they may weigh and criticise. Speak as wisely as thou wilt out of thine own store, there will always be among them men wiser than thou, or men who think that they are wiser, and their pride will prevent thee from convincing them; they can be convinced only by the wisdom of God."

With regard to the form of the sermon, he objects Form of the sermon. vehemently to "the heathen rhetoric of the schools, with all its rules and methods." He would substitute for it a Christian *Laletik*—he is fond of coining words. By this protest, however, he means no more than that truth and reality should underlie the forms of oratory. Quintilian had said as much; and Stier's fellow-countryman, Theremin, had enforced the same obligation.* Still, Stier gives some special hints of his own. Each sermon, he says, should have an exordium, which should generally be a view of the connection of the text, or a justification of the use that is to be made of it. In the sermon itself the first point is to make clear what is in the text, not merely in its original reference but in its principle, for every text contains some principle of permanent application. The preacher should be very clear in this, for he will be surprised, when he comes into contact with people, how confused and misty they are in their knowledge of Bible principles. But, after reaching the understanding, he must bring home the principle to the heart, the conscience, and the life ; without this there can be no edification. Every sermon should have these two qualities—should be both Scriptural

* For a fuller notice of Theremin, see page 373.

and personal, taken from the Bible and coming
home to the hearers.   He prefers, as might be
expected, textual divisions, but he is not rigid, and
is quite willing that the different parts of the text
should be taken together, or that one leading topic
should be selected, if unity cannot otherwise be
gained.   The close of the sermon should be a brief
summary for the final stroke, in which we must
take care that we do not draw back from the truth
stated in the sermon with the view of making it
milder and more pleasing.

Pulpit lan-
guage.
The speech of the pulpit should have for its
basis the language of the Bible.   This is the best
mould for the truth, and it is the language which
the mass of the people comprehend and feel.   A
man should not try to say things new and beautiful
and deep.   If these come to him naturally, good
and well ; but the truth itself, if properly stated,
is deep and beautiful, and will be always new if
drawn from the variety of God's Word.   Upon this
he again and again insists, that whether preaching
be topical or textual, it should keep close to the
thought and to the language of the Bible.*

* In this, as in many other points, Stier resembles our ven-
erated professor of exegesis, the late Dr. John Brown.   We
do not append any sketches of his sermons, as they chiefly

The principles of Stier may be sometimes one- His faults.
sided and extreme, but they certainly deal with the
most important side of preaching. If he himself
was not always successful, it was from neglect of
his own maxims about bringing home the truth in
concrete shapes. He also shows a tendency to
undue repetition and prolixity, and to bringing too
much of the apparatus of the exegete into the
sermon. Yet, where these errors are avoided, such
preaching will be not only the most profitable but
the most interesting. We turn now to one who
succeeded where Stier failed.

Friedrich Wilhelm Krummacher was born at Krummacher,
Mörs, near Clèves, on the Rhine, and died at $^{1796-1868.}$
Potsdam. He was perhaps the most popular
German preacher of his day, and resembled the
late Dr. Thomas Guthrie, in appearance and in
his pulpit manner, as well as in the tone of his
mind.

Both on his father's and on his mother's side he Early
belonged to a family of preachers. His father, who influences.
was rector of the town school at Mörs, was a man

follow the lines of his text, dealing largely with exposition,
and applying the subject as he proceeds. But his commentaries give a fair idea of his style. He cannot be reckoned
among the popular preachers of Germany.

of faith and poetic nature, the author of a book on
the Parables which is still popular in Germany, and
has been translated into English. His uncle,
Gottfried Daniel Krummacher, was also an author
and a noted preacher, and his words on his death-
bed made an ineffaceable impression on Friedrich
and his brother : " Yes, my young friends, we must
all lie here, you and I.   We were born to die.   See
that you learn early to believe on the Lord Jesus,
for without Him we are the most miserable of all
creatures."

Krummacher studied first at Halle and then at
Jena.   Both places were under the influence of cold
rationalism and tame orthodoxy, but he kept
his spirit alive by reading Schleiermacher's *Reden*
(the book which quickened Harms), Matthias
His ministry. Claudius, and, above all, Luther.   His first settlement was at Frankfurt-on-the-Main, where he
became the intimate friend of a young French
minister, named Manuel, who died young.   The
latter was a man of great insight and culture, and
Krummacher learned from him how to read and
use the Scriptures.   But here he first began to
find his own manner, and to strike out boldly in
it.   From Frankfurt he went to Gemarke in the
Wüpperthal, and thence to Elberfeld, in the same

neighbourhood. That district, which is full of manufacturing towns and villages, has long been one of the chief centres of religious life in Germany. It had a band of faithful and able ministers; and Krummacher says he does not think that there was a place in Europe where at that time the Gospel showed itself with so much living power. He describes with enthusiasm the imposing Sabbath and week-day assemblies—head behind head, men as well as women; the mighty waves of song that seemed to lift the preacher above himself; the deep earnestness and sympathy reflected on the faces of the audience; the solemn Communions; the praise heard in the houses during the week, living echoes of the Sabbath sermons; the joyful welcome to the minister on his visits; and the manifest effect of the Gospel upon the living and the dying.

It was here that in 1828 he published his first book, *Glimpses into the Kingdom of Grace*, of which Goethe wrote a somewhat scoffing review —a proof that Krummacher was becoming a man of note. He continued here for a number of years, till he was called to Berlin to take the place of the well-known theologian, Marheineke. The soil there was very different from that of the

Wüppertnal; for Berlin had been the centre of
the Illuminism, and, for many years, perhaps the
most bleak region of Protestantism in the world.
The ordinary Berliner recognised religion only by
the registration of baptisms and funerals. The
great Church of the Trinity, to which Krummacher went, was nearly empty, but ere long he
drew to it from all quarters of Berlin, and from all
classes of society, a congregation so large that a
seat could be secured only by an early visit. He
was also the means of a considerable revival of
interest in mission work. In 1853 the King called
him to the Court-church at Potsdam, with a view
to giving him relief, and from personal liking for
his preaching. He died there suddenly at the age
of seventy-two.

His preaching. His *Elijah the Tishbite*, translated by Dr. Cairns,
who was also his interpreter at the Berlin meet-
ing of the Evangelical Alliance, his *Elisha the
Prophet*, and his *David King of Israel* give a clear
idea of his style of lecturing or preaching; for
these were delivered to popular audiences, and all
his discourses have their characteristics. Every
student should read them as specimens of the
picturesque treatment of Bible history, which was
his favourite subject. His manner is highly dram-

atic; he has the power of making scenes and persons visible and present. They seem to come nearer and nearer the hearers, as he shows that men of the past were like ourselves, with the same heart under the antique Eastern robe. His language is full of colour and imagery, with a rich varied flow that winds round every subject and suits itself either to the lofty or to the tender. Within these pictures we have constantly the great doctrines of grace, the New Testament being poured back into the bosom of the Old, Jesus Christ walking amid the seven golden candlesticks of the Jewish Temple, the still small voice speaking from Horeb of sin and salvation, of death and life eternal. It may be added that in Krummacher all the externals were those of an orator; his voice was powerful, rich, and flexible, able to sink to a soft whisper or rise to the roll of thunder. His look and gesture were so expressive that deaf people, it is said, followed the course of his preaching with intelligence. His power continued to the end of his life, becoming mellowed and more mature, but not less attractive.

As to his opinions about preaching, he refuses His opinion all rules, like Stier, and wishes that every man about preaching. should take his own natural bent. Such a refusal

will be generally found to proceed from some
previous excess of formalism. The logical method
of Reinhard had been pressing hard on the freedom
of German preachers ; and Krummacher is at the
farthest possible recoil from this. In him we see the
complete rebellion of heart and fancy against the
reign of the rigid understanding.

His method. But, notwithstanding this, he has his method
and principles. The introduction is generally
short and vivid, leading right up to the text; the
divisions are briefly expressed and memorable ;
while the close is also brief and telling, the
application being given throughout the discourse.
But his characteristics do not lie in his methods,
but in the carrying of them out. They remind
one of the paintings of Rubens, where the lines of
the sketch are lost in the strong colours and broad
handling of the subject. He was a colourist, and
indeed took lessons for his preaching from a celebrated German painter, Kugelgen, who was married
to his sister, and whose autobiography, *Erinnerungen
eines alten Mannes*, is one of the most delightful
books a student of German can read. The same
feature belonged to Dr. Guthrie. When he was
criticising a picture one day, the artist said, "What
do you know of our art, Dr. Guthrie?" "I do

know about it," he replied, "you paint on canvas, we with words." So Krummacher's sermons are like a gallery of paintings. Every truth is thrown into a figure. Every historical incident is filled up from his fancy with the greatest minuteness. A touch or two of the Bible is to him like a bone to a comparative anatomist; he can reconstruct the whole figure from it and clothe it with flesh and fence it with sinews, till we feel that, whether the facts were so or not, the figure is one of human nature. He recommends the preacher to use three books—the Bible, his own heart, and the people, and he himself draws from these in all his sermons.*

But it must be confessed that he commits faults His faults. in using each of these three books, and that he would have been the better for some of the rules which he despises. In regard to the people, he is apt to cultivate the love for the sensational and to transgress the bounds of good taste; *e.g.*, in describing the death of John the Baptist, he was so minute and vivid as to the manner of the execution that some of the ladies in the audience shrieked and fainted away. How much better to have imitated the wise reserve of the evangelist! In

* Some further notes on Krummacher's preaching will be found in note S, on pages 367-8.

regard to the heart, he lets it carry him away into
digressions that leave the main current of the
discourse and deprive it of concentrated power.
And in regard to the Bible, he overlooks its
historical development, making Elijah and Elisha
as fully acquainted with the doctrines of the New
Testament as the Apostle Paul. He reminds one
of a criticism which Dr. Guthrie used to repeat,
passed by a Unitarian writer upon his own *Gospel
in Ezekiel:* "Dr. Guthrie seems to think that Ezekiel
signed the Confession of Faith." Now it is quite
true that Christ may be found in all the Bible, but
not by the same methods nor in the same light.
There is the morning-star issuing from the bosom
of the night, there is the faint flush, the rosy dawn,
the bright noontide. We must not confuse these.
We lose the truth, the beauty, the harmony of the
Bible, its convincing testimony to its own divinity,
its fitness to all the stages of our humanity, if
we do not trace the goings of our God and King,
like the light that shineth more and more unto the
perfect day.

But notwithstanding such faults, we may even
say because of them, Krummacher deserves the
attention of every student who wishes to carry life
into his exposition of the Bible, to vivify its history,

and to make it everlastingly fresh and new ; and if one could combine the Bible exegesis of Stier with the Bible representation of Krummacher, so that the Christ who was so dear to both of them might be felt in the Old Testament and seen in the New, he would be a Biblical preacher indeed.

NOTE R, see page 350.

J. F. MEYER AND SCHUBERT.

Johann F. von Meyer, who was born at Frankfurt in 1772, and died there in 1849, influenced many preachers by his study of the Scriptures and his religious philosophy, although he was not a theologian by profession. He was a student of law, and rose to a high position as a judge and diplomatist, but he was also a student of universal learning. He devoted himself to poetry and art and natural philosophy; to the drama, ancient and modern. Attached strongly to the stage, he made an effort to raise it to the position of a teacher of morality and a purifier of social life. But his endeavour after this ideal failed in the rude conflict with popular taste. The frequenters of the theatre demanded different entertainment from what his conscience would allow him to give. He was a student of the Bible on the poetic and moral side, but trials taught him to read it for comfort and to enter into its depth. "I learned," he says, "that the doctrine of redemption is the distinguishing and immovable centre of Christianity, and that the Cross is the believer's star to guide him into endless discoveries of wisdom and glory." He did not give up human learning, but sought to use it for the elucidation of Bible truth. He made himself an eminent Hebrew scholar that he might read the Old Testament, to which he directed a great deal of thought. He made a new translation of the Bible. He also wrote a large work *Bibel-Deutungen*, Hints for the Bible, and another, *Blätter für höhere Wahrheit*, Leaves for the higher Truth, somewhat in the manner of M. Claudius, but without his peculiar humour. His views, as those of a layman, had a great effect in turning the thoughts of many to religion, and his writings on the Bible, though fanciful in their allegorising, have opened up fresh paths to students.

G. H. von Schubert (1780-1860) occupied a somewhat different position. He was a medical man, with an all-devouring appetite for knowledge, the friend of Herder, of Schelling, of Karl Ritter, and of most of the eminent men of his time. He studied the Bible in Meyer's spirit, and he made a long journey to the East in order to understand it in its birth-place. His book, *Old and New out of the Inner Region of the Soul,* made a great impression on the young men of his time.

NOTE S, see page 363.

KRUMMACHER'S PREACHING.

Here are two specimens of his brief introductions—

Phil. iii. 20-21—"Our conversation is in heaven," &c.

"What language is this, dear friends! And it is not the language of a perfected saint, but of a sinful son of Adam, a pilgrim of earth like ourselves. We may use it when we become Christians as the apostle was. How was he a Christian? Let us see, first, what light this passage throws upon the answer."

I Kings viii. 65—Solomon's Feast.

"The words we have read place us in one of the happiest times of the history of Israel. They introduce us to a feast. The joyful songs of these fair days have been silenced for thousands of years. But if we listen, they renew themselves in our hearts with loftier tones. Let us try to catch their echoes by thinking, first, of the object of the feast, and, secondly, of the feast itself."

Here is the close of a sermon on Hosea xiv. 5—"I will be as the dew unto Israel : he shall grow as the lily."

" May the Lord then come unto us like the dew ! May He come to those who are still like a withered branch, fit to be cast into the fire and burned, and may He work a wonder like that on Aaron's withered rod, which in a night, through His power, budded and blossomed and bore its almond fruit ! And as often as He comes down to us to call a soul into the eternal world, may it be said in heaven,—He is gone down into His garden to the beds of spices, to feed in the gardens and to gather lilies ! May His kingdom and His flock blossom like the rose. Amen."

He has a celebrated sermon on " Judah's Encampment," taken from Numbers ii. 3. It is divided thus :—

1. The tribe of Judah ; 2. His camp ; 3. Its position ; 4. His standard ; 5. His armies ; 6. His captain—each head being taken as emblematical.

This is not making the Old Testament bear upon the New, but playing with it. His uncle, Gottfried Daniel, was much given to this method of preaching.

LECTURE XX.

IN the latter part of our survey we have seen the decline of the older rationalism, principally through the influence of Schleiermacher and the theology of feeling. The end of this form of rationalism, the rationalism of the superficial understanding and of utilitarian morality, was also hastened by the philosophy of Kant. Kant did not occupy the Christian ground. In his *Critique of Pure Reason,* he denies that reason as such can give any knowledge beyond the finite, but in his *Critique of the Practical Reason,* which is his name for conscience, he recognises the categorical

End of the older rationalism.

Kant.

* [This lecture was written in 1880. Seven years have not only removed some of the preachers mentioned in the lecture, but have changed the attitude of others. Any attempt to bring the lecture up to date would necessarily have expressed the opinions not of Dr. Ker but of the editor.]

imperative, the inexorable "thou shalt" of duty; and from this he deduces three immediate consequences—God, moral freedom, and immortality. Kant was, so far, a Stoic in morality, and therefore he was opposed to the easy self-satisfaction of the old Illuminist school. He held, too, very strongly, the fallen moral condition of human nature, and, thus, though he denied or ignored the doctrines of the Gospel, he took such a high and earnest view of moral law that he may be called a John the Baptist outside the limits of the Bible. We refer not to the purpose, but to the result of his teaching.

Opposed by such influences as these, the Illuminism or Naturalism of last century, having no root in itself, withered away. It produced no great preachers after Zollikofer; and its last theologians were Paulus and Wegscheider, who were all but forgotten before they died. We have noted the revival of Christian teaching through Schleiermacher, Nitzsch and Tholuck, Hofacker and Harms, Stier and Krummacher, who all were men of faith, though they belonged to different schools.

The vessel did not, however, enter the harbour; or when the wind had ceased from one quarter, it

sprang up from another. The chief occasion of
this was the popularity of a new system of philosophy—the system of Hegel. The Hegelian philo- Hegelianism.
sophy professed to take a wider view than that of
Kant, and to explain the universe and everything
in it from the structure and movements of the
mind. It was the development of the universe in
all its fulness and multiplicity from the indifference of being or not-being, from the emptiness of
nothing or less than nothing. It created wonderful excitement throughout Germany, and its force
was felt in almost every region of thought and
action. After the death of Hegel in 1831, his
school divided into two main branches—the Right,
or Christian side, which sought to reconcile his
teaching with positive revelation, and the Left,
which became pantheistic or atheistic. While the
attempts of the Right to reconcile Hegelianism
with Christianity have only kindled *ignes fatui;*
the Left, although it has died away in Germany as
a philosophical system, remains in some of its consequences. One of these has been the formation
of the so-called Historico-critical school of ration- The Historico-
alism, the chief seat of which has been until lately critical school
the university of Tübingen, from which it is
usually named. The early leaders of this school

were the noted David F. Strauss, and Ferdinand C. Baur. Instead of accepting the Bible documents, and explaining away their revelations, they sought to destroy their authenticity, and so to neutralise their contents. Strauss did this by the Mythical, and Baur by the Tendency theory; the one of which is that the early Christians were deceived, the other, that they were deceivers. The controversies that arose out of those theories, and the varied voluminous literature which they produced, interfered much with the progress of the revival.

Controversies about Union.

There was another cause of disturbance. From the time of the Reformation, there have been two churches in Germany, the Lutheran and the Calvinistic or Reformed. King William III., the father of the present Emperor, with that imperious spirit which seems to belong to Prussian rule, ordered the union of those churches, and enforced it under penalty. His example was followed by other German Governments, but resistance was offered, specially on the side of the Lutherans; and when more liberty was granted, there came to be three churches instead of two, the Lutheran, the Reformed, and the Union which comprised a portion of both. This question has caused much friction of feeling, and has checked the flow of Christian life.

Still there has been progress. A large proportion of the theological professors, and of the
ministers in all the three churches, maintain positive Christian principles ; and at no period, perhaps,
since the time of Spener has there been a greater
number of earnest and eloquent preachers of the
Gospel. I shall to-day give the names and characteristics of some of them, noting some features of
the style of preaching which prevails at present.

Before coming to our own time, however, we Theremin,
may mention a name which would have had a 1780-1846.
separate place at an earlier period in this course,
had time permitted. Franz Theremin, for a long
time the most popular preacher in Berlin, was born
in Germany, although of Huguenot descent, and
was educated at Berlin, Halle, and Geneva. He
preached for several years in French, first at
Geneva and afterwards at Berlin ; but in 1814 he
accepted a call to the chief German church in
Berlin, where he continued till his death in 1846,
discharging latterly the additional duties of professor at the university, besides lecturing on homiletics. Many of his sermons have been published,
and they are considered models of a certain kind
of eloquence, which we may call the Classical-
Christian. He was a believing man, and the spirit

of his preaching was evangelical and warm. He was a lover of method, and studied diligently the ancient models, while the form of his sermons shows traces of his French origin. He has written a book on preaching, which is well worth reading, *Beredsamkeit eine Tugend,* "Eloquence a virtue." The object of it is to show that rhetoric is a branch of ethics. The public speaker, especially the minister, should be a good man,* convinced of the truth and righteousness of his cause, and animated by his conviction. His preparation, his choice of materials, his arrangement, and his delivery should all be regulated by the highest principles, and should constantly aim at a pure end. Theremin carries out this line of thought into all the details of preaching, and he himself acted on it.

The other German preachers to whom I shall refer are either now alive, or have died recently. Instead of taking them in chronological order, we shall glance at them according to the schools which they represent.

Modern Rationalists— Schwarz. We may mention, first, Karl Schwarz, of the modern rationalistic school, who stands at its head as a preacher; if we do not name others, it is not because rationalists are not abundant, but

* *Decet oratorem bonum virum esse.*—QUINTILIAN.

because this school does not produce many eminent
preachers. Schwarz is the exponent of *The New-
est Theology*, a kind of manifesto of his party, and
his sermons have already passed through several
editions. He is a man of sharp intellect, ready
and eloquent of utterance, while a breeze of imagination fills the sails of his speech, and makes up
for the want of real warmth and light. His principle is that a preacher must translate the spirit of
Christ into the wants and feelings of his time, by
which he means the adaptation, not of language,
but of the substance of Christian doctrines. He
would take the ideas of sin and atonement, the
death, resurrection, and ascension of Christ, and,
having stripped them of what he calls their mythical dress, he would apply them to the human
nature of our day. Thus for the Holy Spirit, he
substitutes "the higher reason of Christianity;" for
the sinful heart, "the laxity of modern life;" for
regeneration, "the beginning of nobler impulses;"
instead of Christ's ascension, we have "the elevation
of humanity;" instead of personal immortality, we
have "corporate immortality." The old words are
very often so skilfully used that the superficial
hearer thinks he is getting the Bible, and it is only
the hungry heart which feels the want of living

bread. There is at the same time a constant repetition of scorn for traditionalism and Pharisaism, with a claim to superior enlightenment and culture. But it is simply the old rationalism aerated—Hegel in the pulpit instead of Wolf—and when it stands a while, or comes from an unskilful imitator, it is as dead as such teaching was in the middle of last century.

Modern Lutherans—

The modern Lutheran school stands at the opposite extreme. It is to be found both in the separate community which has tried to base itself on the old Confession of the church, and in the United church, which has more or less adopted its views. It includes a number of distinguished names; Kahnis and Delitzsch of Leipzig are its men of learning; Ludwig Harms and Kliefoth are its popular preachers; while Kögel is more, being one of the most eloquent Christian orators in Germany. We cannot characterise them all, but we may refer briefly to Harms and Kögel.

L. Harms, 1808-1865.

Ludwig Harms, though not related to Claus Harms, had much of the same character. He assisted and succeeded his father, who was minister at Hermannsburg in the Lüneburg. The population of that district is of the Low-German type, the same race as the Angles, Jutes, and Saxons, who

peopled our shores 1400 years ago, strong, persevering, and realistic, but ready to sink into the
animal. It has been qualified in Scotland by the
Celtic admixture, which brought in elements of the
ideal, and also by religion ; else we had been more
of the earth earthy than we are. Harms found a
low and sensuous moral tone, resembling that
of our own country where the abominable bothy
system prevails. By his persevering labours and
ardent preaching, he made a green spot in the
desert, formed schools, prayer-meetings, home
missions, and even sent out several missionaries to
the shores of Africa. He himself was a genuine
Nether-Saxon, hard, rugged, and practical, with a
deep vein of tenderness beneath. He says of
himself, " I belong by nature and training to the
rough kind. I was taught by my father not to cry
though my head should be knocked to pieces, but
when I first.saw my sins against God I wept like
a child." The grace of God softened his heart, but
left the same strong bold nature. He threw himself with all his force against the indifference and
vice by which he was surrounded, preached in
plain straightforward language, and wrought a real
reformation in the district. His ideas of preaching
and his own style will be best understood by

his advice, which is as follows: "I have only one theory, that of the Holy Ghost. With the power of the Holy Ghost fresh from the Bible, driven by the love of Christ, let us speak right on to the people as our tongue is made, and because we cannot help it. To see in every soul a soul bought by the blood of Christ, which should belong to Him, and which we must strive to win back for Him—that, I take it, is the fresh road of life. Do you preach without scruple God's Word? Have no fear of consequences, chastise the sins and godlessness of the lairds and farmers, whether they are present or not, and the sins and godlessness of the labourers, whether they are present or not, and whether both alike take it ill or not; God's Word never comes back empty. Picture to them Jesus Christ—this before all things; set Him before their eyes in the full form of His Cross and of His glory, and pray among the people with all your heart for the Holy Spirit. Do not manufacture your sermons, but pray them out on your knees.* When the people are sleeping, wrestle with the Lord for the souls of men; sacrifice time, strength, and comfort, everything, everything, to the Lord and to the salvation of souls. Again, I say, preach

* "*Bene precasse est bene studuisse.*"

the Word of God, whether it be justification by
faith or the sanctification of the Sabbath, the
Gospel or the law, preach it so that there be no
back-door left for mistake or escape. Everything
must bend to God's Word, and nothing can relieve
you from the duty of plain dealing with it. Call
everything by its right name, that men may get
hold of your meaning with their hands, and that
nothing may fly over their heads. With all this
I entreat you walk holily, and avoid everything
that tastes or smells of the world ; preach nothing
that you do not practise."

Harms carried out this fully, so much so that, in
the meetings he held after the regular service, he
spoke to the people in the Low-German dialect,
which corresponds to our Lowland Scottish.*

R. Kögel is as different as well may be from Kögel.
Harms. He has fancy and feeling of the highest
order, and is perhaps the most brilliant preacher
in Germany at the present time. He is a man of
learning and cultivation, with wide knowledge of
history and literature ; a man of the world, also, in
his acquaintance with human nature. He resembles
Harms in this, that he is fearless in rebuking sin,

* This reminds us how Dr. Chalmers explained to an old
woman the meaning of faith by the word "lippen."

whether it be in the court or in the cottage, and
that he aims at plain intelligible speech. But he
is, besides, a poet in the pulpit, with command over
the whole range of feeling. Many of his sermons
have been published, and they are widely read,
especially the series named, *From the Fore-court to
the Most Holy Place.* He preaches very often from
the Old Testament; but his power lies not so much
in going into the depths of the Bible, as in reaching
the depths of the human heart. He is well aware
that, with all the talk in our day of intellectual
difficulties, the real obstacle with most men is the
aversion of the heart to the humble, self-denying
character of the Gospel, and therefore he aims at
the heart. He is incisive and aggressive in his
preaching; borrowing the words of the old orator,
he says that every sermon must be a battle.

Scriptural—   The next group of preachers may be called the
Scriptural. Among these we may rank Julius
Müller, and Beck of Tübingen, lately dead, Luthardt,
Steinmeyer, Gerok, and Uhlhorn, who are still
alive.

J. Müller,   Julius Müller was one of the greatest theologians
1801-1878.
of modern Germany, and is in this respect to be
placed beside Nitzsch. His chief book, *The Christian Doctrine of Sin,* in spite of one or two excres-

cences, makes a true appeal, on the one hand to
Scripture, and on the other to conscience. As a
liber classicus it will not soon give place to any
other, and is indeed one of those books which
make an epoch by fresh criticism and masterly
analysis of the deepest spiritual facts. His preaching, however, is quite different. It is so plain and
natural, that one would fail to find the great
theologian in it, were it not for his clearness and
simplicity. He lays down two principles for his
own guidance. First, the preacher is above all
things an expositor of the Word of God, not a
philosopher with a system of human wisdom,
nor an imaginative painter of ideal creations.
He has charge of the divine oracles, and must
stand aside and let them speak, or rather they
must speak through him, warmed by his heart
and verified by his experience. His second
principle is that the preacher's language should
be such as to reach all his hearers, or at least that
it should not be his fault if it does not. If there
are those who come to the house of God to have
their vanity flattered or their ears tickled, the
preacher cannot on their account neglect the
great work of speaking to the hearts of the sinful
and suffering. The house of God is a place where

the rich and poor should meet together on the
same level, with the words, "Behold, we are here
present before God, to hear the things that are
commanded us of God;" and the preacher must
address himself to this state of mind, or he must
seek to bring the hearers to it.   Müller's own
•sermons are constructed on this principle; while a
profound and philosophical theologian, he preaches
to the capacity of plain people.   The use of his
learning seems, in the language of Usher, to be
"the making of things plain."

Two notable preachers of this school are to be
found in Würtemberg.

Gerok.   Karl von Gerok is the most popular preacher in
the south of Germany, holding a place like that of
Kögel in Berlin.   He deals, however, more with
the meaning of Scripture than Kögel.   He has
published four volumes of sermons, and in the preface to the second he defines his developed idea
of preaching.   The first volume, he says, may
seem to have more youthful fire and fancy, but his
endeavour is more and more to apply the text
of the Bible to the heart and life, in the spirit of
the teaching of the Evangelical Confession, with
language suited to the various necessities of the
community.   His wish is to make the narrow way

no broader than God has made it, and yet not to exclude art or science or any other aspect of life, nor to keep back those who are still astray, or in search of the truth. Gerok holds a high position in the superintendence of the Würtemberg church, and he is the author of some of the best modern hymns, breathing a deep and fine Christian feeling.

We must say something of Johann Tobias Beck, J. T. Beck, whose influence is still powerful in Würtemberg 1804-1879. and indeed throughout Germany. In 1842 he was appointed professor at Tübingen, where Strauss and Baur had assailed the Bible with the most persevering ingenuity and with the keenest weapons of learned criticism. When Baur spoke, it was considered the last word of the destructive school. In the New Testament he left standing as unassailable the epistles to the Romans, Corinthians, and Galatians ; all the rest he attacked. Beck was one of the most decided believers in the inspiration of the Bible, and, when he was appointed to succeed Baur, the change which he wrought at Tübingen was wonderful. His class-room was soon crowded by students from all parts of Germany and from foreign lands. He did not exercise influence so much by the apparatus of learning—though he was a distinguished scholar ; he carried home conviction

by the way in which he dealt with the Bible morally
and spiritually.   He had laid not only his understanding but his heart, his conscience, his spirit,
close to the Bible, having made it the unbroken
study of his life.   He knew it as a man knows the
home in which he has lived for years, and was "a
man of the Word" as few have been since the days
of the apostles.   His own studies had begun with
Bengel's *Gnomon,* and along with this he had
caught from Oetinger a flavour of mysticism, which
was congenial to the German students with their
love of the uncommon.   But it was a mere stray
twig of his doctrine; the stem and the root were
deep in the Word of God as the book given for
man.   This was his teaching in the professor's
chair, and he preached as he taught; indeed it was
often said of him that he preached from the chair
and taught from the pulpit.   He tells us that he
learned his academical theology in ten years of an
active pastorate, that he found then the difference
between broken cisterns and the living fountain,
and became convinced that the great error of the
time was to place *ideæ academicæ* instead of *ideæ
Scripturariæ.*   The academy and science are good,
but when the life of the Bible leaves them they
yield only pieces of dead scholasticism.   Strauss,

Baur, and Renan, he says, are mere anatomists. The Bible is not only light but life ; it is a seed that sends forth fresh buds and blossoms for every man who comes to it, and for every generation. In this spirit he taught and preached to the end, and left a class of scholars who may do something to repair the evil wrought by the destructive historical critics.

Luthardt, the well-known professor at Leipzig, Luthardt. is also a distinguished preacher who never fails to find an audience. His aim is to reach the heart and conscience, but his sermons are marked by a union of simplicity with elevation, and by thoughtfulness compressed often into short sententious sayings.

Steinmeyer, professor in Berlin, was, in his earlier Steinmeyer. years, spoken of as "the young Schleiermacher." He resembles Schleiermacher in the way in which he builds up his materials, and in the steady step with which he advances to his purpose ; but he differs from him in this, that he occupies himself much more with his text and with the meaning of Scripture. His views are always fresh and original, and few men are better fitted for penetrating below the surface of the text, and opening up new and at the same time true lines of thought.

2 C

Uhlhorn.

Uhlhorn is a man who has been rising of late in reputation. His sphere of labour is Göttingen and Hanover. He is a man of deep and extensive theological learning, and belongs to the school of Nitzsch, with more of clearness and oratorical power in his mode of representation.

The Bremen School.

There are parts of Germany where evangelical preaching has a long established hold. We have spoken of Würtemberg, and have also referred to Elberfeld and the Wüpperthal; we may mention here the city of Bremen, which is a centre of missionary effort. The Christian life of Bremen has owed much to Menken, a preacher of marked individuality, who died in 1831; to Friedrich Mallet, whose published sermons have met with a very favourable reception; and more recently to Funcke who, besides being a telling preacher, is the author of a number of books, somewhat in the style of Claudius, which are widely read. This part of Germany has a type of mind closely resembling the Dutch, strong in mother wit and practical sagacity, with a vein of realistic poetry. It is shown fully in the Dutch and Flemish schools of painting, and in the noted animal epic of *Reineke Fuchs*, Reynard the Fox, which had a Nether-Saxon origin. When carried into preaching by such men as Claudius, Harms, and Funcke, it produces sermons of a singularly clear, impressive, and sagacious character, to which, perhaps, the nearest English resemblance is in Spurgeon's preaching; there were elements of it in the late William Arnot and William Anderson.

Before closing this lecture, we may briefly indicate some general features of present German preaching. Features of modern German preaching.

It has lately been striving after more simplicity and clearness, without becoming less instructive. Almost all the recent writers on homiletics dwell on the necessity of studying the language of the people, and speaking to them in it, rather than in the language of the schools.

In form, it varies between the textual and the topical methods, according to the mental structure of the preacher; but, on the whole, the tendency has been to leave Schleiermacher's manner for a closer use of the text—*i.e.*, the preaching has become more Scriptural.

The substance is largely evangelical. We would not have you to infer that the amount of rationalistic preaching is to be measured by the names which we have given. Far from it. But the most distinguished preachers are those of the evangelical school. Their sermons attract the largest audiences and are the most widely read, and it is quite natural that it should be so. Their themes are not only most divine, but most human, reaching into the deepest affections of the heart, and rising with the highest aspirations of the spirit. If this preaching is at any time superseded by superficial views of Christianity, it is only when preachers deal unworthily with the truths which are committed to their trust. There is no theme which so attracts men, or so moves them in their whole nature, as the glorious Gospel of the blessed God.

LECTURE XXI.

LESSONS FOR OUR PREACHING.

W E propose to-day to gather together some
counsels for guidance in preaching, drawn Guidance for
chiefly from our survey of German preaching be- our preaching—
tween the Reformation and our own time. There
are two aspects of preaching : the form of the sermon, and its matter or contents. Taking these in
order, observe, first, what we may learn as to the 1. As to form.
form.

I. At an early stage in this course of lectures we Textual and
topical
saw that the first form of Christian preaching was methods.
the homily, in which a portion of Scripture was
explained and applied, and that this method, when
used in the exposition of a single verse, developed into what is technically called the Textual
method ; for a Textual sermon is a homily on a
single verse. We also saw that very early in the
history of the pulpit there came to be discourses

upon saints or martyrs, delivered either at the time
of their death or on the anniversaries of their death.
These took the form of the oration of the Greeks
and Romans, and, when Christianity had gained
power among the more educated classes, this became a favourite method of preaching, and
developed into what we term the Topical method.
Preaching has constantly varied between these two
—the Textual or analytic, in which the preacher
follows his text faithfully, dealing with its several
parts; and the Topical or synthetic, in which he
selects the chief points, and expands or impresses
it by reasons, suggestions, and illustrations not contained in the text.

Luther, as a rule, preferred the Textual method,
though he did not adhere to it strictly; Melancthon, the Topical; Spener, the Textual; the
rationalists and men like Reinhard, the Topical.

Their gradual approximation.
In later times the two methods have drawn
closer to each other, leading thus to forms of
preaching which we cannot accurately describe by
either of those names. The Textual treatment has
approached the Topical by seeking to use the leading thought of the text as the centre of the sermon,
and to group the other parts round it; while the
Topical has approached the Textual by seeking

for a text which really contains the topic, and by adhering to the original meaning of the text throughout the sermon. There have thus come to be methods termed Textual-topical and Topical-textual. It may seem as if these were the same, but there is a real difference between them. If you look for a text, or are attracted by one, and make the chief topic in it the centre of your sermon, you take the Textual-topical. On the other hand if you select a topic—say, Missions, or the New Year, or the Teaching of Christ—and go to the Bible for a text to strike the note of your discourse, your method is Topical-textual.

Now, so far as there has been progress in German preaching, it has been in the direction of these two mixed methods. Latterly, the most impressive and successful preachers have avoided both extremes, both the slavish adherence to verbal exposition of the Bible, and the unchartered liberty which disregards the need of a Scriptural basis. Whatever your special bent may be, you will be cautioned against error by observing that this has been a line of real progress, and has guided recent preachers to produce better sermons than men who were probably their superiors in power and in resources. If you are drawn towards the Topical

Lesson from this.

method, then seek for a true Scriptural ground,
attach your topic to a real text, that so your sermon may be Scriptural.   If you are drawn towards
the Textual method, which is upon the whole the
more useful and the more suitable for most men,
then seek for concentration, and do not let the
parts straggle.   This rule applies in part even to
the lecture upon a continuous passage, which can
rarely be subjected to Topical treatment.   Even
there, wherever it is possible, try to find the order
of the thoughts in the passage, so as to sustain the
interest of your hearers and to leave a single
impression.   Indeed it is usually desirable to select
one verse, either from the passage itself or from
some other part of Scripture, which contains the
kernel of the lecture, or will at least serve your
hearers as an index-finger.

2. As to sub-
stance.

II. When we turn from the form to the substance
of the sermon, we find that almost all preachers
and homiletes admit that it should be drawn from
the Scriptures.   But we may draw from the Scriptures in many different ways, and the special way
we take gives our preaching its distinctive character.

Reformers.

The early Reformers went to the Bible on the
principle that the great thing is to preach faith—
faith in Christ, faith in Christ as the ground of the

sinner's justification in the sight of God. The doctrine of justification by works—by ceremonial, by penance, or at the best by moral conduct—was so prevalent that they set over against it such texts as, " Being justified freely by His grace ; " " Being justified by faith we have peace with God ; " " In whom we have redemption through His blood." They offered free and full salvation to all sinners who would believe in Christ, and the effect of such preaching, coming as it did from their hearts and from strong conviction, was very great, as it will always be.

But in time, faith, instead of being a means Dogmatists. leading to Christ, became an end in itself, and instead of Christ there were certain doctrines about Christ—logical propositions contained in the creed and founded on proof-texts. The great thing then for a Christian man was orthodoxy, and salvation was to be found by being sound in the faith—*i.e.*, in the creed. Religion ran into a surface-shell and became hard and crustaceous. It was not so with all ; there were many exceptions, many quiet, earnest preachers, and hearers also, whose names have not come down to us ; but as a whole, the seventeenth century was one of hard, dry dogmatism.

Pietists.   There came then the desire on the part of good men for life. They said, " Religion does not consist in holding doctrines, however true and Scriptural they may be ; it consists in living a life of faith in the Son of God, and in order to live we must be born." These men drew from the Bible the great doctrines of regeneration and the work of the Holy Ghost. Their texts were, "Verily, verily, I say unto you, ye must be born again;" " Awake, thou that sleepest, and arise from the dead, and Christ shall give thee light ; " "If we live in the Spirit, let us also walk in the Spirit." These were the Pietists—men like Spener and Francke, as holy and devoted men as ever lived ; and they produced a great effect. Under their preaching there was a revival of religion throughout Germany. The Bible was read and studied, fellowship-meetings prevailed, books of devotion were written, warm, fervid hymns were composed and sung, and Christians rejoiced in the dawning of a new day.

Later Pietists.   This lasted for more than two generations ; but by-and-by the Pietists came to set too much value upon feeling ; they made it everything ; they studied their hearts, felt their pulses, cultivated temperaments and emotions, and were in despair when they could not find what they sought. Their hearts did not look out to see the great living Christ of the Bible ; they tried to trace His image in the troubled watery reflection of their own emotion. Religion became subjective and sentimental — sometimes too sweet when they were pleased with themselves, and sometimes very sour when they compared themselves with the common world. Now, pride of any kind brings punishment, and spiritual pride is never more offensive to God than in the spirit which says, " Stand by ; I am holier than thou." So there arose a wide-spread cry : " Let us be done with words and phrases and moods and mysticism, let us have reality and plainness ; come out of this sultry, misty region into the light of common day, the light which we call reason. If there be anything in the Bible, it ought to explain itself distinctly, and to prove itself to our natural understanding. Man is the measure of the universe ; he is to measure it by his reason, and his reason is the growth of his senses, the outcome of what he sees and handles and feels."

Taking this principle to the Bible, the Rational- Rationalists. ists sought by it to uproot all the supernatural, that the Church might have a simple, easy book which would perplex and trouble nobody. The preaching of their generation took this character. It disregarded the divine nature of Christ, and spoke of His humanity; it denied or overlooked His atonement, and dwelt upon His example. It rejected doctrine and insisted on morality; it smiled at regeneration and sanctification as antiquated and mystical notions, and maintained the sole need for moral improvement. It was all for charity or toleration (except of Pietists), and lukewarm about truth. Some of its preachers attracted large audiences by their rhetorical power, and showed much ingenuity in the use of their scanty materials; but the majority, not being great orators, tried to keep up the interest of the people by taking secular and social subjects, and preaching upon the trivial events of domestic or municipal affairs. Soon the people wearied of such nine days' wonders, and missed the things that made them thrill and weep and tremble and rejoice. Not the Bible only, but the whole world of human life seemed so stale and flat and unprofitable. The soul was ready to die of inanition, and the church became a more tiresome place than it had been in the old orthodox time. This was the hour of midnight, a Greenland midnight, and the German church took a chill, from which she has not yet recovered.

Then came men who said, " But after all there is Ratio-pietists. more in man than the bare understanding, there is a soul, and the soul has wants and desires which the understanding can nèither explain nor satisfy. The soul is conscious of weakness, and must have something or some one to lean on. It is conscious of sin, and it needs pardon and purity, or the power that will give it hope of purity ; it can conceive of an infinity and an eternity, and it must turn to these. What can meet its wants but Christ ? That which you give us for Him is not merely beneath the Bible view, it is beneath the cry of the soul in man's nature. Whatever you make of the Bible, we feel there must be a Christ."

The first of these men was Schleiermacher. His Schleier-macher. was the religion of feeling, feeling in a different sense from the Pietistic, not the feeling that follows conversion, but the feeling in man's nature that seeks for a God and finds Him in Christ. It arose from the necessity of going deeper than the bare understanding and senses—to the soul, that religion might have a basis there ; and it expressed the important truth that we should commend ourselves to every man's conscience (συνείδησις) in the sight of God, try to get at the deepest things in human nature, and bring them up into the light of the divine.

Mediating school.

This was a starting-point of a new style of preaching in Germany—the study of man's inmost nature, and the bringing of the Gospel to bear on it. But Schleiermacher only gave the starting-point; he was too subjective and shadowy, and those who followed him have dealt more with the personal Christ. Such is the preaching of Nitzsch, Tholuck, Julius Müller, and others, who have in the main returned to the preaching of the Reformation, and of Spener and Francke. They preach justification by faith as Luther did, and they preach regeneration with Spener and Francke ; *i.e.*, they hold by doctrine, and they hold also by the religion of the heart, while their aim is to present these to the soul of man with self-evidencing power, the power that makes a man say, Come and see. This is really the ground taken long before by men like John Howe and Pascal, and in recent days by such French preachers as Vinet and Adolph Monod ; but in Germany it has been reached after a long struggle, which was forced on by rationalism, and the need of finding a deep foundation on which to meet it.

What then are the conclusions which we should draw from these things, in regard to the subject-matter of preaching?

1. First, we should preach justification by faith. This was the doctrine that made the early Reformers strong, and it is the only form in which you can offer a free Gospel, and give men a foundation on which they can stand to begin the great work of building up a new life.

Yet we must beware of letting this preaching run into the mere rehearsal of a creed. We must keep it living; and the way to keep it living is to connect it always with a personal Christ. Carry all the doctrines up to Him—the rays of light to the Sun of Righteousness—*in whom* we have redemption through His blood.

2. Secondly, we should preach conversion and re- generation—the need of a great change, and of the work of God's Holy Spirit. Religion is nothing unless it is a life, an inward life given from above.

But we must not allow our preaching, or the lives of Christian people, to drift into mere emotion, which will surely become unhealthy and morbid. We must turn the heart out upon the life, and show that the evidence of Christianity is to be given by reflecting the image and the character of

Christ. If we live by the Spirit, we shall walk in
the Spirit, and a straight, steadfast walk is the way
to gain deeper spiritual peace and to prove our
religion to the world.

Of the Media-
ting school.
3. We may learn from the present Mediating
school that we require to study, not merely the
Bible but human nature, and to bring these two
together. We must make our hearers feel that
Christ still knows what is in man, and that, when
He comes in His Gospel, He discloses truths which
they could not indeed have found without Him,
but which they now know to be real, not on
His authority alone but by inward testimony,
as a patient's symptoms confirm a wise doctor's
diagnosis of his case; and not only this, but that
He can cure their nature and lift it up to a height
they knew not of before.

Of the Illum-
inists.
4. But have we nothing to learn from the Illuminists? Yes; we may learn from them the duty of
using plain, direct speech, and a language which
men can understand. The truths of the Gospel
reach away into the infinite and eternal, else they
would not be suited to an immortal nature; but
the first elements of them can be made so plain
that he who runs may read. I may see a pathway
up a mountain-side that ascends and winds under

deep rock shadows and through thick forests, till it disappears in the far heights on which the sunshine gleams, and earth and heaven meet. I should be a rationalist if I said, "The path leads no further than the little terminus you see;" but I should be an obscurantist, if I did not set the traveller on the road, saying, "This is the way, walk ye in it."

And we have this, further, to learn from the Illuminists, that the preacher has to deal with all man's nature and all man's life. As Tholuck says, "Every sermon should have heaven for its father, and earth for its mother." It is not needful that we should tell men about ploughing and bee-keeping and gardening and weaving; but we can bring home to them the great rule, "Whatsoever ye do, do all to the glory of God."

Let us, then, preach salvation by faith, and regeneration through the Holy Spirit; let us seek to search the depths of the soul with the Gospel of Christ; let us bring all God's truth to bear on the life of men in plain, practical speech; and we shall be workmen that need not be ashamed.

INDEX.

403

THE MIRACULOUS ELEMENT IN THE GOSPELS.

By ALEXANDER BALMAIN BRUCE, D.D., Author of "The Parabolic Teaching of Christ." 8vo, cloth. $2.50.

This work, though constructed on a different method, may be regarded as a companion to my work on THE PARABOLIC TEACHING OF CHRIST, published a few years ago. In the Fifth and Sixth Lectures I have considered from my point of view, at considerable length, a large number of the miraculous narratives, and made observations on nearly the whole of the narratives of this character contained in the Gospels. My object in these portions of the work is not to expound homiletically the whole narrative in which a miracle is recorded, but to inquire whether the event recorded be indeed a miracle.

" *It will take rank at once among the standard treatises upon its always important and engrossing theme. It is an elaborate study—the fruit of wide-reaching and profound research and patient reflection. The result of these studies is that the volume is a powerful defense of the miracles as an essential feature of the religion of Christ. It is a cause of congratulation to the whole Christian public that so valuable course of lectures has been given to the whole world in so available shape,"*—BOSTON CONGREGATIONALIST.

"An exhaustive discussion of the New Testament Miracles. The topics are candidly, lucidly, and very ably considered. The volume is a rich addition to our apologetic literature, which every Biblical student will desire to add to his library."—*Zion's Herald.*

The Parabolic Teaching of Christ.

A Systematic and Critical Study of the Parables of our Lord. By Rev. Prof. A. B. BRUCE, D.D. 1 vol., 8vo, cloth, 527 pp. Price, $2.50.

"A work which will at once take its place as a classic on the Parables of our Saviour. No minister should think of doing without it."—*American Presbyterian Review.*

American Literary Churchman says: " We recommend this book with the most confident earnestness. It is a book to be bought and kept; it has both depth and breadth and minute accuracy; it has a living sympathy with the teaching of the Parables and with the spirit of the Master."

ENGLISH NOTICES.

" Prof. Bruce brings to his task the learning and the liberal and finely sympathetic spirit which are the best gifts of an expositor of Scripture. His treatment of his subject is vigorous and original, and he avoids the capital mistake of overlaying his exegesis with a mass of other men's views."—*Spectator.*

" The studies of the Parables are thorough, scholarly, suggestive and practical. Fullness of discussion, reverence of treatment, and sobriety of judgment, mainly characterize this work."—*Christian World.*

" Each Parable is most thoughtfully worked out, and much new light is thus thrown on the difficulties which surround many of these beautiful and suggestive examples of Divine teaching."—*Clergymen's Magazine.*

" This volume has only to be known to be welcomed, not by students alone, but by all earnest students of Christ's oracles. On no subject has Dr. Bruce spoken more wisely than on the question why Jesus spoke in parables. The one end the author sets before himself is, to find out what our Lord really meant. And this he does with a clearness and fullness worthy of all praise. **Familiar as we are with some of the best and most popular works on the Parables, we do not know any to which we could look for so much aid in our search after the very meaning which Christ would have us find in His words.**"—*Nonconformist.*

Copies sent by mail, postpaid, on receipt of price.

A. C. ARMSTRONG & SON, 714 Broadway, New York.

5

TALKS WITH YOUNG MEN.

By J. THAIN DAVIDSON. 12mo, in handsome cloth binding, illuminated cover. Price, $1.25.

"These talks are direct, practical and pungent, such as young men like to hear. They are crowded with points of counsel and direction ; they will be invaluable to any young man, and all so plainly and forcibly told, and so fully illustrated, that one can but pursue the reading of them to the end. The graphic descriptions of human nature, and sharp laying open of motive in worldly and selfish living, show an unusually keen sense of observation and understanding of the human heart. It should have a wide circulation."—*N. Y. Evangelist.*

Rev. Mr. SPURGEON says : " The author gives young men fine advice—full of grace and thought—enlivened by story and proverb, fresh with sympathy, and on fire with zeal. These short talks are just what they should be, and all that they further need is to be largely distributed among the crowds of our advancing manhood. TO BEGIN TO READ IS TO BE BOUND TO CONTINUE; THE TALKS ARE SO SENSIBLE THAT NO ONE WISHES TO SILENCE THE TALKER-BY LAYING ASIDE THE BOOK."

N. Y. Christian Advocate and Journal says : "This volume will find readers wherever it is known. The talks are fervent and DIRECT APPEALS TO THE HEART. THE STYLE IS ANIMATED AND PICTURESQUE. AND THE BOOK WILL BE READ BY ALL WHO BUY IT."

By the same Author.

FOREWARNED—FOREARMED.

In cloth. Uniform with " Talks With Young Men " 12mo. $1.25.

Methodist Recorder : "To young men we would specially recommend this useful, earnest, and interesting book. They will find themselves not preached to, but talked with, and that they have in Mr. Davidson a friend wise, tender and true. Fathers could not do better than place this excellent volume in the hands of their sons at once."

DR. DAVIDSON'S NEW BOOK FOR YOUNG MEN.

THE CITY YOUTH.

Uniform with " Talks With Young Men." 12mo, cloth. $1.25.

It has been the Author's aim, in the preparation of this book, to supply a genial and useful *Friend*, who will talk cheerily yet seriously to the new-comer, and put him on his guard against the moral dangers by which he is certain to be beset.

THE CHURCHETTE :

A Year's Sermons and Parables for the Young.

By the Rev. J. R. HOWATT. Uniform with " Talks With Young Men." Cloth: $1.25.

Literary World: "Short, simple, cheery, colloquial, imaginative, impressive, the sermons yield abundant evidence that, as he says, his ' aim has been to speak to children in the sunshine.' There is also a freshness, not to say an originality, about the subjects selected and their treatment, which gives a special charm to the book."

HOME·WORSHIP
AND

THE USE OF THE BIBLE IN THE HOME.

A Practical Method of Using Scripture and Explanation
FOR
Systematic Study of the Bible by Subjects,
FOR
Readings Suited to Every Special Need,
AND FOR
Ready Reference.
BY
Rev. J. P. THOMPSON, D.D., and Rev. C. H. SPURGEON.
EDITED BY
Rev. JAMES H. TAYLOR, D.D.
WITH SPECIAL CHAPTERS BY

BISHOP SIMPSON.	REV. WM. M. TAYLOR, D.D.
REV. JOHN HALL, D.D.	REV. GEORGE D. BOARDMAN, D.D.

Illustrated with Steel Engravings and Maps.

In placing the present work before the public, special mention should be made of the superior facilities here offered for making THE BIBLE A WORKING POWER IN THE HOME. Combining Scripture and familiar exposition in attractive form for the reading and study of the Bible by *subjects*, it places the whole at *instant command* by a new method of classification and indexing.

The Biblical explanations represent an important part of the life studies of its distinguished authors, and indicate to some extent the character and magnitude of the work. Omitting the dry details of comment which have no spiritual significance, great prominence is given to the *helpful* lessons which are so full of inspiration to a better life. The work commends itself as furnishing an entirely *practical* method, by which families, as they gather at their own firesides, may accomplish a thorough course of Bible study, with some central subject of thought made prominent *for each day*. The means are thus at hand for renewing, in *more effective form*, the grand old custom, so honored and blessed of God in days past, of religious education in the home. These short, attractive readings—requiring but a very short time for each—are admirably adapted to the few minutes which every Christian family has already set apart for worship.

SOLD ONLY BY SUBSCRIPTION.

A. C. ARMSTRONG & SON, 714 Broadway, New York.

22

THE BOOK IN ACTUAL USE.

(EXCERPTS.)

BISHOP SIMPSON.
(M. E. Church.)

" It is superior to any work of the same character which I have ever seen."

Rev. R. S. STORRS, D.D.
(Cong., Brooklyn, N. Y.)

" Family Worship will be enriched and made more delightful by the use of it. "

Rev. HENRY SCUDDER, D.D.
(Cong., Chicago.)

" It meets a *real want* and does it *admirably*."

BISHOP BOWMAN.
(Sen. Bishop M. E. Ch.)

" It is decidedly the best book of the kind I have seen. It must be of much value in the Sunday School as well as in the home."

Rev. WAYLAND HOYT, D.D
(Baptist, Philadelphia, Pa.)

"After a good deal of personal use of this work, I give it my unqualified approval."

RA D. SANKEY.
(Evangelist.)

" I am delighted with the work, and cannot conceive of anything more complete and appropriate. God speed the good book on its mission of light and love."

Rev. J. H. VINCENT, D D.
(Pres. Chautauqua Lit. and Sci. Circle.)

" I think this an *invaluable* home manual."

Rev GEO DANA BOARDMAN, D.D.
(Baptist, Philadelphia, Pa.)

"I am thoroughly delighted with this work. It is rounded in conception and admirable in execution ; a strong helper towards the true eternal home."

BISHOP FOWLER.
(M. E. Church.)

" This thoughtful, spiritual, scriptural work must tone up life on every side. It is a remarkable collection of spiritual stimulants and intellectual incitements."

Rev. ROSS C. HOUGHTON, D.D.
(M. E. Church.)

"I have used this work in my family for some time, and cheerfully give it my unqualified approval. It helps to a systematic study of the Bible. *There is not a dull page in the book, and I deem it especially adapted to the needs of the children in our families.* I commend it most heartily and prayerfully to all

---

. *SOLD ONLY BY SUBSCRIPTION.*

A. C. ARMSTRONG & SON, 714 Broadway, New York.

28 .

HOME WORSHIP AND USE OF THE BIBLE.

Rev. P. S. HENSON, D.D.
(Baptist.)

"Scripture is here made to interpret Scripture, and the notes are very clear, concise and helpful."

Rev. E. H. STOKES, D.D.
(M. E. Church.)

"The whole book is aglow with Divine light."

Rev. GEO. S. CHAMBERS, D.D.
(Pres.)

"The great number of devotional uses of which this book is capable shows that its reverent compilers and authors builded even more wisely than they knew."

Rev. GEO. F. PENTECOST, D.D.

"I have used this work in my own family, and all the household liked it. In thousands of families it must be of unspeakable value and helpfulness."

Rev. JOS. CUMMINGS, D.D., LL.D.
(Pres. Evanston Univ.—M. E.)

"It is a work peculiarly well adapted to secure the object in view—*the best that has come under my notice.*"

Rev. JAS. B. ANGELL, D.D., LL.D.
(Pres. University, Mich.)

"It is *admirably* suited to increase the interest of any household in the daily study of the Scriptures and in family devotions."

Rev. CHAS. F. DEEMS, D.D.
(Church of the Strangers, N. Y.)

"The revival most needed now is the revival of home worship. More than all the sensational evangelistic efforts would be the permanent and growing influence of the church in the house."

Rev. E. P. GOODWIN, D.D.
(Cong., Chicago.)

"This volume is aimed at securing for God's word a more *general*, because a more *intelligent* use. The only possible method of searching the Scriptures, of finding out what they teach, and of getting the light, cheer and help they are meant to give, is the *topical* one, taking a given truth or subject and finding what the word of God teaches as to that."

SPECIAL OFFER.

We are introducing this work by CHURCHES, giving each member the advantage of a

SPECIAL RATE AT THE TIME OF INTRODUCTION.

If you will kindly give us the name of some person whom you consider well qualified to introduce the work in your vicinity, we will see that you have

A COPY OF THE WORK FREE,

when he shall have ordered ten books.

SOLD ONLY BY SUBSCRIPTION.

A. C. ARMSTRONG & SON, 714 Broadway, New York.